COLLECTED PAPERS OF KENNETH J. ARROW

Volume **4** The Economics of
Information

COLLECTED PAPERS OF KENNETH J. ARROW

The Economics of Information

The Belknap Press of Harvard University Press

Cambridge, Massachusetts   1984

Library of Congress Cataloging in Publication Data

(Revised for volume 4)

Arrow, Kenneth Joseph, 1921-
   Collected papers of Kenneth J. Arrow.

   Includes bibliographical references and indexes.
   Contents: v. 1. Social choice and justice—
—v. 4. The economics of information.
   1. Welfare economics—Addresses, essays, lectures.
2. Social choice—Addresses, essays, lectures. 3. Social
justice—Addresses, essays, lectures. 4. Distributive
justice—Addresses, essays, lectures. 5. Information
theory in economics—Addresses, essays, lectures.
I. Title.
HB846.A7725 1983   330.1   83-2688
ISBN 0-674-13760-4 (v. 1)
ISBN 0-674-13763-9 (v. 4)

Preface

The work of Jerzy Neyman and Egon Pearson ("On the Problem of the Most Efficient Tests of Statistical Hypotheses," *Philosophical Transactions of the Royal Society of London,* series A, 231:289–337, 1933) gave an economic cast to the foundations of statistical method. They presented criteria of performance and sought to optimize them. Abraham Wald (*Statistical Decision Functions,* New York: Wiley, 1950) gave a more explicitly economic account. Even earlier, statistical methodology in acceptance inspection and quality control had been based on explicitly economic concepts (producers' and consumers' risks). Statistical method was an example for the acquisition of information. In a world of uncertainty it was no great leap to realize that information is valuable in an economic sense. Nevertheless, it has proved difficult to frame a general theory of information as an economic commodity, because different kinds of information have no common unit that has yet been identified. In different ways the papers in this volume have sought to set out the dimensions of the problem or problems and have proposed approaches in certain specific cases. But a general approach is still elusive.

I should like to thank Mary Ellen Geer for her careful and thorough editing and Michael Barclay and Robert Wood for preparation of the index.

Contents

The Economics of
Information

1 Bayes and Minimax Solutions of Sequential Decision Problems

Abraham Wald developed the idea and methods of testing statistical hypotheses by sequential analysis at the Statistical Research Group, formed to develop statistical methods for use in the national defense in World War II. No doubt, as in other such efforts, many of the fruits were not available for use until after the emergency that called them forth was over. The memorandum (Statistical Research Group, 1945), originally marked "Confidential," was circulated, and some of us at the Weather Division of Air Force headquarters were using it within a few months to test whether or not the long-range weather forecasts produced there were significantly bet-

This chapter was written with D. Blackwell and M. A. Girshick. Reprinted from *Econometrica,* 17 (1949): 213–244. The research for this paper was carried on at the RAND Corporation, a nonprofit research organization under contract with the United States Air Force. It was presented at a joint meeting of the Econometric Society and the Institute of Mathematical Statistics at Madison, Wisconsin, September 9, 1948, under the title "Statistics and the Theory of Games." Many of the results in this paper overlap with those obtained previously by Wald and Wolfowitz (1948), and also with some prior unpublished results of Wald and Wolfowitz, announced by Wald at the meeting of the Institute of Mathematical Statistics at Berkeley, California, June 22, 1948. Sections 3 and 6 of the present paper contain analogues of lemmas 1–4 of Wald and Wolfowitz (1948), though both the statements and the proofs differ because of the generally different approach. The proof that the sequential probability ratio test of a dichotomy minimizes the expected number of observations under either hypothesis, in Section 5 of the present paper, follows from Section 3 in the same way that the proof of the same theorem follows from lemmas 1–8 in Wald and Wolfowitz. The previously mentioned unpublished results of Wald and Wolfowitz include the main result of Section 2 (structure of the optimum sequential procedure for the finite multidecision problem) in the special case of linear cost functions.

ter than chance. (They were not.) I became especially interested in Wald's more general formulations of statistical decision theory, both nonsequential and sequential (Wald, 1947b).

While at the RAND Corporation in the summer of 1948, I worked especially with Meyer A. Girshick. About that time, Girshick had attended a meeting of the Institute of Mathematical Statistics at which Wald and Jacob Wolfowitz presented some new results about the structure of sequential analysis when there were more than two alternative hypotheses. He returned with great excitement and stimulated David Blackwell and myself to join him in attempting to reconstruct the results in a more transparent form; the original presentation was certainly hard to understand, and its underlying logic unclear. The three of us grasped that the essential idea was the repetition of the decision situation at each step, though with varying values of the parameters. Hence the decision rule consisted in specifying regions in the parameter space, the same for all time. This point of view was of course implicit in the studies of Wald (1947a) and of Wald and Wolfowitz (1948) but had not been made central.

An unpleasant episode was connected with this paper: a version was circulated that had inadequate acknowledgment to the work of Wald and Wolfowitz, and they felt that there was a challenge to their priority. The published version presents the relation between the papers fairly.

The paper sets forth explicitly the notion of recursive optimization. It provided me with a model argument to be applied to the determination of optimal inventories in work done jointly with Theodore E. Harris and Jacob Marschak. More important, it helped to suggest to Richard Bellman (1957) the general principle of dynamic programming, which has found so many applications.

The problem of statistical decisions has been formulated by Wald (1947b) as follows. The statistician is required to choose some action a from a class A of possible actions. He incurs a loss $L(u,a)$, a known bounded function of his action a and an unknown state u of Nature. What is the best action for the statistician to take?

If u is a chance variable, not necessarily numerical, with a known a priori distribution, then $\mathcal{E}L(u,a) = R(a)$ is the expected loss from action a, and any action, or randomized mixture of actions, which minimizes $R(a)$ has been called by Wald a *Bayes solution* of the decision problem, corresponding to the given a priori distribution of u.

Now suppose there is a sequence x of chance variables $x_1, x_2, \ldots$, whose joint distribution is determined by u. Instead of choosing an action immediately, the statistician may decide to select a sample of x's since this will yield partial information about u, enabling him to make a wiser selection of a. There will be a cost $c_N(x)$ of obtaining the sample $x_1, \ldots,$ x_N and, in choosing a sampling procedure, the statistician must balance the expected cost against the expected amount of information to be obtained.

Formally, the possibility of making observations leaves the situation unchanged, except that the class A of possible actions for the statistician has been extended. His action now consists of choosing a sampling procedure T and a decision function D specifying what action a will be taken for each possible result of the experiment. The expected loss is now $R(T,D) = l(T,D) + c(T)$, where $l(T,D)$ is the expected value of $L(u,a)$ for the specified sampling procedure and decision rule, and $c(T)$ is the expected cost of the sampling procedure. A Bayes solution is now a pair (T,D), or randomized mixture of pairs (T,D), for which $R(T,D)$ assumes its minimum value.

The minimizing $T = T^*$ has been implicitly characterized by Wald and may be described by the following rule: At each stage, take another observation if and only if there is some sequential continuation which reduces the expected risk below its present level. The main difficulty here is that various quantities which arise are not obviously measurable: for instance, if the first observation is x_1, we must compare our present risk level, say $w_1(x_1)$, with $z(x_1) = \inf w(x_1,T,D)$, where $w(x_1,T,D)$ is the expected risk for any possible continuation (T,D); we take another observation if and only if $w_1 > z$. It is not a priori clear that z will be a measurable function of x_1, so that the set of points x_1 for which we stop may not be measurable. Actually, z always is measurable, as will be shown.[1]

A characterization of the minimizing $T = T^*$ is obtained for hypotheses involving a finite number of alternatives under the condition of random sampling. It consists of the following. We are given k hypotheses $H_i (i = 1,2, \ldots, k)$ which have an a priori probability g_i of occurring, a risk matrix $W = (w_{ij})$ where w_{ij} represents the loss incurred in choosing H_j when H_i is true, and a function $c(n)$ which represents the cost of taking n observations. It is shown that for each sample size N, there exist k convex regions S_j^* in the

---

1. The possibility of nonmeasurability is not considered in Wald (1947a) or Wald and Wolfowitz (1948).

$(k-1)$-dimensional simplex spanned by the unit vectors in Euclidean k-space whose boundaries depend on the hypotheses H_i, the risk matrix W, and the cost function $c_N(n) = c(N+n) - c(n)$. These regions have the property that if the vector $\mathbf{g}(N)$ whose components represent the a posteriori probability distribution of the k hypotheses lies in S_j^*, the best procedure is to accept H_j without further experimentation. However, if $\mathbf{g}(N)$ lies in the complement of $\cup_{j=1}^k S_j^*$, the best procedure is to continue taking observations. At any stage, the decision whether to continue or terminate sampling is uniquely determined by this sequence of k regions, and moreover, this sequence of regions completely characterizes T^*.

A method for determining the boundaries of these convex regions is given for $k=2$ (dichotomy) when the cost function is linear. It is shown that in this special case, T^* coincides with Wald's sequential probability ratio test.

The minimax solution to multivalued decision problems is considered, and methods are given for obtaining them for dichotomies. It is shown that in general, the minimax strategy for the statistician is pure, except when the hypotheses involve discrete variates. In the latter case, mixed strategies will be the rule rather than the exception. Examples of double dichotomies, binomial dichotomies, and trichotomies are given to illustrate the construction of T^* and the notion of minimax solutions.

It may be remarked that the problem of optimum sequential choice among several actions is closely allied to the economic problem of the rational behavior of an entrepreneur under conditions of uncertainty. At each point in time, the entrepreneur has the choice between entering into some imperfectly liquid commitment and holding part or all of his funds in cash pending the acquisition of additional information, the latter being costly because of the foregone profits.

1. Construction of Bayes Solutions

The Decision Function

We have seen that the statistician must choose a pair (T,D). It turns out that the choice of D is independent of that of T.

LEMMA. *There is a fixed sequence of decision functions D_m such that*

$$(1\text{-}1) \qquad R(T,D_m) \to \inf R(T,D) = w(T) \quad \text{for all } T.$$

This will be the main result of this section. It follows that the expected loss from a procedure T may be taken as $w(T)$, since this loss may be approximated to arbitrary accuracy by appropriate choice of D_m, and a best sequential procedure T^* of a given class will be one for which $w(T^*) = \inf w(T)$, where the infimum is taken over all procedures T of the class under consideration.

We are considering, then, a chance variable u and a sequence x of chance variables $x_1, x_2, \ldots$. A *sequential procedure* T is a sequence of disjunct sets $S_0, S_1, \ldots, S_N, \ldots$, where S_N depends only on $x_1, \ldots, x_N$ and is the event that the sampling procedure terminates with the sample $x_1, \ldots, x_N$; we require that $\Sigma_{N=0}^{\infty} P(S_N) = 1$. S_0 is the event that we do not sample at all, but take some action immediately; it will have probability either 0 or 1.

A *decision function* D is a sequence of functions $d_0, d_1(x_1), \ldots, d_N(x_1, \ldots, x_N), \ldots$, where each d_N assumes values in A and specifies the action taken when sampling terminates with $x_1, \ldots, x_N$. We admit only decision functions D such that $L[u,d_N(x)]$ is for each N a measurable function.

Proof of Lemma. The loss from (T,D) is $G(u,x;T,D) = L[u,d_N(x)] + c_N(x)$ for $x \in S_N$, and $\mathscr{E}G = R(T,D)$. Here, $c_N(x)$ depends only on $x_1, \ldots, x_N$. Then, denoting by $\mathscr{E}_N$ the conditional expectation given $x_1, \ldots, x_N$, we have $\mathscr{E}_N G = \mathscr{E}_N L[u,d_N(x)] + c_N(x)$ for $x \in S_N$, and

(1-2) $$R(T,D) = \sum_{N=0}^{\infty} \int_{S_N} \mathscr{E}_N L(u,d_N) \, dP + c(T).$$

Now fix N; we shall show that we can choose a sequence of functions $d_{Nm}(x)$, $m = 1, 2, \ldots$, such that

(a) $\mathscr{E}_N L(u,d_{Nm}) \geqq \mathscr{E}_N L(u,d_{N,m+1})$ for all x,

(b) $\mathscr{E}_N L(u,d_N) \geqq r_N$ for all d_N and all x, where

$$r_N(x) = \lim_{m \to \infty} \mathscr{E}_N L(u,d_{Nm}).$$

(c) $r_N \geqq \mathscr{E}_N r_n$ if $n \geqq N$.

First choose a sequence d'_{Nm} such that

$$\mathscr{E} L(u,d'_{Nm}) \to \inf_{d_N} \mathscr{E} L(u,d_N) = r.$$

Now define d_{Nm} inductively as follows: $d_{N1} = d'_{N1}$; $d_{Nm} = d'_{Nm}$ for those values of x such that $\mathcal{E}_N L(u,d'_{Nm}) \leq \mathcal{E}_N L(u,d_{N,m-1})$, otherwise $d_{Nm} = d_{N,m-1}$. Then certainly (a) holds, so that $\lim\limits_{m \to \infty} \mathcal{E}_N L(u,d_{Nm}) = r_N(x)$ exists. Also $\mathcal{E}_N L(u,d_{Nm}) \leq \mathcal{E}_N L(u,d'_{Nm})$, so that $\mathcal{E} r_N = r$. Choose any d_N and any $\delta > 0$, and let S be the event $\{\mathcal{E}_N L(u,d_N) < r_N(x) - \delta\}$. Then, defining $d^*_{Nm} = d_N$ on S, $d^*_{Nm} = d_{Nm}$ elsewhere, we have

$$\mathcal{E} L(u,d^*_{Nm}) \leq \int_S r_N(x)\, dP + \int_{CS} \mathcal{E}_N L(u,d_{Nm})\, dP - \delta P(S),$$

so that $\lim\limits_{m \to \infty} \mathcal{E} L(u,d^*_{Nm}) \leq r - \delta\, P(S)$, and $P(S) = 0$. This establishes (b).

Finally, (c) follows from the fact that every $d_N(x)$ is also a possible $d_n(x)$ if $n > N$. This means that, defining $d^*_n = d_N$, we have $\mathcal{E}_N L(u,d_N) = \mathcal{E}_N[\mathcal{E}_n L(u,d^*_n)] \geq \mathcal{E}_N r_n$ for all d_N, and consequently (c) holds.

Now define $D_m = \{d_{Nm}\}$. Since $\mathcal{E}_N L(u,d_{Nm})$ decreases with m, (1-2) yields that

$$R(T,D_m) \to \sum_{N=0}^{\infty} \int_{S_N} r_N(x)\, dP + c(T) = w(T),$$

and, using (b), that $R(T,D) \geq w(T)$ for all D. Thus we have reduced the problem of finding Bayes solutions to the following. We are given a sequence x of chance variables $x_1, x_2, \ldots$, and a sequence of nonnegative expected loss functions $w_0, \ldots$, where $w_N = r_N(x_1, \ldots, x_N) + c_N(x_1, \ldots, x_N)$. c_N is the cost of the first N observations, and r_N is the loss due to incomplete information. With each sequential procedure $T = \{S_N\}$ there is associated a risk $w(T) = \Sigma_N \int_{S_N} w_N(x)\, dP$. How can T be chosen so that $w(T)$ is as small as possible?

The Best Truncated Procedure

Among all sequential procedures not requiring more than N observations, there turns out to be a best, that is, one whose expected risk does not exceed that of any other. Moreover, the procedure can be explicitly described, by induction backwards, in such a way that its measurability is clear. After $N - 1$ observations $x_1, \ldots, x_{N-1}$, we compare the present risk w_{N-1} with the conditional expected risk $\mathcal{E}_{N-1} w_N$ if we take the final observation. Thus, by choosing the better course, we can limit our loss to $\alpha_{N-1} = \min(w_{N-1}, \mathcal{E}_{N-1} w_N)$, which may be considered as the attainable risk with the observations $x_1, \ldots, x_{N-1}$. We can then decide, on the basis of $N-2$ observations, whether the $(N-1)$st is worth taking by comparing the present risk, w_{N-2}, with $\mathscr{E}_{N-2}\alpha_{N-1}$, the attainable risk if x_{N-1} is observed. Continuing backwards, we obtain at each stage an expected attainable risk α_k for the observations $x_1, \ldots, x_k$, and a description of how to attain this risk, that is, of when to take another observation. This is formalized in the following theorem.

THEOREM 1. *Let* $x_1, \ldots, x_N; w_0, \ldots, w_N$ *be any chance variables,* $w_i = w_i(x_1, \ldots, x_i)$. *Define* $\alpha_N = w_N$, $\alpha_j = min\ (w_j, \mathscr{E}_j\alpha_{j+1})$ *for* $j < N$, $S_j = \{w_i > \alpha_i$ *for* $i < j$, $w_j = \alpha_j\}$. *Then for any disjoint events* $B_0, \ldots, B_N$, B_i *depending only on* $x_1, \ldots, x_i$, $\Sigma_{i=0}^N P(B_i) = 1$, *we have*

$$\sum_{j=0}^N \int_{S_j} w_j\, dP \le \sum_{i=0}^N \int_{B_i} w_i\, dP.$$

Proof. We shall show that, for fixed i and any $(x_1, \ldots, x_i)$-set A,

(1-3)
$$\sum_{j\ge i} \int_{AS_j} \alpha_j\, dP = \sum_{j\ge i} \int_{AS_j} \alpha_i\, dP,$$

and that, for fixed j, and any disjoint sets $A_j, \ldots, A_N$ with A_i depending only on $x_1, \ldots, x_i$ and $\cup_{i=j+1}^N A_i$ depending only on $x_1, \ldots, x_j$,

(1-4)
$$\sum_{i>j} \int_{A_i} \alpha_j\, dP \le \sum_{i>j} \int_{A_i} \alpha_i\, dP.$$

Choosing $A = B_i$ in (1-3) and summing over i, choosing $A_i = B_iS_j$ in (1-4) and summing over j, and adding the results yields

(1-5)
$$\sum_{i,j=0}^N \int_{B_iS_j} \alpha_j\, dP \le \sum_{i,j=0}^N \int_{B_iS_j} \alpha_i\, dP.$$

Now on S_j, $\alpha_j = w_j$, and always $\alpha_i \le w_i$. Making these replacements in (1-5) yields the theorem.

We now prove (1-3) and (1-4). The relationship (1-3) is clear for $i = N$; for $i < N$,

$$\sum_{j\ge i} \int_{AS_j} \alpha_i\, dP = \int_{AS_i} \alpha_i\, dP + \int_{A(S_{i+1}\cup\ldots\cup S_N)} \alpha_i\, dP.$$

But on $S_{i+1} \cup \ldots \cup S_N$, $\alpha_i = \mathscr{E}_i\alpha_{i+1}$; making this replacement in the final integral and using induction backwards on i completes the proof. The relationship (1-4) is clear for $j = N$; for $j < N$,

$$\sum_{i>j} \int_{A_i} \alpha_j \, dP = \int_{A_{j+1}\cup\ldots\cup A_N} \alpha_j \, dP \leq \int_{A_{j+1}\cup\ldots\cup A_N} \alpha_{j+1} \, dP$$

$$= \int_{A_{j+1}} \alpha_{j+1} \, dP + \sum_{i>j+1} \int_{A_i} \alpha_{j+1} \, dP,$$

where the inequality is obtained from the fact that always $\alpha_j \leq \mathcal{E}_j \alpha_{j+1}$. An induction backwards on j now completes the proof of (1-4).

The Best Sequential Procedure

We are given now a sequence of functions $w_0, w_1, \ldots, w_N, \ldots$, where $w_N = r_N(x_1, \ldots, x_N) + c_N(x_1, \ldots, x_N)$. The sequence $r_N(x)$ is uniformly bounded, since we supposed the original loss function $L(u,a)$ to be bounded, and we have shown that $r_n \geq \mathcal{E}_N r_n$ for $n > N$. We shall suppose that $c_N(x)$ is a nondecreasing sequence, $c_N(x) \to \infty$ as $N \to \infty$ for all x. We now construct a best sequential procedure.[2]

The best sequential procedure is obtained as a limit of the best truncated procedures given in the preceding section.

We first define $\alpha_{NN} = w_N$, $\alpha_{jN} = \min(w_j, \mathcal{E}\alpha_{j+1,N})$, $S_{jN} = \{w_i > \alpha_{iN}$ for $i < j$, $w_j = \alpha_{jN}\}$. For fixed j, α_{jN} is a decreasing sequence of functions; say $\alpha_{jN} \to \alpha_j$ as $N \to \infty$. Then $\alpha_j = \min(w_j, \mathcal{E}_j\alpha_{j+1})$. Define $S_j = \{w_i > \alpha_i$ for $i < j$, $w_j = \alpha_j\}$. We shall prove that $T^* = \{S_j\}$ is a best sequential procedure, that is, T^* is a sequential procedure, and for any sequential procedure $T = \{B_j\}$,

$$w(T^*) = \sum_{j=0}^{\infty} \int_{S_j} w_j \, dP \leq \sum_{i=0}^{\infty} \int_{B_i} w_i \, dP = w(T).$$

Now

$$\sum_{i=N+1}^{\infty} \int_{B_i} w_i \, dP \geq \int_{\underset{i>N}{\cup} B_i} c_N \, dP \geq \int_{\underset{i>N}{\cup} B_i} w_N \, dP - M \sum_{i>N} P(B_i),$$

---

2. The assumption made here is somewhat weaker than condition 6 in Wald (1947a, p. 297). The only other assumption made, that $L(u,a)$ is bounded, is condition 1 in Wald (1947a, p. 297).

where M is the uniform upper bound of $r_1(x)$, $r_2(x)$, . . . Thus

$$\sum_{i=0}^{N-1} \int_{B_i} w_i \, dP + \int_{B_N} w_N \, dP + \int_{\underset{i>N}{\cup B_i}} w_N \, dP$$

$$\leq w(T) + MP(B_{N+1} \cup \ldots),$$

so that $w(T_N) \leq w(T) + MP(B_{N+1} \cup \ldots)$, where T_N is the truncated test $B_0, \ldots, B_{N-1}, B_N \cup B_{N+1} \cup \ldots$. From the preceding section,

$$\sum_{j=0}^{N} \int_{S_{jN}} w_j \, dP \leq w(T_N)$$

for all N. Then

$$\sum_{j=0}^{\infty} \int_{S_j} w_j \, dP \leq w(T),$$

letting $N \to \infty$, and using Lebesgue's convergence theorem and the easily verified fact that the characteristic function of S_{jN} approaches that of S_j, and therefore $w(T^*) \leq w(T)$.

It remains to prove that T^* really is a sequential test, that is,

$$\sum_{N=0}^{\infty} P(S_N) = 1.$$

Write $A_N = C(S_0 + \ldots + S_N)$, $\Pi_{N=1}^{\infty} A_N = A$; we show that $P(A) = 0$. It is easily verified by induction that $\alpha_{jN} \geq c_j$ for all N. The relation (1-3), with $i = 0$, A = sample space, yields that

$$\alpha_{0N} \geq \sum_{j=m+1}^{N} \int_{S_{jN}} c_m \, dP = \int_{C(S_{0N} + \ldots + S_{mN})} c_m \, dP$$

for all $m < N$. Then

$$\alpha_0 \geq \int_{A_m} c_m \, dP \geq \int_A c_m \, dP$$

for all m. Since $c_m \to \infty$, $P(A) = 0$.

We now prove that $w(T^*) = \alpha_0$. If T_N^* denotes the truncated test $S_0, S_1, \ldots, S_N + S_{N+1} + \ldots$, the proof that $w(T_N) \to w(T)$ shows that

$w(T_N^*) \rightarrow w(T^*)$. Also (1-3), with $i = 0$, $A =$ sample space, shows that

$$\alpha_{0N} = \sum_{j=0}^{N} \int_{S_{jN}} w_j \, dP.$$

Since $\{S_{0N}, \ldots, S_{NN}\}$ is the best of all procedures truncated at N, and T^* is the best of all sequential procedures, $w(T^*) \leq \alpha_{0N} \leq w(T_N^*)$. Letting $N \rightarrow \infty$ yields $w(T^*) = \alpha_0$.

Now $S_0 = \{w_0 \leq \alpha_0\}$; that is, the best procedure T^* is to take no observations if and only if there is no sequential procedure which reduces the risk below its present level. This remark, which identifies our procedure with that characterized by Wald, at least at the initial stage, will be useful in the next section.

2. Bayes Solutions for Finite Multivalued Decision Problems

In this section we shall seek a characterization of the optimum sequential procedure developed in Section 1 in cases where the number of alternative hypotheses is finite. It will be shown that the optimum sequential test for a k-valued decision problem is completely defined by k (or a sequence of k) convex regions in a $(k-1)$-dimensional simplex spanned by the unit vectors. No procedure has yet been developed for determining the boundaries of these regions in the general case. However, for $k = 2$ (dichotomy) and for a linear cost function, a method for determining the two boundaries has been found and the optimum test is shown to be the sequential probability ratio test developed by Wald (1947b).

Statement of the Problem

We are given k hypotheses $H_1, H_2, \ldots, H_k$, where each H_i is characterized by a probability measure u_i defined over an R-dimensional sample space E_R and has an a priori probability g_i of occurring. We are also given a risk matrix $W = (w_{ij})$, $(i, j = 1, 2, \ldots, k)$, where w_{ij} is a nonnegative real number and represents the loss incurred in accepting the hypothesis H_j when in fact H_i is true. (We shall assume that $w_{ii} = 0$ for all i. This is based on the supposition, which appears reasonable, that the decision maker is not to be penalized for selecting the correct alternative, no matter how unpleasant its consequences may be.) In addition to the risk matrix (w_{ij}) we shall assume that the cost of experimentation depends only on the number (n) of observations taken and is given by a function $c(n)$ which approaches infinity as n approaches infinity. The problem is to characterize the procedure for deciding on one of the k alternative hypotheses which results in a minimum average risk. This risk is defined as the average cost of taking observations plus the average loss resulting from erroneous decisions.

Structure of the Optimum Sequential Procedure

Let G_k stand for the convex set in the k-dimensional space defined by the vectors $\mathbf{g} = (g_1, g_2, \ldots, g_k)$ with components $g_i \geq 0$ and $\Sigma_{i=1}^k g_i = 1$; and let $H = (H_1, H_2, \ldots, H_k)$ represent the k hypotheses under consideration. Then every vector $\mathbf{g}$ in G_k may be considered as a possible a priori probability distribution of H.

For any $\mathbf{g}$ in G_k and for any sequential procedure T (see the definition in Section 1), let $R(\mathbf{g}|T)$ represent the average risk entailed in using the test T when the a priori distribution of H is $\mathbf{g}$. Then

$$(1\text{-}6) \qquad R(\mathbf{g}|T) = \sum_{i=1}^k g_i \mathscr{E}_i[c(n)|T] + \sum_{i=1}^k \sum_{j=1}^k g_i w_{ij} P_{ij}(T),$$

where $\mathscr{E}_i[c(n)|T]$ is the average cost of observations when the sequential test T is used and H_i is true, and $P_{ij}(T)$ is the probability that the sequential test T will result in the acceptance of H_j when H_i is true. The risk involved in accepting the hypothesis H_j prior to taking any observations will be designated by $R_j(j = 1, 2, \ldots, k)$ and is given by

$$(1\text{-}7) \qquad R_j = \sum_{i=1}^k g_i w_{ij}.$$

We now define k subsets $S_1^*, S_2^*, \ldots, S_k^*$ of G_k as follows. A vector $\mathbf{g}$ of G_k will be said to belong to S_j^* if (a) min $(R_1, R_2, \ldots, R_k) = R_j$ and (b) $R(\mathbf{g}|T) \geq R_j$ for all T. We observe that since the unit vector with 1 in the jth component belongs to S_j^*, the subsets S_j^* are nonempty. We now prove the following theorem.

THEOREM 2. *The sets S_j^* are convex. That is, if $\mathbf{g}_1$ and $\mathbf{g}_2$ belong to S_j^* so does $\mathbf{g} = a\mathbf{g}_1 + (1 - a)\mathbf{g}_2$ for all a, $0 \leq a \leq 1$.*

Proof. Assume the contrary. Then there exists a sequential procedure T such that

$$(1\text{-}8) \qquad R(\mathbf{g}|T) = \sum_{i=1}^k g_i \mathscr{E}_i[c(n)|T] + \sum_{i=1}^k \sum_{j=1}^k g_i w_{ij} P_{ij} < \sum_{i=1}^k g_i w_{ij}.$$

But by definition, if either $\mathbf{g}_1$ or $\mathbf{g}_2$ represents the a priori distribution of the hypotheses H, we must have for all sequential procedures and hence for T,

(1-9) $$R(\mathbf{g}_1|T) = \sum_{i=1}^{k} g_{1i}\mathscr{E}_i[c(n)|T] + \sum_{i=1}^{k}\sum_{j=1}^{k} g_{1i}w_{ij}P_{ij} \geq \sum_{i=1}^{k} g_{1i}w_{ij},$$

and

(1-10) $$R(\mathbf{g}_2|T) = \sum_{i=1}^{k} g_{2i}\mathscr{E}_i[c(n)|T] + \sum_{i=1}^{k}\sum_{j=1}^{k} g_{2i}w_{ij}P_{ij} \geq \sum_{i=1}^{k} g_{2i}w_{ij}.$$

If we now multiply (1-9) by a and (1-10) by $(1 - a)$ and add, we see that the resulting expression contradicts (1-8). This proves the theorem.[3]

It is easily seen that for given hypotheses H the shape of the convex regions S_j^* will depend on the cost function $c(n)$ and the risk matrix W. Thus if the cost of taking a single observation were prohibitive, the region S_j^* in G_k would simply consist of all vectors $\mathbf{g}$ for which min $(R_1, R_2, \ldots, R_k) = R_j$. On the other hand, if the cost of taking observations were negligible and the risk of making an erroneous decision large, the regions S_j^* would shrink to the vertices of the polyhedron G_k. To exhibit the dependence of the regions S_j^* on H, $c(n)$, and W, we shall use the symbol $S_j^*[H,c(n),W]$. We shall also use the symbol $S^*[H,c(n),W]$ to represent the region consisting of all vectors $\mathbf{g}$ in G_k which belong to the complement of $\cup_{j=1}^{k} S_j^*[H,c(n),W]$.

We now define $c_N(n) = c(N + n) - c(N)$ for all $N = 0, 1, 2, \ldots$. Thus $c_N(n)$ represents the cost of taking n observations when N observations have already been taken. It will now be shown that, for random sampling, the problem of characterizing the optimum sequential procedure T^* for a given H, $c(n)$, and W reduces itself to the problem of finding the boundaries of the regions $S_j^*[H,c_N(n),W]$ for all N. The truth of this can be seen from the following considerations.

We are initially given a vector $\mathbf{g}$ in G_k as the a priori distribution of the hypotheses H. Initially we are also given a matrix W and a function $c(n) = c_0(n)$. Now assume we have taken N independent observations ($N = 0,1,2,\ldots,$). These N observations transform the initial state into one in which (a) the vector $\mathbf{g}$ goes into a vector $\mathbf{g}^{(N)}$ in G_k where each component $g_i^{(N)}$ of $\mathbf{g}^{(N)}$ represents the new a priori probability of the hypothesis H_i (that

---

3. A similar proof shows the convexity of the corresponding regions in cases where the number of alternatives is infinite.

is, the a posteriori probability of H_i given the values of the N observations), (b) the risk matrix W remains unchanged, and (c) the cost function $c(n)$ goes into the function $c_N(n)$.

Assume now that the boundaries of the regions $S_j^*[H,c_N(n),W]$ are known for each j and N. Then, if we take the observations in sequence, we can determine at each stage $N(N = 0,1,2, \ldots)$ in which of the $k + 1$ regions the vector $\mathbf{g}^{(N)}$ lies. If $\mathbf{g}^{(N)}$ lies in $S^*[H,c_N(n),W]$, then, by definition of this region, there exists a sequential test T which, if performed from this stage on, would result in a smaller average risk than the risk of stopping at this stage and accepting the hypothesis corresponding to the smallest of the quantities $R_j^{(N)} = \Sigma_{i=1}^k g_i^{(N)} w_{ij} (j = 1,2, \ldots, k)$. But it has been shown in Section 1 that if any sequential test T is worth performing, the optimum test T^* is also worth performing. Now T will coincide with T^* for at least one additional observation. But when that observation is taken $\mathbf{g}^{(N)}$ will become $\mathbf{g}^{(N+1)}$ and $c_N(n)$ will become $c_{N+1}(n)$. Again if $\mathbf{g}^{(N+1)}$ lies in $S^*[H,c_{N+1}(n),W]$, the same argument will show that it is worth taking another observation. However, if $\mathbf{g}^{(N+1)}$ lies in $S_j^*[H,c_{N+1}(n),W]$ for some j, it implies that there exists no sequential test T which is worth performing, and hence the optimum procedure is to stop sampling and accept H_j.

Thus we see that the optimum sequential test T^* is identical with the following procedure. Let $N = 0, 1, 2, \ldots$, represent the number of observations taken in sequence. For each value of N we compute the vector $\mathbf{g}^{(N)}$ representing the a posteriori probabilities of the hypotheses H. As long as $\mathbf{g}^{(N)}$ lies in $S^*[H,c_N(n),W]$ we take another observation. We stop sampling and accept $H_j(j = 1,2, \ldots, k)$ as soon as $\mathbf{g}^{(N)}$ falls in the region $S_j^*[H,c_N(n),W]$.

We have as yet no general method for determining the boundaries of $S_j^*[H,c_N(n),W]$ for arbitrary H, $c_N(n)$, and W. However, in the case of a dichotomy $(k = 2)$ and a linear cost function, such a method has been found and will be discussed here in detail. Some illustrative examples of the optimum sequential test for trichotomies $(k = 3)$ will also be given.

3. Optimum Sequential Procedure for a Dichotomy when the Cost Function is Linear

We are given two alternative hypotheses H_1 and H_2, which, for the sake of simplicity, we assume are characterized respectively by two probability densities $f_1(x)$ and $f_2(x)$ of a random vector X in an R-dimensional Euclidean space. (If X is discrete, $f_1(x)$ and $f_2(x)$ will represent the probability under the respective hypotheses that $X = x$.) We assume that the a priori probability of H_1 is g and that of H_2 is $1 - g$, where g is known. (Later we shall show how to construct the minimax sequential procedure whose average risk is independent of g.) We are also given two nonnegative numbers w_{12} and w_{21}, where $w_{ij}(i \neq j = 1,2)$ represents the loss incurred in accepting H_j when H_i is true. In addition we shall assume that the cost per observation is a constant c which, by a suitable change in scale, can be taken as unity. We also assume that the observations taken during the course of the experiment are independent. We define $P_{1n} = \Pi_{i=1}^{n} f_1(x_i)$ and $P_{2n} = \Pi_{i=1}^{n} f_2(x_i)$, where $x_1, x_2, \ldots ,$ x_n represent the first observation, second observation, and so on.

If we apply the discussion of the previous section to the dichotomy under consideration, we see that the convex regions $S_j^*(j = 1,2)$ reduce themselves to two intervals, I_1 and I_2, where I_1 consists of points g such that $0 \leq g \leq \underline{g}$ and I_2 consists of points g such that $\bar{g} \leq g \leq 1$ where $\underline{g} \leq \bar{g}$. Moreover, in view of the assumption of constant cost of observations, the boundaries $\underline{g}$ and $\bar{g}$ of these two intervals are independent of the number of observations taken but depend only on w_{12} and w_{21} (and, of course, c, which is taken as unity).[4]

The intervals I_1 and I_2 have the following properties. If the a priori probability g for H_1 belongs to I_1, then there exists no sequential procedure which will result in a smaller average risk than the risk $R_1 = w_{12}g$ of accepting H_2 without further experimentation. If the a priori probability g for H_1 belongs to I_2, there exists no sequential procedure which will result in a smaller average risk than the risk $R_2 = w_{21}(1 - g)$ of accepting H_1 without any further experimentation. However, in case $\underline{g} < g < \bar{g}$, then there exists a sequential test T whose average risk will be less than the minimum of R_1 and R_2.

Using the argument of the previous section, we see that if in the initial stage $g \leq \underline{g}$, the optimum procedure is to accept H_2 without taking any observations. Similarly, if in the initial stage $g \geq \bar{g}$, the optimum procedure is to accept H_1 without taking any observations. However, if $\underline{g} < g < \bar{g}$, then there exists a sequential test T worth performing, and this test will coincide with the optimal test T^* for at least the first observation. Now suppose the

---

4. It is assumed here that the intervals are closed; this assumption has not yet been justified. It will be shown later in this section that it is a matter of indifference whether the endpoints are included or not.

first observation x_1 is taken. We then compute the a posteriori probability g_1 that H_1 is true, where g_1 is given by

$$(1\text{-}11) \qquad g_1 = \frac{gf_1(x_1)}{gf_1(x_1) + (1-g)f_2(x_1)}.$$

We are now in the same position as we were initially. If $g_1 \leqq \underline{g}$, the best procedure is to stop sampling and accept H_2. If $g_1 \geqq \bar{g}$, the best procedure is to stop sampling and accept H_1. However, if $\underline{g} < g_1 < \bar{g}$, then there exists a sequential test T' and hence T^* which is worth performing, and we take another observation.

We thus see that the optimum sequential test T^* for a dichotomy must coincide with the following procedure. For any w_{12} and w_{21} we determine $\underline{g}$ and $\bar{g}$ by a method to be described later. Let $n = 0, 1, 2, \ldots$, represent the number of observations taken in sequence. At each stage we compute g_n, where g_n is given by

$$(1\text{-}12) \qquad g_n = \frac{gP_{1n}}{gP_{1n} + (1-g)P_{2n}}.$$

We continue taking observations as long as $\underline{g} < g_n < \bar{g}$. We stop as soon as, for some n, either $g_n \leqq \underline{g}$ or $g_n \geqq \bar{g}$. In the former case we accept H_2, in the latter case we accept H_1.

The optimum test T^* described above is identical with the sequential probability ratio test developed by Wald (1947a). Wald's test is defined as follows. Let $L_n = P_{2n}/P_{1n}$ and let A and B be two positive numbers with $B \leqq 1$ and $A \geqq 1$. Observations are taken in sequence, and sampling continues as long as $B < L_n < A$. Sampling terminates as soon as for some sample size n, either $L_n \geqq A$ or $L_n \leqq B$. In the former case H_2 is accepted, and in the latter case H_1 is accepted. This procedure, however, is the same as T^* provided T^* requires at least one observation and provided we set

$$(1\text{-}13) \qquad B = \frac{1-\bar{g}}{\bar{g}} \frac{g}{1-g} \quad \text{and} \quad A = \frac{1-\underline{g}}{\underline{g}} \frac{g}{1-g}.$$

We now define

$$(1\text{-}14) \qquad z_i = \log \frac{f_2(x_i)}{f_1(x_i)},$$

$$(1\text{-}15) \qquad a = \log A, \quad -b = \log B.$$

In terms of these quantities, the sequential procedure T^* can be defined as follows. Continue sampling as long as $-b < \sum_{i=1}^{n} z_i < a$. Terminate sampling and accept the appropriate hypothesis as soon as for some n, $\sum_{i=1}^{n} z_i \geq a$ or $\sum_{i=1}^{n} z_i \leq -b$.

A Method for Determining $\underline{g}$ and $\bar{g}$

From the above considerations we see that the optimum sequential test for a dichotomy with a constant cost function is completely determined by $\underline{g}$ and $\bar{g}$. We shall therefore turn our attention to the problem of determining these quantities for any given w_{12} and w_{21}. However, before we consider this problem we state the following theorem, which will be proved in Section 6.

THEOREM 3. *Let Σ be any class of sequential tests T for a dichotomy H_1, H_2. Let $R(g|T)$ be the average risk of test T when the a priori probability of H_1 is g. Then $\inf_{T \in \Sigma} R(g|T)$ is a continuous function of g in the open interval $0 < g < 1$.*

Theorem 3 implies that the risk of the sequential test T^*, which is best among the class of tests involving taking at least one observation, is a continuous function of g. Hence it follows that at the boundaries $g = \underline{g}$ as well as $g = \bar{g}$, the risk incurred when the appropriate decision is made with no observations must equal the average risk when observations are taken, and the optimal procedure is used thereafter. Thus if we equate these two risks at $g = \underline{g}$ and also at $g = \bar{g}$, we get two equations from which we can obtain these quantities, provided, of course, we are able to compute the operating characteristics of the sequential probability ratio test. Since the two risks are equal at $g = \underline{g}$ and at $g = \bar{g}$, it follows, as previously noted, that it makes no difference whether or not those points are included in the intervals I_1 and I_2, respectively, where no further observations are taken.

When $g = \underline{g}$, the risk of accepting H_2 with no observations is given by

(1-16) $R_2 = w_{12}\underline{g}$.

On the other hand, if we set $g = \underline{g}$ in (1-15) we obtain a sequential probability ratio test $T_{\underline{g}}^*$ defined by the boundaries

(1-17) $\underline{a} = \log A = 0$ and $-\underline{b} = \log B = \log \dfrac{1 - \bar{g}}{\bar{g}} \dfrac{\underline{g}}{1 - \underline{g}}$.

We are therefore led to the problem of determining the average risk $R(g|T_g^*)$, where T_g^* is defined by (1-17).

It is clear that for this test, the first observation will either terminate the sampling or result in a new sequential test with boundaries $a' = -z_1$ and $-b' = -(b + z_1)$, where z_1 is given by (1-14) with $i = 1$, and $-b < z_1 < 0$. Let $P_i(z)$ be the probability distribution of $z = \log f_2(x)/f_1(x)$ when H_i is true, $(i = 1,2)$. Moreover, for any sequential probability ratio test defined by boundaries $-b'$ and a', let $L(a',b'|H_i) = P(\Sigma_{j=1}^n z_j \leq -b')$ when H_i is true. Then $1 - L(a',b'|H_i) = P(\Sigma_{j=1}^n z_j \geq a')$ when H_i is true. We also define $\mathcal{E}(n|a',b'; H_i)$ as the average number of observations required to reach a decision with this test when H_i is true.

Under the hypothesis H_1, the average risk when T_g^* is used is given by

(1-18)
$$R_1(T_g^*) = 1 + w_{12} \int_0^\infty dP_1(z) + \int_{-b}^0 \mathcal{E}(n|-z,\underline{b} + z; H_1) \, dP_1(z)$$
$$+ w_{12} \int_{-b}^0 [1 - L(-z,\underline{b} + z|H_1)] \, dP_1(z).$$

Under the hypothesis H_2, the average risk with T_g^* is given by

(1-19)
$$R_2(T_g^*) = 1 + w_{21} \int_{-\infty}^{-b} dP_2(z) + \int_{-b}^0 \mathcal{E}(n|-z, \underline{b} + z; H_2) \, dP_2(z)$$
$$+ w_{21} \int_{-b}^0 L(-z, \underline{b} + z, H_2) \, dP_2(z).$$

Hence the total risk using T_g^* when $g = \underline{g}$ is

(1-20)
$$R(g|T_g^*) = \underline{g}R_1(T_g^*) + (1 - \underline{g})R_2(T_g^*).$$

Equating (1-20) to (1-16), we get

(1-21)
$$\underline{g}R_1(T_g^*) + (1 - g)R_2(T_g^*) = w_{12}\underline{g}.$$

By symmetry, we get

(1-22)
$$\bar{g}R_1(T_g^*) + (1 - \bar{g})R_2(T_g^*) = w_{21}(1 - \bar{g}).$$

Equations (1-21) and (1-22) determine $\underline{g}$ and $\bar{g}$ uniquely. In general, it will be very difficult to compute the operating characteristics involved in these equations. However, it is possible to employ the approximations developed by Wald (1947b), which will usually result in values of g and $\bar{g}$ close to the true values, especially if the hypotheses H_1 and H_2 do not differ much from each other.

Exact Values of $\underline{g}$ and $\bar{g}$ for a Special Class of Double Dichotomies

We are given two binomial populations π_1 and π_2 defined by two parameters p_1 and p_2, where $p_i = P(x = 1)$ and $q_i = 1 - p_i = P(x = 0)$ for $i = 1, 2$ and $p_1 < p_2$. Let H_1 stand for the hypothesis that p_1 is associated with π_1 and p_2 is associated with π_2, and let H_2 stand for the hypothesis that p_2 is associated with π_1 and p_1 is associated with π_2. Let w_{12} be the risk of accepting H_2 when H_1 is true, and w_{21} be the risk of accepting H_1 when H_2 is true. We assume that the cost per observation is constant and, without loss of generality, is taken as unity. Let g be the a priori probability that H_1 is true, and hence $1 - g$ is the a priori probability that H_2 is true. The problem is to determine $\underline{g}$ and $\bar{g}$ which define the optimum procedure T^* for testing these hypotheses.

It is easily shown that if $\underline{g}$ and $\bar{g}$ are known, T^* is defined as follows. We set

$$(1\text{-}23) \quad a = \left\{ \frac{\log \left(\dfrac{1 - \bar{g}}{\bar{g}} \dfrac{g}{1 - g} \right)}{-\log \dfrac{p_2 q_1}{q_2 p_1}} \right\}, \quad b = \left\{ \frac{\log \left(\dfrac{1 - \underline{g}}{\underline{g}} \dfrac{g}{1 - g} \right)}{\log \dfrac{p_2 q_1}{q_2 p_1}} \right\},$$

where the symbol $\{y\}$ stands for the smallest integer greater than or equal to y. Let $x_{11}, x_{12}, \ldots$, be a sequence of observations obtained from π_1 and $x_{21}, x_{22}, \ldots$, a sequence of observations obtained from π_2. We continue sampling as long as $-b < \sum_{i=1}^{n}(x_{2i} - x_{1i}) < a$. We terminate sampling as soon as for some sample size n either $\sum_{i=1}^{n}(x_{2i} - x_{1i}) = a$ or $\sum_{i=1}^{n}(x_{2i} - x_{1i}) = -b$. In the former case we accept H_1, in the latter case we accept H_2.

Let $L(a,b|H_i) = P[\sum_{i=1}^{n}(x_{2i} - x_{1i}) = a]$ when H_i is true and let $\mathcal{E}(n|a,b;H_i)$ be the expected number of observations required to reach a decision when H_i is true. Then, without any approximation (see Girshick, 1946), we have

$$(1\text{-}24) \quad L(a,b|H_1) = \frac{u^{a+b} - u^b}{u^{a+b} - 1},$$

$$(1\text{-}25) \quad L(a,b|H_2) = \frac{\left(\dfrac{1}{u} \right)^{a+b} - \left(\dfrac{1}{u} \right)^b}{\left(\dfrac{1}{u} \right)^{a+b} - 1},$$

$$(1\text{-}26) \quad \mathcal{E}(n|a,b;H_1) = \frac{(a + b)L(a,b|H_1) - b}{p_1 q_2 - p_2 q_1},$$

(1-27) $\qquad \mathcal{E}(n|a,b;H_2) = \dfrac{(a + b)L(a,b|H_2) - a}{p_2q_1 - p_1q_2},$

(1-28) $\qquad$ where $\quad u = \dfrac{p_2q_1}{p_1q_2}.$

Now let $g = \underline{g}$. Then $T^*_{\underline{g}}$ is defined by the boundaries $a = \bar{a}$ and $b = 0$, where $\bar{a}$ is obtained from (1-23) with $g = \underline{g}$.

Using the same considerations as those leading to (1-18) and (1-20), we find the average risk of $T^*_{\underline{g}}$ to be

(1-29) $\qquad R(\underline{g}|T^*_{\underline{g}}) = 1 + \underline{g}w_{12}(1 - p_2q_1)$
$\qquad\qquad + \underline{g}p_2q_1\{\mathcal{E}(n|\bar{a} - 1,1;H_1) + w_{12}[1 - L(\bar{a} - 1,1|H_1)]\}$
$\qquad\qquad + (1 - \underline{g})p_1q_2[\mathcal{E}(n|\bar{a} - 1,1,H_2) + w_{21}L(\bar{a} - 1,1|H_2)].$

If we equate (1-29) to $w_{12}\underline{g}$, the risk of accepting H_2 with no observations, and simplify, we get

(1-30) $\qquad 1 + p_1q_2\mathcal{E}(n|\bar{a} - 1,1;H_2) + p_1q_2w_{21}L(\bar{a} - 1,1|H_2)$
$\qquad\qquad + \underline{g}\{p_2q_1[\mathcal{E}(n|\bar{a} - 1,1;H_1) - w_{12}L(\bar{a} - 1,1|H_1)]$
$\qquad\qquad - p_1q_2[\mathcal{E}(n|\bar{a} - 1,1;H_2) + w_{21}L(\bar{a} - 1,1|H_2)]\} = 0.$

If we now let $g = \bar{g}$, then $T^*_{\bar{g}}$ is defined by the boundaries $a = 0$ and $b = \bar{a}$. Hence the average risk of going on with the optimum procedure when $g = \bar{g}$ is given by

(1-31) $\qquad R(\bar{g}|T^*_{\bar{g}}) = 1 + \bar{g}p_1q_2\{\mathcal{E}(n|1,\bar{a} - 1;H_1)$
$\qquad\qquad + w_{12}[1 - L(1,\bar{a} - 1;H_1)]\} + (1 - \bar{g})w_{21}(1 - p_2q_1)$
$\qquad\qquad + (1 - \bar{g})p_2q_1[\mathcal{E}(n|1,\bar{a} - 1;H_2) + w_{21}L(1,\bar{a} - 1|H_2)].$

Equating (1-31) to $w_{21}(1 - \bar{g})$ and simplifying, we get

(1-32) $\qquad 1 - p_2q_1w_{21} + p_2q_1\mathcal{E}(n|1,\bar{a} - 1;H_2) + p_2q_1w_{21}L(1,\bar{a} - 1|H_2)$
$\qquad\qquad + \bar{g}[p_1q_2\mathcal{E}(n|\bar{a} - 1,1;H_1) + w_{12}p_1q_2$
$\qquad\qquad - p_1q_2w_{12}L(1,\bar{a} - 1;H_1) + w_{21}p_2q_1$
$\qquad\qquad - p_2q_1\mathcal{E}(n|1,\bar{a} - 1;H_2) - w_{21}p_2q_1L(1,\bar{a} - 1;H_2)] = 0.$

The following procedure may be used for computing $\underline{g}$ and $\bar{g}$ from Eqs. (1-30) and (1-32). Guess an integer $\bar{a}$ and compute $\underline{g}$ from (1-30) and $\bar{g}$ from (1-32). Substitute these values in the formula

(1-33) $\qquad a = \left\{ \dfrac{\log \dfrac{\bar{g}(1 - \underline{g})}{\underline{g}(1 - \bar{g})}}{\log \dfrac{p_2q_1}{p_1q_2}} \right\}.$

If the resulting quantity has a value equal to the guessed $\bar{a}$, the computed $\underline{g}$ and $\bar{g}$ are correct. If not, repeat the process.

Equations (1-30) and (1-32) can also be used to compute w_{12} and w_{21} for given values of $\underline{g}$ and $\bar{g}$. This can be accomplished as follows. For the given $\underline{g}$ and $\bar{g}$, compute a from (1-33). Set $\bar{a} = a$ in (1-30) and (1-32) and solve for w_{12} and w_{21}.

The average risk of the optimum sequential procedure under consideration can be computed as a function of g as soon as $\bar{g}$ and $\underline{g}$ are determined and is given by

$$(1\text{-}34) \qquad R(g|T^*) = g\mathscr{E}(n|a,b;H_1) + (1 - g)\mathscr{E}(n|a,b;H_2) \\ + gw_{12}[1 - L(a,b|H_1)] + (1 - g)w_{21}L(a,b|H_2),$$

where for the given g, a and b are determined from (1-23). Since a and b are integers, the curve obtained by plotting $R(g|T^*)$ against g will consist of connected line segments.

4. Multivalued Decisions and the Theory of Games

The finite multivalued decision problem can be considered as a game with Nature playing against the statistician. Nature selects a hypothesis $H_i(i = 1,2, \ldots ,k)$, and the statistician selects a test procedure. The payoff function involved in this game is the risk function which consists of the average cost of experimentation plus the average loss incurred in making erroneous decisions under the test procedure selected by the statistician.

From the point of view of the theory of games, the existence of the optimum sequential procedure T^* for multivalued decisions means this: For every mixed strategy (a priori distribution) of Nature, the statistician has a pure strategy which is optimum against it. Thus, if Nature's mixed strategy were known, the statistician's problem would be solved, except for the problem of characterizing T^*. But often Nature's mixed strategy is completely unknown. In that case Wald suggests that the statistician play a minimax strategy: that is, the statistician should select that decision procedure which minimizes the maximum risk. This procedure has the property that if it is consistently employed, the resulting average risk will be independent of Nature's a priori distribution, provided Nature's best strategy is completely mixed.

Examples of Dichotomies

In terms of the multivalued decision problem, say the dichotomy with a constant cost function, the minimax strategy of the statistician consists of the following. For a given H_1, H_2, w_{12}, w_{21}, and cost per observation c (which we take as unity), the statistician computes $\underline{g}$ and $\bar{g}$ and then finds that $g = g^*$ for which the risk function $R(g^*|T_{g^*}^*)$ is a maximum. He then proceeds as if Nature always selects g^* for its a priori distribution. If the hypotheses H_1 and H_2 involve continuous random variables, this procedure will always result in an average risk $R(g|T_{g^*}^*)$ which is independent of g. However, if H_1 and H_2 involve discrete random variables, this is no longer generally true and the statistician may have to resort to mixed strategies.

As an illustration, consider the double dichotomy discussed in the preceding section. Suppose we have obtained $\underline{g}$ and $\bar{g}$ and found that $R(g|T^*)$ given

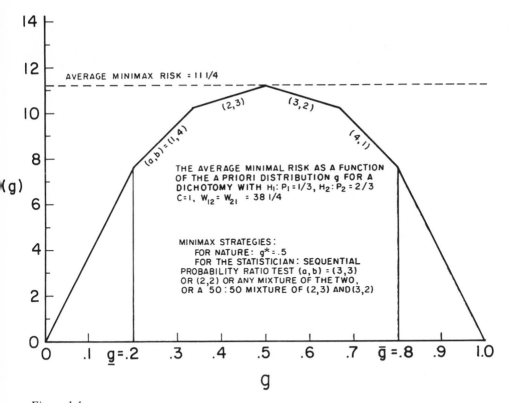

Figure 1.1

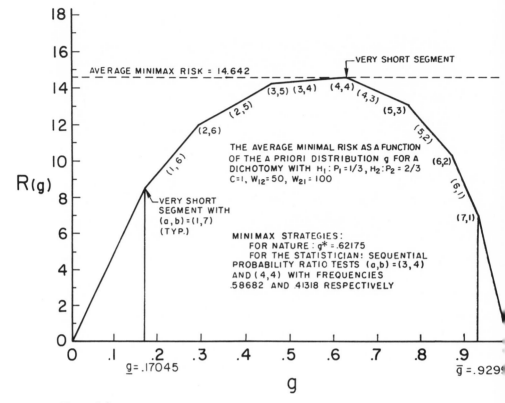

Figure 1.2

in (1-34) has a maximum at $g = g^*$. Let the a and b corresponding to g^* be designated by a^* and b^*. Then, in order that the sequential test $T_{g^*}^*$ (defined by the boundaries a^* and $-b^*$) be independent of g, we must have (see 1-34)

(1-35) $\mathcal{E}(n|a^*,b^*;H_1) + w_{12}[1 - L(a^*,b^*|H_1)]$
$$= \mathcal{E}(n|a^*,b^*;H_2) + w_{21}L(a^*,b^*|H_2).$$

But since a^* and b^* are necessarily integers, this equation will usually not be satisfied. This implies that Nature's strategy g^* must have the property that when we set $g = g^*$ in (1-23) (removing the braces), either a is exactly an integer, or b is exactly an integer, or both are integers. Suppose, for example, that $a = a^*$ is an integer but not $b = b^*$. This means that when $\sum_{i=1}^{n}(x_{2i} - x_{1i}) = a^*$ we have two courses of action to follow: we can either stop and accept H_1 or go on experimenting with the best sequential test defined by the boundaries $a = a^* + 1$ and $b = b^*$. But these two procedures

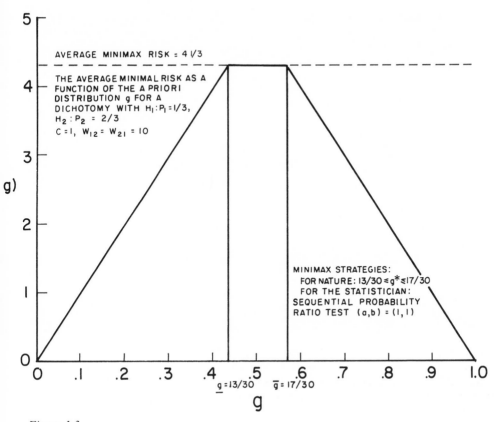

AVERAGE MINIMAX RISK = 4 1/3

THE AVERAGE MINIMAL RISK AS A
FUNCTION OF THE A PRIORI
DISTRIBUTION g FOR A
DICHOTOMY WITH $H_1:P_1 = 1/3$,
$H_2:P_2 = 2/3$
$C = 1$, $W_{12} = W_{21} = 10$

MINIMAX STRATEGIES:
FOR NATURE: $13/30 \leq g^* \leq 17/30$
FOR THE STATISTICIAN:
SEQUENTIAL PROBABILITY
RATIO TEST $(a,b) = (1,1)$

$g = 13/30$ $\bar{g} = 17/30$

g

Figure 1.3

will not always have the same risk for $g \neq g^*$. Thus in order to make the average risk independent of g, we shall have to employ a mixed strategy. That is, we shall have to employ one procedure some specified fraction f of the times and the other procedure $1 - f$ of the times, where $0 < f < 1$.

To illustrate these concepts, we have computed four examples of binomial dichotomies all with the same hypotheses $H_1:p_1 = \frac{1}{3}$, $H_2:p_2 = \frac{2}{3}$, but varying w_{12} and w_{21}. The risk function $R(g|T^*)$ as well as the minimax strategies are given for each of these examples[5] in Figures 1.1 through 1.4.

---

5. The optimum sequential test T^* for any symmetric binomial dichotomy (that is, $p_1 + p_2 = 1$) becomes identical with the test described in Section 5 when the following substitutions are made: write q_1 for $p_1 q_2$, q_2 for $p_2 q_1$, $\Sigma_{i=1}^{N} x_i$ for $\Sigma_{i=1}^{N}(x_{2i} - x_{1i})$, where each x_i takes on the value of 1 with probability p_i and -1 with probability $q_i = 1 - p_i(i = 1,2)$.

It can be shown that for all symmetric binomial dichotomies there always exists a pure minimax strategy for the statistician if $w_{12} = w_{21}$. However, this is no longer true if $w_{12} \neq w_{21}$. This phenomenon is illustrated in the tables below.

Examples of Trichotomies

Example 1. Assume that the random variables x_1, x_2, . . . are independently distributed and all have the same distribution. Each x_n takes on only the values 1, 2, 3 with probabilities specified by one of the following alternative hypotheses.

	Event		
Hypothesis	1	2	3
H_1	0	$\frac{1}{2}$	$\frac{1}{2}$
H_2	$\frac{1}{2}$	0	$\frac{1}{2}$
H_3	$\frac{1}{2}$	$\frac{1}{2}$	0

Let w_{ij} be the loss if H_j is accepted when H_i is true; the values are given by the following table.

	Hypothesis accepted		
State of nature	H_1	H_2	H_3
H_1	0	4	6
H_2	6	0	4
H_3	4	6	0

Note that both of these matrices are invariant under a cyclic permutation of the hypotheses and events. Finally, assume that the cost of each observation is 1.

Let g_i be the a priori probability of H_i. An a priori distribution $\mathbf{g} = (g_1, g_2, g_3)$, with $g_1 + g_2 + g_3 = 1$, may be represented by a point in an equilateral triangle with unit altitudes; the distances from the point to the three sides are the values of g_1, g_2, and g_3. P_i is the point where $g_i = 1(i = 1,2,3)$ (see Figure 1.5).

Let $R(\mathbf{g}|T)$ be the average risk under sequential procedure T when the a priori probabilities are g_1, g_2, g_3. Let T_0 be the best sequential procedure

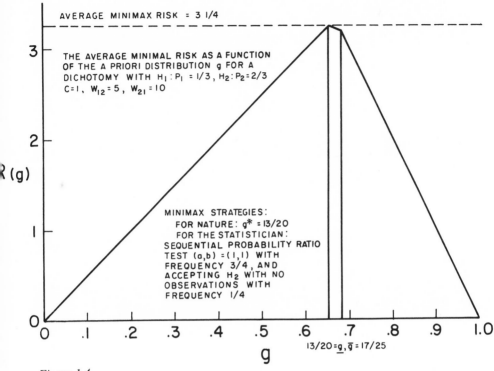

AVERAGE MINIMAX RISK = 3 1/4

THE AVERAGE MINIMAL RISK AS A FUNCTION
OF THE A PRIORI DISTRIBUTION g FOR A
DICHOTOMY WITH $H_1 : P_1 = 1/3$, $H_2 : P_2 = 2/3$
$C = 1$, $W_{12} = 5$, $W_{21} = 10$

MINIMAX STRATEGIES:
  FOR NATURE: $q^* = 13/20$
  FOR THE STATISTICIAN:
  SEQUENTIAL PROBABILITY RATIO
  TEST $(a,b) = (1,1)$ WITH
  FREQUENCY 3/4, AND
  ACCEPTING H_2 WITH NO
  OBSERVATIONS WITH
  FREQUENCY 1/4

$13/20 = \underline{g}, \overline{g} = 17/25$

Figure 1.4

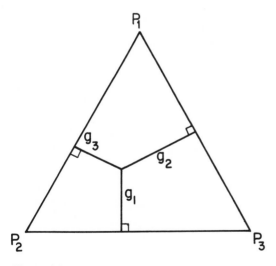

Figure 1.5

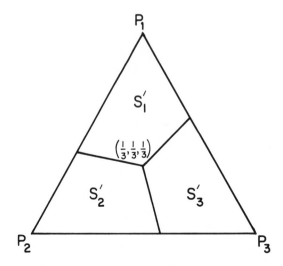

Figure 1.6

where no observations are taken; let S'_i be the region in g-space where H_i is accepted under T_0. Let $L_j(\mathbf{g})$ be the loss in accepting H_j when the a priori distribution is $\mathbf{g}$. Then

$$(1\text{-}36) \qquad L_j(\mathbf{g}) = \sum_{i=1}^{3} w_{ij} g_i.$$

S'_1 is defined by the inequalities $L_1 \leqq L_2$, $L_1 \leqq L_3$, or

$$6g_2 + 4g_3 \leqq 4g_1 + 6g_3, \qquad 6g_2 + 4g_3 \leqq 6g_1 + 4g_2.$$

That is,

$$(1\text{-}37) \qquad g_1 \geqq \max\left(\tfrac{3}{2}g_2 - \tfrac{1}{2}g_3, \tfrac{1}{3}g_2 + \tfrac{2}{3}g_3\right).$$

At P_1, $g_2 = g_3 = 0$, $g_1 = 1$, so that P_1 belongs to S'_1. When $g_3 = 0$, (1-37) becomes $g_1 \geqq \tfrac{3}{2}g_2$, while $g_1 + g_2 = 1$, so that $g_1 \geqq \tfrac{3}{5}$; when $g_2 = 0$, $g_1 \geqq \tfrac{2}{3}g_3$, $g_1 + g_3 = 1$, so that $g_1 \geqq \tfrac{2}{5}$. Also, the two lower bounding lines for g_1 are equal when $\tfrac{3}{2}g_2 - \tfrac{1}{2}g_3 = \tfrac{1}{3}g_2 + \tfrac{2}{3}g_3 = g_1$, or $g_1 = g_2 = g_3 = \tfrac{1}{3}$. S'_1 contains all points above the boundary defined by the polygon with vertices $(\tfrac{3}{5},\tfrac{2}{5},0)$, $(\tfrac{1}{3},\tfrac{1}{3},\tfrac{1}{3})$, and $(\tfrac{2}{5},0,\tfrac{3}{5})$. S'_2 and S'_3 can be obtained by successive cyclic permutations of these coordinates (Figure 1.6).

Let $T^*(\mathbf{g})$ be the optimum sequential procedure for a given a priori distribution. Let g_{ij} be the a posteriori probability of H_i given that $x_1 = j$;

$$(1\text{-}38) \qquad g_{ij} = \frac{g_i p_{ij}}{\sum\limits_{k=1}^{3} g_k p_{kj}},$$

where p_{ij} is the probability that $x_1 = j$ under H_i. Let $T_1^*(\mathbf{g})$ be the sequential procedure defined as taking one observation and then using procedure $T^*(g_{1j},g_{2j},g_{3j})$ when $x_1 = j$. $T_1^*(\mathbf{g})$ is the best sequential procedure which involves taking at least one observation. In the present case, $p_{jj} = 0$, so that $g_{jj} = 0$ by (1-38); therefore, $T^*(g_{1j},g_{2j},g_{3j})$ is the optimum sequential test for a dichotomy.[6]

Let S_i^* be the region in g-space for which H_i is accepted without any observation under $T^*(\mathbf{g})$. As has been shown, the regions S_i^* are essentially all that is needed to determine all the tests $T^*(\mathbf{g})$. Further, the regions S_i^* are convex sets whose boundaries are characterized by the relations

$$(1\text{-}39) \qquad R[\mathbf{g}|T_1(\mathbf{g})] = L_i(\mathbf{g}), \qquad L_i(\mathbf{g}) = \min_j L_j(\mathbf{g}),$$

so that

$$(1\text{-}40) \qquad S_i^* \subset S_i'.$$

It is first necessary to find the optimum tests for each of the dichotomies formed by taking pairs from the trichotomy H_1, H_2, H_3. Consider the dichotomy H_1, H_2. Then $g_1 + g_2 = 1$. Suppose g_1 is such that it pays to take at least one observation. From (1-38), since $p_{i3} = \frac{1}{2}(i = 1,2)$,

$$(1\text{-}41) \qquad g_{i3} = \frac{g_i}{g_1 + g_2} = g_i.$$

Hence, if $x_1 = 3$, the a posteriori probabilities are unchanged, and, as shown previously, the optimum test calls for taking another observation. On the other hand, $p_{11} = 0$, so that $g_{21} = 1$. Therefore, if $x_1 = 1$, the process should be terminated and H_2 accepted. Similarly, if $x_1 = 2$, the process should be terminated and H_1 accepted. It follows that if g_1 is such that the best sequential procedure calls for taking at least one observation, then the best procedure is to sample indefinitely until $x_n = 1$ or 2; in the former case, accept H_2, in the latter, H_1. The probability of accepting the wrong hypoth-

---

6. It is to be pointed out that, for any trichotomy, the intersection of the regions S_i^* with the sides of the triangle may be determined by computing $\underline{g}$, $\bar{g}$ (see Section 3) for the appropriate dichotomy.

esis is zero under either hypothesis; the risk is then the expected number of observations, which is 2 under either hypothesis.

The boundaries $\underline{g}_{12}$ and $\bar{g}_{12}$ of the interval of g_1's in which it pays to go on are then determined by the equation

(1-42)
$$w_{12}\underline{g}_{12} = 2, \text{ or } \underline{g}_{12} = \tfrac{1}{2},$$
$$w_{21}(1 - \bar{g}_{12}) = 2, \text{ or } \bar{g}_{12} = \tfrac{2}{3}.$$

Returning to the specification of $T_1^*(\mathbf{g})$, we note that if $x_1 = 3$,

$$g_{i3} = \frac{g_i p_{i3}}{\displaystyle\sum_{k=1}^{3} g_k p_{k3}}.$$

As $p_{33} = 0$, $p_{i3} = \tfrac{1}{2}$ for $i = 1, 2$,

$$g_{i2} = \frac{g_i}{g_1 + g_2} \; (i = 1, 2).$$

Therefore, $T_1^*(\mathbf{g})$ can be described as follows. If $x_1 = 3$, H_3 is rejected entirely; if $g_1/(g_1 + g_2) \le \tfrac{1}{2}$, stop and accept H_2; if $g_1/(g_1 + g_2) \ge \tfrac{2}{3}$, stop and accept H_1; if $\tfrac{1}{2} < g_1/(g_1 + g_2) < \tfrac{2}{3}$, continue sampling until $x_n = 1$ or 2, at which point stop and accept H_2 or H_1, respectively. The three conditions on $g_1/(g_1 + g_2)$ can be written in the simpler form,

(1-43) $g_1 \le g_2, \qquad g_1 \ge 2g_2, \qquad g_2 < g_1 < 2g_2,$

respectively. The cases where $x_1 = 1$ or 2 can be obtained from the preceding case by cyclic permutation of the numbers 1, 2, 3.

Let $R_j^*(\mathbf{g})$ be the conditional expected risk associated with $T_1^*(\mathbf{g})$ when the a priori probability distribution is $\mathbf{g}$, given that $x_1 = j$; and let p_j be the a priori probability that $x_1 = j$. Then

(1-44) $R[\mathbf{g}|T_1^*(\mathbf{g})] = \displaystyle\sum_{j=1}^{3} p_j R_j^*(\mathbf{g}),$

(1-45) $p_j = \displaystyle\sum_{i=1}^{3} p_{ij} g_i,$

(1-46) $R_3^*(\mathbf{g}) = \begin{cases} 1 + w_{12}\dfrac{g_1}{g_1 + g_2} = 1 + \dfrac{4g_1}{g_1 + g_2} & \text{if } g_1 \le g_2, \\[2mm] 3 & \text{if } g_2 \le g_1 \le 2g_2, \\[2mm] 1 + w_{21}\left(1 - \dfrac{g_1}{g_1 + g_2}\right) = 1 + \dfrac{6g_2}{g_1 + g_2} & \text{if } g_1 \ge 2g_2. \end{cases}$

$R_1^*(\mathbf{g})$ and $R_2^*(\mathbf{g})$ can be obtained from (1-46) by cyclic permutation of the subscripts.

The region S_1^* can now be determined by the relations (1-39)–(1-40) and (1-44)–(1-46). First note that when $g_3 = 0$, the problem reduces to the dichotomy between H_1 and H_2 already discussed, so that the interval from $g_1 = 1$ to $g_1 = \frac{2}{3}$ on the line $g_3 = 0$ belongs to S_1^*. Hence the point $(\frac{2}{3},\frac{1}{3},0)$ lies on the boundary of S_1^*. This point satisfies the conditions

(1-47) $\qquad g_2 \leqq g_1 \leqq 2g_2, \qquad g_2 \geqq 2g_3, \qquad g_3 \leqq g_1.$

Consider the intersection, if any, of the boundary of S_1^* with the region R_1 defined by (1-47). Using (1-44)–(1-45), (1-39),

(1-48) $\qquad \dfrac{g_1 + g_2}{2} R_3^*(\mathbf{g}) + \dfrac{g_2 + g_3}{2} R_1^*(\mathbf{g}) + \dfrac{g_1 + g_3}{2} R_2^*(\mathbf{g}) = L_1(\mathbf{g}).$

From (1-47)–(1-48), (1-46), and (1-36),

$$3\frac{g_1 + g_2}{2} + \frac{g_2 + g_3}{2}\left(1 + \frac{6g_3}{g_2 + g_3}\right)$$
$$+ \frac{g_1 + g_3}{2}\left(1 + \frac{4g_3}{g_1 + g_3}\right) = 6g_2 + 4g_3,$$

or

(1-49) $\qquad g_2 = \frac{1}{3}.$

The intersection of (1-49) with the line $g_2 = 2g_3$ occurs at the point $(\frac{1}{2},\frac{1}{3},\frac{1}{6})$, which satisfies the conditions (1-47) and so lies on the boundary of the region R_1. As R_1 is convex, it follows that the boundary of S_1^* actually does intersect R_1 and there coincides with the line segment joining $(\frac{2}{3},\frac{1}{3},0)$ and $(\frac{1}{2},\frac{1}{3},\frac{1}{6})$. The latter point satisfies also the conditions

(1-50) $\qquad g_2 \leqq g_1 \leqq 2g_2, \qquad g_3 \leqq g_2 \leqq 2g_3, \qquad g_3 \leqq g_1.$

Let R_2 be the region defined by (1-50). Then we can find as before the intersection of the boundary of S_1^* with R_2; the boundary hits the line $g_2 = g_3$ at the point $(\frac{3}{7},\frac{2}{7},\frac{2}{7})$, which point lies in R_2. Hence the boundary of S_1^* actually does intersect R_2 and there coincides with the segment joining $(\frac{1}{2},\frac{1}{3},\frac{1}{6})$ to $(\frac{3}{7},\frac{2}{7},\frac{2}{7})$. If we continue this method, it can be shown that S_1^* is bounded by the polygon with vertices $(\frac{2}{3},\frac{1}{3},0)$, $(\frac{1}{2},\frac{1}{3},\frac{1}{6})$, $(\frac{3}{7},\frac{2}{7},\frac{2}{7})$, $(\frac{2}{5},\frac{1}{5},\frac{2}{5})$, $(\frac{1}{2},0,\frac{1}{2})$, and $(1,0,0)$. It is easily verified that S_1^* is actually a subset of S_1', as demanded by (1-40). The vertices of the polygons bounding S_2^* and S_3^* can be obtained by cyclic permutation of the coordinates.

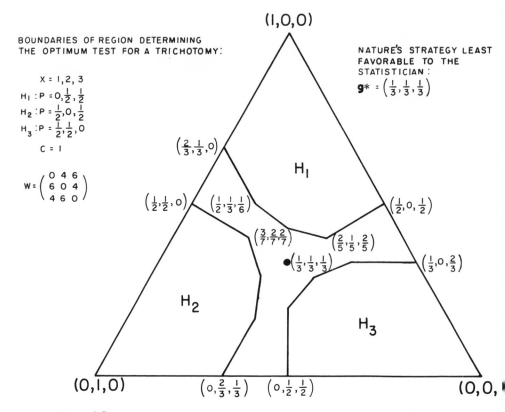

Figure 1.7

For any given **g**, the regions S_1^*, S_2^*, and S_3^* completely define the optimal procedure. It remains to find the minimax procedure.

As shown by (1-46), the maximum conditional expected risk given that $x_1 = 1$ is 3, and this occurs when $g_3 \leq g_2 \leq 2g_3$. Similarly, the maximum conditional expected risks given that $x_1 = 2$ and 3, respectively, are both equal to 3, and they occur when $g_1 \leq g_3 \leq 2g_1$, $g_2 \leq g_1 \leq 2g_2$, respectively. Any **g*** satisfying these three conditions will be a least favorable a priori distribution; clearly, the only set of values is $g_1 = g_2 = g_3 = \frac{1}{3}$. If $x_1 = 1$, the corresponding a posteriori distribution is $(0,\frac{1}{2},\frac{1}{2})$. This is on the boundary of S_3^*, so the optimum procedure is to stop after one observation and choose H_3. In general, then, the minimax procedure is to take one observation, stop, and accept H_3 if $x_1 = 1$, H_1 if $x_1 = 2$, and H_2 if $x_1 = 3$. The risk associated with this test is 3, of which the cost of observation is 1, and the

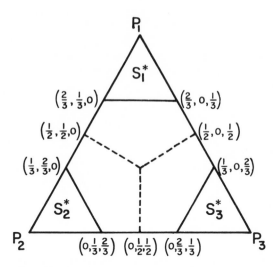

Figure 1.8

expected loss due to incorrect decision is 2, independent of the true a priori distribution.

It may be of interest to note that the minimax test is not unique, the lack of uniqueness corresponding exactly to the inclusion or exclusion of the boundaries of S_1^*, S_2^*, and S_3^* in those sets. If we exclude the boundaries, then, when $x_1 = 1$, we continue. As long as $x_n = 1$, the a posteriori probabilities remain at $(0,\frac{1}{2},\frac{1}{2})$; when $x_n = 2$ (3), the a posteriori probability of $H_3(H_2)$ becomes 1. Therefore, a second minimax test is to stop the first time $x_n \neq x_{n-1}$, and then accept that hypothesis whose subscript equals neither x_n nor x_{n-1}. The maximum risk is again 3; all of this is represented by the expected number of observations which is the same for all a priori distributions (see Figure 1.7).

Example 2. The boundaries of the regions S_i^* might also be straight lines, as shown by the following example (Figure 1.8). Let $x_1, x_2, \ldots$, be independently distributed with the same distribution, and x_n takes on the values 1, 2, or 3. Let H_i be the hypothesis that $x_n = i$ with probability 1 ($i = 1,2,3$), and let $w_{ij} = 3$ for $i \neq j$, $w_{ii} = 0$. Assume that the cost of each observation is 1. Then the best test involving at least one observation is clearly to take exactly one observation and accept H_i if $x_1 = i$. The expected loss due to incorrect decision is 0, so that the risk of this test is 1. Hence the boundary of S_1^* is characterized by the relation $w_{21}g_2 + w_{31}g_3 =$

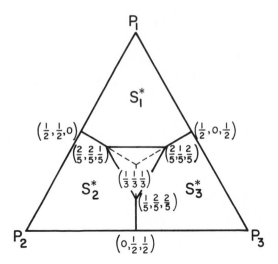

Figure 1.9

$3(g_2 + g_3) = 1$, or $g_1 = \frac{2}{3}$. Similarly, S_2^*, S_3^* are defined by the inequalities $g_2 \geq \frac{2}{3}, g_3 \geq \frac{2}{3}$, respectively.

If no observations are taken, the region S_1' in which H_1 is accepted is characterized by $w_{21}g_2 + w_{31}g_3 \leq \min(w_{12}g_1 + w_{32}g_3, w_{13}g_1 + w_{23}g_2)$ or $1 - g_1 \leq \min(g_1 + g_3, g_1 + g_2)$, $2g_1 \geq \max(1 - g_2, 1 - g_3)$.

The boundary is the polygonal line with vertices $(\frac{1}{2},\frac{1}{2},0)$, $(\frac{1}{3},\frac{1}{3},\frac{1}{3})$, and $(\frac{1}{2},0,\frac{1}{2})$. The boundaries of S_2' and S_3' are found similarly. The regions S_1^*, S_2^*, S_3^* clearly lie inside S_1', S_2', S_3', respectively.

Example 3. In both previous examples, inner boundaries of the regions S_i^* were found by equating the risk of accepting H_i if no observations are taken with the risk under the best procedure calling for taking at least one observation. The regions so found were in both cases subsets of S_i'. However, this relation need not hold in general, as shown by the following example (Figure 1.9).

Let all conditions be the same as in Example 2 except that $w_{ij} = \frac{2}{3}$ for $i \neq j$. Then the risk of accepting H_1 without observations is equal to the risk of the best test taking at least one observation when $g_1 = \frac{2}{3}$. But the region $g_1 \geq \frac{2}{3}$ is not a subset of S_1' (which is the same here as in Example 2). S_1^* is the intersection of S_1' and the region $g_1 \geq \frac{2}{3}$. S_1^* is bound from below by the polygonal line with vertices $(\frac{1}{2},\frac{1}{2},0)$, $(\frac{2}{5},\frac{2}{5},\frac{1}{5})$, $(\frac{2}{5},\frac{1}{5},\frac{2}{5})$, and $(\frac{1}{2},0,\frac{1}{2})$.

5. Another Optimum Property of the Sequential Probability Ratio Test

In Section 3 it was shown that the sequential probability ratio test is optimum in the sense that for a given a priori distribution g, it minimizes the average risk. We shall now prove a further result.

THEOREM 4. *For fixed probabilities of making erroneous decisions, the sequential probability ratio test minimizes the average number of observations when H_1 is true as well as when H_2 is true.*

Proof. For a fixed $A \geq 1$ and $B \leq 1$, let α be the probability of accepting H_2 when H_1 is true if the sequential probability ratio test T^* with these boundaries is used. Similarly, let β be the probability of accepting H_1 when H_2 is true. The quantities α and β are uniquely determined by A and B.

Choose any g such that $0 < g < 1$, solve for $\underline{g}$ and $\bar{g}$ from (1-13) and then compute $w_{12} = w_{12}(\underline{g}, \bar{g})$ and $w_{21} = w_{21}(\underline{g}, \bar{g})$ from (1-21) and (1-22). The quantity $\underline{b}$ entering in (1-21) and (1-22) is given by $\log(A/B)$.

The three quantities $w_{12}(\underline{g}, \bar{g})$, $w_{21}(\underline{g}, \bar{g})$ and g have the property that if the a priori distribution is g and if the risk of accepting H_2 when H_1 is true is $w_{12}(\underline{g}, \bar{g})$ and the risk of accepting H_1 when H_2 is true is $w_{21}(\underline{g}, \bar{g})$, then the sequential test T^* has minimum average risk. The average risk under T^* is given by

$$(1\text{-}51) \qquad R(g|T^*) = g\mathcal{E}(n|T^*;H_1) + (1-g)\mathcal{E}(n|T^*;H_2)$$
$$+ gw_{12}(\underline{g},\bar{g})\alpha + (1-g)w_{21}(\underline{g},\bar{g})\beta.$$

Now let T be any other test procedure which results in probabilities $\alpha' \leq \alpha$ and $\beta' \leq \beta$ of making erroneous decisions. Then for the same triplet g, $w_{12}(\underline{g}, \bar{g})$, and $w_{21}(\underline{g}, \bar{g})$ the average risk under T is given by

$$(1\text{-}52) \qquad R(g|T) = g\mathcal{E}(n|T;H_1) + (1-g)\mathcal{E}(n|T;H_2)$$
$$+ gw_{12}(\underline{g},\bar{g})\alpha' + (1-g)w_{21}(\underline{g},\bar{g})\beta'.$$

Now since $R(g|T^*) \leq R(g|T)$, we must have

$$(1\text{-}53) \qquad g\mathcal{E}(n|T^*;H_1) + (1-g)\mathcal{E}(n|T^*;H_2)$$
$$\leq g\mathcal{E}(n|T;H_1) + (1-g)\mathcal{E}(n|T;H_2).$$

But the inequality (1-53) must hold for all values of g, $0 < g < 1$. Hence from continuity considerations we must have

$$(1\text{-}54) \qquad \mathcal{E}(n|T^*;H_1) \leq \mathcal{E}(n|T;H_1)$$

and

(1-55) $\mathcal{E}(n|T^*;H_2) \leq \mathcal{E}(n|T;H_2).$

This proves the theorem.

6. Continuity of the Risk Function of the Optimum Test

THEOREM 3. *Let Σ be any class of sequential tests of a multiple decision involving a finite number of alternative hypotheses, and let $R(\mathbf{g}|T)$ be the risk of test T when the a priori distribution of the hypotheses is $\mathbf{g}$. Then $\inf_{T \in \Sigma} R(\mathbf{g}|T)$ is a continuous function of $\mathbf{g}$ in the region for which $g_i > 0$ for all i, provided that for some T_0 in Σ, $R(\mathbf{g}|T_0)$ is everywhere finite.*[7]

Proof. For each hypothesis H_i and each test procedure T there is a non-negative risk which is the sum of the expected cost of observations and the expected loss due to failure to make the best decision; call this risk $A_i(T)$. Then

(1-56) $R(\mathbf{g}|T) = \sum_i g_i A_i(T).$

Let $\mathbf{g}_0$ be any a priori distribution for which $g_{0i} > 0$ for all i, and choose $0 < \delta_0 < \min_i g_{0i}$. Let G be the region in $\mathbf{g}$-space for which $\Sigma_i |g_i - g_{0i}| \leq \delta_0$; then $g_i > 0$ for all i and all $\mathbf{g}$ in the compact set G. Let T_0 be the test referred to in the hypothesis.

(1-57) $\sup_{\mathbf{g} \in G} \inf_{T \in \Sigma} R(\mathbf{g}|T) \leq \sup_{\mathbf{g} \in G} R(\mathbf{g}|T_0) = K < +\infty,$

the last inequality following since $R(\mathbf{g}|T_0)$ is linear and hence continuous on the compact set G.

Let Σ' be the subclass of Σ for which $\inf_{\mathbf{g} \in G} R(\mathbf{g}|T) \leq K + 1$. As Σ' is a subset of Σ, $\inf_{T \in \Sigma'} R(\mathbf{g}|T) \geq \inf_{T \in \Sigma} R(\mathbf{g}|T)$. Suppose for some $\mathbf{g}'$ in G,

$$\inf_{T \in \Sigma'} R(\mathbf{g}'|T) > \inf_{T \in \Sigma} R(\mathbf{g}'|T).$$

Then

(1-58) $\inf_{T \in \Sigma} R(\mathbf{g}'|T) = \inf_{T \in \Sigma - \Sigma'} R(\mathbf{g}'|T).$

---

7. The essential features of the proof of this theorem are due to George Brown.

But if T belongs to $\Sigma - \Sigma'$,

(1-59) $R(g'|T) \geq \inf_{g \in G} R(g'|T) > K + 1.$

From (1-59) and (1-57),

$$\inf_{T \in \Sigma - \Sigma'} R(g'|T) \geq K + 1 > \sup_{g \in G} \inf_{T \in \Sigma} R(g|T) \geq \inf_{T \in \Sigma} R(g'|T),$$

contradicting (1-58). Hence,

(1-60) $\inf_{T \in \Sigma'} R(g|T) = \inf_{T \in \Sigma} R(g|T)$

everywhere in G, and it suffices to consider only tests in Σ'.

$R(g|T)$ assumes its minimum in G. Hence,

$$\inf_{g \in G} R(g|T) = R(g''|T) = \sum_i g_i'' A_i(T).$$

As $g_i'' > 0$, $A_i(T) \geq 0$ for all i,

(1-61) $g_i'' A_i(T) \leq R(g''|T) = \inf_{g \in G} R(g|T) \leq K + 1,$

since T belongs to Σ'. Although g_i'', may vary with T, it must have a positive lower bound because of the compactness of G and the fact that $g_i > 0$ for all g in G. As i takes on only a finite number of values, g_i'' has a positive uniform lower bound. Then (1-61) implies that $A_i(T)$ is bounded from above uniformly in i and T. Let C be this upper bound.

Choose any $\delta < \delta_0$, and any g such that $\Sigma_i |g_i - g_{0i}| < \delta$.

$$|R(g|T) - R(g_0|T)| < C\delta,$$
$$R(g|T) - R(g_0|T) < C\delta.$$
$$\inf_{T \in \Sigma'} R(g|T) \leq \inf_{T \in \Sigma'} R(g_0|T) + C\delta.$$

Similarly, $\inf_{T \in \Sigma'} R(g_0|T) \leq \inf_{T \in \Sigma'} R(g|T) + C\delta$, so that $\inf_{T \in \Sigma'} R(g|T)$, and therefore, by (1-60), $\inf_{T \in \Sigma} R(g|T)$ is continuous at g_0.

The continuity of $\inf_{T \in \Sigma} R(g|T)$ does not extend in general to the boundary of g-space where $g_i = 0$ for some i, as is shown by the following example.

Let $x_1, x_2, \ldots$, be independently distributed variates with a common distribution, each x_n taking on only the values 1, 2, 3. Let H_1 be the hypothesis $P(x_n = 1) = p_1$, $P(x_n = 2) = 1 - p_1$, $P(x_n = 3) = 0$; H_2 the hypothesis $P(x_n = 1) = p_2$, $P(x_n = 2) = 1 - p_2$, $P(x_n = 3) = 0$; H_3 the hypothesis $P(x_n = 1) = P(x_n = 2) = 0$, $P(x_n = 3) = 1$. Let the cost of each observation be 1.

Let T_0 be the minimax test of the dichotomy H_1, H_2. Let $c = \Sigma_{n=1}^{\infty} 1/n^2$. Let q_n be defined inductively, as follows:

$$q_1 = \frac{1}{c}, \qquad q_n = \frac{1}{cn^2 \prod_{i=1}^{n-1} (1 - q_i)}.$$

Then test T_1 is defined as follows. If $x_n = 1$ or 2, and the process has not stopped before n, form the sequence $y_1, \ldots, y_m$ consisting of all those elements of the sequence $x_1, \ldots, x_n$ for which $x_k \neq 3$. Then either go on or stop and make a decision in accordance with T_0 applied to the sequence $y_1, \ldots, y_m$. If $x_n = 3$, stop and accept H_3 with probability q_n, go on with probability $1 - q_n$.

T_0 has a certain risk R for all $\mathbf{g}$ such that $g_1 + g_2 = 1$. Choose $N > R$. Let T_2 be the test consisting of taking N observations and then making the best decision.

Clearly, under H_1 or H_2, x_n is never equal to 3, so that $y_1, \ldots, y_m$ is the same as $x_1, \ldots, x_n$, and T_1 coincides with T_0. The expected loss for T_1 under H_1 or H_2 is thus R. Under H_3, $x_n = 3$ for all n; hence, the probability of stopping at m is $1/cm^2$, so that the probability of stopping is 1 but the expected cost and therefore the expected risk are infinite. Therefore, if $g_3 = 0$, $R(\mathbf{g}|T_1) = R$; but if $g_3 > 0$, $R(\mathbf{g}|T_1) = +\infty$. On the other hand, $R < N \leq R(\mathbf{g}|T_2) < +\infty$, everywhere.

If Σ contains the two tests T_1 and T_2, $\inf_{T \in \Sigma} R(\mathbf{g}|T) = R(\mathbf{g}|T_1) = R$ for $g_3 = 0$, but $\inf_{T \in \Sigma} R(\mathbf{g}|T) = R(\mathbf{g}|T_2) \geq N > R$ for $g_3 \neq 0$. Hence, $\inf_{T \in \Sigma} R(\mathbf{g}|T)$ is not continuous at any point for which $g_3 = 0$.

References

Arrow, K. J., T. E. Harris, and J. Marschak. 1951. "Optimal Inventory Policy," *Econometrica,* 19:250–272 (to appear in a later volume of these Collected Papers).

Bellman, R. E. 1957. *Dynamic Programming.* Princeton, N.J.: Princeton University Press.

Girshick, M.A. 1946. "Contributions to the Theory of Sequential Analysis. I," *Annals of Mathematical Statistics,* 5:123–143.

Statistical Research Group. 1945. *Sequential Analysis of Statistical Data.* New York: Columbia University Press.

Wald, A. 1947a. *Sequential Analysis.* New York: Wiley.

Wald, A. 1947b. "Foundations of a General Theory of Sequential Decision Functions," *Econometrica,* 15:275–312.

Wald, A., and J. Wolfowitz. 1948. "Optimum Character of the Sequential Probability Ratio Test," *Annals of Mathematical Statistics,* 19:326–339.

2   Admissible Points of Convex Sets

With strong departments of statistics at both Stanford and the University of California at Berkeley beginning about 1947, there was a great deal of interaction in the form of joint seminars. The concept of admissibility of statistical procedures was one of the chief topics; clearly there was some relation between admissible procedures and those that were optimal Bayesian for some prior distribution. For convex sets, the relation was essentially mathematically identical to that between optimal resource allocations and supporting price systems. However, the duality was not perfect. A few informal discussions among Edward Barankin and David Blackwell, of Berkeley, and myself led to an improved characterization.

A point s of a closed convex subset S of k-space is *admissible* if there is no $t \in S$ with $t_i \leq s_i$ for all $i = 1, \ldots, k$, $t \neq s$. An example is given in which the set A of admissible points is not closed. Let P be the set of vectors $p = (p_1, \ldots, p_k)$ with $p_i > 0$, $\Sigma_1^k p_i = 1$, let $B(p)$ be the set of $s \in S$ with $(p,s) = \min_{t \in S} (p,t)$, let $B = \cup B(p)$, so that B consists of exactly those points of S at which there is a supporting hyperplane whose normal has positive components, and let $\bar{B}$ be the closure of B.

This chapter was written with E. W. Barankin and D. Blackwell. Reprinted from *Contributions to the Theory of Games,* Vol. 2, ed. H. W. Kuhn and A. W. Tucker. Copyright 1953, © renewed 1981 by Princeton University Press. Excerpt, pp. 87–91, reprinted by permission of Princeton University Press.

THEOREM 1. $B \subset A \subset \bar{B}$. *If S is determined by a finite set, there is a finite set* $\mathbf{p}_1, \ldots, \mathbf{p}_N$, $\mathbf{p}_j \in P$, *such that* $B = \cup_{j=1}^N B(\mathbf{p}_j)$, *so that, since* $B(\mathbf{p})$ *is closed for fixed* $\mathbf{p}$, $B = A = \bar{B}$.

That $B \subset A \subset \bar{B}$ when S is determined by a finite set was noted, in the language of convex cones, by Gale (1951).

A consequence of Theorem 1 is that, in a two-person zero-sum game in which each player has only a finite number of pure strategies, every pure strategy which yields the value of the game against every minimax strategy of the opponent enters with positive probability into some minimax strategy, a result due to Bohnenblust, Karlin, and Shapley (1950).

Proof of Theorem 1. Suppose first that S is bounded. If $\mathbf{s} \in S$, $\mathbf{s} \notin A$, there is a $\mathbf{t} \in S$ with $t_i \leq s_i$ for all i and $\mathbf{t} \neq \mathbf{s}$. Then $(\mathbf{p},\mathbf{t}) < (\mathbf{p},\mathbf{s})$ for every $\mathbf{p} \in P$, so that $\mathbf{s} \notin B$. Thus $B \subset A$.

To show that $A \subset \bar{B}$, let $\mathbf{a} \in A$. We may achieve $\mathbf{a} = (0,0, \ldots, 0)$ by translating the coordinate system. For any ϵ, $0 < \epsilon \leq \dfrac{1}{k}$, let $P(\epsilon)$ be the set of $\mathbf{p} \in P$ with $p_i \geq \epsilon$ for $i = 1, \ldots, k$. For any two closed bounded convex sets R, S of k-space, there are vectors $\mathbf{r}^* \in R$, $\mathbf{s}^* \in S$ with $(\mathbf{r}^*,\mathbf{s}) \geq (\mathbf{r}^*,\mathbf{s}^*) \geq (\mathbf{r},\mathbf{s}^*)$ for all $\mathbf{r} \in R$, $\mathbf{s} \in S$; this fact may be proved as follows. Let $\mathbf{r}_n \in R$, $\mathbf{s}_n \in S$ be sequences dense in R, S respectively. The finite game whose $N \times N$ matrix is $(\mathbf{r}_i,\mathbf{s}_j)$, $1 \leq i, j \leq N$, has a value $V(N)$ and good strategies $(\lambda_{N1}, \ldots, \lambda_{NN})$, $(\mu_{N1}, \ldots, \mu_{NN})$; thus if $\mathbf{r}_N^* = \Sigma_{i=1}^N \lambda_{Ni}\mathbf{r}_i$, $\mathbf{s}_N^* = \Sigma_{j=1}^N \mu_{Nj}\mathbf{s}_j$, we have $(\mathbf{r}_N^*,\mathbf{s}_j) \geq V(N) \geq (\mathbf{r}_i,\mathbf{s}_N^*)$ for $1 \leq i, j \leq N$. Letting $N \to \infty$ through a subsequence for which $\mathbf{r}_N^*$, $\mathbf{s}_N^*$ converge, say to $\mathbf{r}^*$, $\mathbf{s}^*$, yields $(\mathbf{r}^*,\mathbf{s}_j) \geq (\mathbf{r}_i,\mathbf{s}^*)$ for all i, j, and $\mathbf{r}^*$, $\mathbf{s}^*$ have the required property. We apply this result to $P(\epsilon)$, S, obtaining $\mathbf{p}(\epsilon) \in P(\epsilon)$, $\mathbf{s}(\epsilon) \in S$ such that $(\mathbf{p}(\epsilon),\mathbf{s}) \geq (\mathbf{p}(\epsilon),\mathbf{s}(\epsilon)) \geq (\mathbf{p},\mathbf{s}(\epsilon))$ for all $\mathbf{p} \in P(\epsilon)$, $\mathbf{s} \in S$, and note that $(\mathbf{p}(\epsilon),\mathbf{s}(\epsilon)) \leq (\mathbf{p}(\epsilon),\mathbf{a}) = 0$. Choose a sequence $\epsilon_n \to 0$ for which $\mathbf{s}(\epsilon_n)$ converges, say to $\mathbf{s}^* \in S$. For all $\mathbf{p} \in P$, $(\mathbf{p},\mathbf{s}(\epsilon_n)) \leq 0$ for sufficiently large n, so that $(\mathbf{p},\mathbf{s}^*) \leq 0$. Thus $s_i^* \leq 0$ for all i and, since $\mathbf{a} = (0,0, \ldots, 0)$ is admissible, $\mathbf{s}^* = \mathbf{a}$. Finally $\mathbf{s}(\epsilon_n) \in B(\mathbf{p}(\epsilon_n)) \subset B$, so that $\mathbf{a} \in \bar{B}$.

For unbounded S, we use the following lemma.

LEMMA. *Let C be a convex set, N a neighborhood, and* $\mathbf{s}_0$ *minimize* $(\mathbf{p},\mathbf{s})$ *for* $\mathbf{s} \in C \cap N$. *Then* $\mathbf{s}_0$ *minimizes* $(\mathbf{p},\mathbf{s})$ *for* $\mathbf{s} \in C$.

Proof. Suppose, for some $\mathbf{s}_1 \in C$, $(\mathbf{p},\mathbf{s}_1) < (\mathbf{p},\mathbf{s}_0)$. Let $\mathbf{s}_2 = \alpha\mathbf{s}_0 + (1 - \alpha)\mathbf{s}_1$;

for $0 < \alpha < 1$, $s_2 \in C$, $(\mathbf{p}, s_2) < (\mathbf{p}, s_0)$. But for α sufficiently small, $s_2 \in N$, which contradicts the hypothesis.

It follows from the Lemma that Theorem 1 holds without the condition that S be bounded. Let S be any closed convex set, $\mathbf{a}$ an admissible point of S. Let N be a closed neighborhood of $\mathbf{a}$. Then $\mathbf{a}$ is admissible in $S \cap N$. By Theorem 1, $\mathbf{a} = \lim_{n \to \infty} s_n$, where s_n minimizes $(\mathbf{p}_n, s)$ for $s \in S \cap N$ for some $\mathbf{p}_n$ in P. Then, by the Lemma, s_n minimizes $(\mathbf{p}_n, s)$ for $s \in S$ for the same $\mathbf{p}_n$.

Now suppose that S is determined by a finite set $s_1, \ldots, s_m$. A subset U of $s_1, \ldots, s_m$ will be called *usable* if there is a $\mathbf{p} \in P$ for which $U \subset B(\mathbf{p})$. Let $U_1, \ldots, U_N$ be the usable subsets of $s_1, \ldots, s_m$, and let $\mathbf{p}_1, \ldots, \mathbf{p}_N$ be corresponding $\mathbf{p}$'s so that $U_j \subset B(\mathbf{p}_j)$. Let $s \in B$, say $s \in B(\mathbf{p})$, $s = \Sigma_1^m \lambda_i s_i$. Then if U is the set of s_i for which $\lambda_i > 0$, $U \subset B(\mathbf{p})$, since $(\mathbf{p}, s_i) > \min_{t \in S}(\mathbf{p}, t)$ for $s_i \in U$ would imply $(\mathbf{p}, s) = \Sigma \lambda_i (\mathbf{p}, s_i) > \min_{t \in S}(\mathbf{p}, t)$. Thus U is usable, say $U = U_j$. Then $s \in B(\mathbf{p}_j)$, and $B = \Sigma_1^N B(\mathbf{p}_j)$. This completes the proof.

An Example

If $k = 2$, it is easily shown that A is closed; in our example $k = 3$ and A is not closed. Let U be the closed arc consisting of all points $(x, y, 1)$ with $(x - 1)^2 + (y - 1)^2 = 1$, $0 \le x, y \le 1$; let $\mathbf{e} = (1, 0, 0)$; and let S be the convex set determined by U and $\mathbf{e}$. The point $f = (1, 0, 1) \in S$ is not admissible; we show that every point $s_0 = (x_0, y_0, 1)$ with $x_0, y_0 > 0$ and $(x_0 - 1)^2 + (y_0 - 1)^2 = 1$ is admissible, in fact, that it is an element of B.

There is a vector $\mathbf{p}_0 = (u_0, v_0, 0)$ with $u_0 > 0$, $v_0 > 0$, $u_0 + v_0 = 1$ such that $(\mathbf{p}_0, s) > (\mathbf{p}_0, s_0)$ for all $s \in S$, $s \ne s_0$. Let $\mathbf{p} = (1 - \epsilon)\mathbf{p}_0 + \epsilon(0, 0, 1)$, $0 < \epsilon < 1$. Then $\mathbf{p} \in P$, and $(\mathbf{p}, s) = (1 - \epsilon)(\mathbf{p}_0, s) + \epsilon$ for $s \in U$, so that $(\mathbf{p}, s_0) < (\mathbf{p}, s)$ for $s \ne s_0$, $s \in U$. Also $(\mathbf{p}, \mathbf{e}) = (1 - \epsilon)(\mathbf{p}_0, \mathbf{e}) > (1 - \epsilon)(\mathbf{p}_0, s_0) + \epsilon = (\mathbf{p}, s_0)$ for ϵ sufficiently small. Thus $s_0 \in B(\mathbf{p})$ for ϵ sufficiently small, completing the proof.

We remark incidentally that $\mathbf{e} \in A$ but $\mathbf{e} \notin B$, so that $A \ne B$, $\overline{B} \ne A$ in our example.

An Application

A consequence of our theorem is the following result of Bohnenblust, Karlin, and Shapley (1950).

THEOREM 2. *Let $A = \|a_{ij}\|$ be an $m \times n$ matrix, considered as the payoff of a zero-sum two-person game, and let D be the set of all i for which $A(i, \mathbf{q}) =$*

$\sum_{j=1}^{n} a_{ij} q_j = v$ *for every minimax strategy* $\mathbf{q}$ *for player II, where* v *is the value of the game. Then there is a minimax strategy* $\mathbf{p}$ *for player I with* $p_i > 0$ *for* $i \in D$.

Proof. If we delete from A the rows for which $i \notin D$, the resulting game has value v, and every minimax strategy for player I in the new game is minimax in the original game. Moreover, $A(i,\mathbf{q}) = v$ for every $i \in D$ and every minimax strategy $\mathbf{q}$ for player II in the new game, for if $A(i_0,\mathbf{q}_0) < v$ for some $i_0 \in D$ and some minimax $\mathbf{q}_0$ in the new game, $A(i_0,\mathbf{q}^*) < v$ for every $\epsilon > 0$, where $\mathbf{q}^* = \epsilon \mathbf{q}_0 + (1 - \epsilon)\mathbf{q}_1$ and $\mathbf{q}_1$ is minimax in the original game. Since $\mathbf{q}_1$ may be chosen so that $A(i,\mathbf{q}_1) < v$ for $i \notin D$, $\mathbf{q}^*$ will be minimax in the original game for sufficiently small $\epsilon > 0$, and $i_0 \notin D$. Thus we may suppose $i \in D$ for $i = 1, \ldots, m$.

Let S be the convex set in m-space determined by the columns of A. The point $\mathbf{s}_0 = (v,v, \ldots, v) \in S$ and is admissible, so that, by Theorem 1, there is a $\mathbf{p} \in P$ with $\mathbf{s}_0 \in B(\mathbf{p})$. That is, $(\mathbf{p},\mathbf{s}_0) = v \leqq (\mathbf{p},\mathbf{s})$ for all $\mathbf{s} \in S$. Thus $\mathbf{p}$ is a minimax strategy for player I, and $p_i > 0$ for $i \in D$.

Implications for Statistics and Economics

Suppose we have a *statistical* problem with a finite number of possible states of nature. To each possible strategy of the statistician, there can be assigned a vector whose components are the risks of the strategy under each of the possible states of nature. Let S be the set of such vectors; S will be convex if mixed strategies of the statistician are admitted and closed under very general assumptions. Then if we define the distance between two strategies as the Euclidean distance between their risk vectors, Theorem 1 asserts that every admissible strategy is the limit of a sequence of strategies, each of which is a Bayes solution against an a priori probability distribution which assigns positive probability to every state of nature. If S is determined by a finite set (for example, if the sample size is bounded, the variables observed take on only a finite set of values, and the number of actions among which choice is to be made is finite), then there is a finite set of such a priori distributions such that a strategy is admissible if and only if it is Bayes against one of these distributions.

In an *economic* context, it is assumed that production is made up by carrying on different *activities* at varying levels of intensity. An activity is characterized by a vector $\mathbf{a}$ whose components are amounts of the different commodities passing through the activity, being positive for outputs and negative for inputs. If the activity is carried on at level x, the amount of commodity i produced is xa_i (which is negative for inputs). If there are a finite number of activities a^j, then the amount of commodity i produced is $\Sigma_j x_j a_i^j$. Let commodities $1, \ldots, k$ be final or desired outputs; let $k + 1, \ldots, m$ be primary inputs. If the negative of the total available supply of commodity $i(i > k)$ is η_i, then the activity levels x_j must satisfy the conditions

$$\sum_j a_i^j x_j \geqq \eta_i, \quad (i > k).$$

The image of this set in x-space under the transformation $y_i = \Sigma_j a_i^j x_j (i = 1, \ldots, k)$ is then the set S of all possible combinations of final commodities possible with the given technology and resource limitations. S is clearly closed, bounded, and convex. A point $\mathbf{s}$ of S is said to be *efficient* if there is no $\mathbf{t} \in S$ such that $t_i \geqq s_i$ for all i, $\mathbf{t} \neq \mathbf{s}$. By Theorem 1 applied to efficient points, there is a finite set of vectors $\mathbf{p}$, with $p_i > 0$ for all i, such that $\mathbf{s}$ is efficient if and only if $\mathbf{s}$ maximizes $(\mathbf{p},\mathbf{s})$ for $\mathbf{s} \in S$ for some one of those $\mathbf{p}$'s. The vector $\mathbf{p}$ can easily be interpreted as a set of prices for the final commodities, and $(\mathbf{p},\mathbf{s})$ is the profit arising from the choice of activity levels leading to $\mathbf{s}$. Hence, any efficient point can be arrived at by instructing producers to maximize profits for a suitable set of positive prices. (See Koopmans, 1951, especially theorem 4.3.)

In the more general case where the number of activities is not finite, the activity levels will in general be replaced by a measure over the space of activities. The set S is still convex and, under suitable assumptions, closed. Then Theorem 1 tells us that we can approximate any given efficient point arbitrarily closely by instructing producers to maximize profits given a suitably chosen set of *positive* prices.

References

Bohnenblust, F., Karlin, S., and Shapley, L.S., "Solutions of discrete, two-person games," *Annals of Mathematics,* Study no. 24 (Princeton, 1950), pp. 51–72.

Gale, D., "Convex polyhedral cones and linear inequalities," Activity Analysis of Production and Allocation (Cowles Commission Monograph no. 13: New York, John Wiley and Sons, 1951), pp. 287–297.

Koopmans, T. C., "Analysis of production as an efficient combination of activities," Activity Analysis of Production and Allocation (Cowles Commission Monograph no. 13: New York, John Wiley and Sons, 1951), pp. 33–97.

3 Statistics and Economic Policy

The government may be regarded as a decision-making entity. Among the decisions it makes are the formation of economic policy and the collection of economic-statistical information. In all modern nations the economic policies of the government are significant activities, if for no other reason than the high proportion of national income which passes through the Treasury; but of course in many countries much more ambitious economic planning is aimed at, though not necessarily achieved. Economic statistics, on the other hand, if one is to judge by expenditures, form only an insignificant proportion of a government's activities and are the least developed precisely in those underdeveloped countries which have the greatest felt needs for economic plans. In this chapter I will stress the relation between these two activities, economic policy and economic statistics, classify the connections between them, and suggest the presumption that the marginal productivity of investment in statistical information is very high in all countries and especially in those countries where, for one reason or another, the primary responsibility for economic growth has been assumed by the government. I will use some language suggested by developments in statistical and economic decision theory. The discussion will be abstract, but the nature of the problems was suggested by a study of the statistical problems in economic planning in Western European countries made in the 1950s.[1]

Reprinted from *Econometrica*, 25 (1957):523–531. Delivered as the presidential address before the Econometric Society at Cleveland, Ohio, December 27, 1956.

1. During the tenure of a Social Science Research Fellowship.

Any decision problem can be thought of as having four parts: (1) an *objective function* which indicates the relative desirability of different possible outcomes; (2) a range of policy alternatives, or *instruments,* to use Tinbergen's felicitous term (see Tinbergen, 1952, p. 7) among which the decision maker (the government in this case) must choose; (3) the *model,* which specifies the empirical relations connecting the instruments, the variables entering into the objective function, and other relevant variables; and (4) the *computational methods* by which the decision maker chooses the values of the instruments so as to maximize the objective function subject to the conditions implied by the model. The last problem has indeed been the main content of the work on decision theory; in one sense, at least, the role of the price system as a computing device for achieving an economic optimum has been one of the main strands of economic theory since the days of Adam Smith. In many respects, the difficulties of computing an optimum (using the term "computation" in a very broad sense) are a limitation on the possible elaboration of a decision problem.

Government economic policy, like almost any realistic decision problem, has two fundamental characteristics: it is *sequential* and it is *uncertain.* By a sequential decision problem is meant one which is extended in time and in which the consequences of decisions made in one period are initial conditions which affect the decisions to be made in the next. By being uncertain is meant that the model does not permit perfect predictability, a condition which is all too obviously true of economics. In a formal model, uncertainty may take the form of random terms in the equations or of ignorance about the values of the structural parameters or, more generally, about the form of the structure.[2]

---

2. The importance in economics of decision problems which are both sequential and uncertain seems to have been first given strong recognition by A. G. Hart in his pioneering monograph (1951), especially chapter 4, and, in a more explicit form, in Hart (1942). Classical capital theory has in effect been concerned with sequential decision problems in which uncertainty does not enter. Hart's work shows the fallacy of attempting to treat sequential decision problems in general by finding a certainty equivalent. Thus Hicks (1946, p. 135) suggests that an individual planning future purchases and sales with uncertain prices will act as if the prices were certain but less favorable to him than the expected values, that is, he will act as if the prices at which he buys are known prices which are larger than the mathematical expectations of the random prices while those at which he sells are smaller. In general, behavior under prices assumed to be known at whatever levels is qualitatively different from behavior under uncertainty.

Theil (1954) and Simon (1956) have shown that when the profit function is quadratic, there is a certainty equivalent; that is, at any moment of time, even in a sequential decision problem,

For the moment assume the latter kind of uncertainty absent; that is, in any period we have a system of equations with random components, some of the variables entering being outcomes of the previous time period. An excellent example of a sequential decision problem under certainty is that of holding inventories (see Arrow, Harris, and Marschak, 1951.) The stock of inventories at the beginning of a period is in part a reflection of decisions and events occurring earlier.

It is clear that in such a system information about the current magnitudes of the variables is valuable. To the extent that variables, such as the stock of inventories, are not perfectly predictable, acquiring knowledge about them increases the possibility of an optimum allocation, or, more precisely, it increases the expected payoff. Of course, this increase in returns has to be balanced against the cost of acquiring the information. This type of information, that is, a knowledge of those parts of the present state of the system which have relevance for the next set of decisions in each period, may be termed *sequential information.*

In a true sequential decision problem, the consequences of any decision extend to infinity. In many such problems, the decisions to be made in any period are of the same form; this repetitive nature makes it possible at times to treat the simpler sequential decision problems by analytic methods.

To proceed formally, let x be the information available at any time period, y a decision variable for the next time period, u a random variable, $P(y,x,u)$ the payoff in a single period, a a discount rate (assumed constant), and $\bar{x}(y,x,u)$ the information transmitted to the next period. Since the action y can depend only on the information x, the sequential decision problem consists of choosing a function $y(x)$ so as to maximize the expected value of discounted future returns,

$$(3\text{-}1) \qquad \sum_{t=0}^{\infty} a^t E\{P[y(x_t),x_t,u_t]\} = Q[y(x),x_0],$$

where x_0 is given initially, $x_t = \bar{x}[y(x_{t-1}),x_{t-1},u_{t-1}]$ for $t \geq 1$, and u_t is the value of the random variable at time t. From the nature of Eq. (3-1), or from general considerations, one can easily see that when time 1 arrives, the situation is essentially the same; the expected value of future returns, looked at from time 1, is the same

---

the acts taken in the immediately next period are the same as they would be if future prices were known with certainty to be equal to their mathematical expectations. However, in the next period, as one more observation has been made, a new set of decisions must still be undertaken, though according to the same scheme; hence even here it remains true that the acquisition of information has value, which it would not have in a world of certainty.

function, but with a new value, x_1, for the initial information, so that it is given by $Q[y(x),x_1]$. From the viewpoint of time 0, this last expression is a random variable, since it depends, through $x_1 = \bar{x}[y(x_0),x_0,u_0]$, on the random variable u_0. Thus at time 0, the expected value of future returns will equal the expected payoff in the immediate period plus the expected value of future returns from the viewpoint of time 1 discounted back one period.

(3-2) $Q[y(x),x_0] = E\{P[y(x_0),x_0,u_0] + aQ[y(x),x_1]\}.$

In particular, let $y^*(x)$ be the *optimal* decision function, and let $Q[y^*(x),x_0] = Q^*(x_0)$ be the corresponding expected value of future returns;

(3-3) $Q^*(x_0) = \max_{y(x)} Q[y(x),x_0].$

Let $y(x) = y^*(x)$ in (3-2).

(3-4) $Q^*(x_0) = E\{P[y^*(x_0),x_0,u_0] + aQ^*(x_1)\}.$

Because $y^*(x)$ is the optimal policy, as indicated in (3-3), the value of $Q^*(x_0)$ cannot be increased by changing the immediate decision $y^*(x_0)$ to any other value y. Hence, we have the fundamental relation, frequently called the *principle of optimality,*

(3-5) $Q^*(x_0) = \max_{y} E\{P(y,x_0,u_0) + aQ^*[\bar{x}(y,x_0,u_0)]\},$

where x_1 has been replaced by its defining formula in order to bring out the dependence of the last term on y. Equation (3-5) is a functional equation which characterizes the function $Q^*(x_0)$ and so determines the maximum possible expected value of future discounted returns for *any* initial value of information x_0. It is curious that the solution for any given x_0 is obtained by considering the problem for all x_0 simultaneously. In most applications, the solution of (3-5) entails the determination of the optimal policy $y^*(x)$; however, the solution is by no means easy in general.

Notice that the above formulation is very general. In most economic applications the initial conditions x_0 include capital assets of all types, as well as information in the strict sense. As noted above, the usual capital theory can be put in the above form in the special case where there are no random variables. It would be easy to show that much of the reasoning used in capital theory has in fact made use of the principle of optimality. The explicit recognition of this principle has stemmed from the work of P. Massé (1946) (though the formulation is somewhat different) and of A. Wald on sequential analysis of statistical data, which can be regarded as a special case (see Wald, 1950, especially theorem 4.2 on p. 105). An application to the theory of inventory holding was given by Arrow, Harris, and Marschak (1951); see also

Dvoretzky, Kiefer, and Wolfowitz (1952). R. Bellman was the first to see the generality of the procedure, to which he has given the name *dynamic programming;* see, among many other publications, Bellman (1953). An elegant formulation is that of S. Karlin (1955).

Usually, though, this explicit solution is not possible computationally even when it is formally manageable. In practice we substitute a one-period decision problem, which I may term a *proximate* decision problem, for the true sequential one. The use of static analysis in economics to deal with dynamic problems which are beyond our capabilities is an illustration of this methodological point; Keynesian income analysis is a recent example. Such a substitution is not merely sloppy thinking (though this may enter); it is a necessity forced upon us by the limitation of our computational (including mental) resources.

Not to be grievously misleading, however, the proximate decision problem must be so described as to reflect some characteristics of the sequential decision problem from which it is abstracted. It would be very wrong to assume that the proximate decision problem is described correctly by considering only one period of the original sequential decision problem; this would amount to assuming that the world is coming to an end after the one period. In the inventory example, inventories left over at the end of a period have a value in meeting future contingencies, even though they have none from the point of view of the one period. In the proximate decision problem, then, the objective function must be modified to give a value to these inventories. Thus a government planning year by year should not aim at setting its end-of-year foreign currency reserves at zero; a positive balance is valuable as a guard against the uncertainty of the future. The British experience after World War II would suggest that failure to heed this elementary point may lead to the necessity of rapid and costly adjustments.

In the same way, the objective function for the proximate decision problem must ascribe a positive value to sequential information even though the information is not used in the current period. The argument is strictly analogous.

Of course, the objective function for the proximate decision problem cannot be perfectly known, for such knowledge would be equivalent to having solved the full sequential decision problem. But we can form some approximation. We have two hopes that our approximation will not be too bad; one is that growing experience will enable us to improve our knowledge of this function, and the other is that the consequences in the far future in any case, because of time preference and uncertainty, do not matter much.[3]

Let us return to the second form of uncertainty mentioned earlier, the uncertainty about the structural equations themselves. Unlike the previous situation, there is a cumulative growth of knowledge; as the number of observations gets larger, there is an increase in the efficiency with which we estimate our parameters. The information used this way may be termed *cumulative information.*

These general considerations on the nature of government economic policy may be put in a slightly different way. There are really three types of time, or, more precisely, three different ways in which time enters into the formulation of optimal policy. First, there is sequential time, the fact that economic events and their consequences are extended in time. Sequential time arises mainly because both stocks and flows are economic variables, though there may be lags due to other reasons; sequential time is the time of classical capital theory. Second, there is computational time; even in a single-period optimization, computation is never instantaneous. Usually computation is iterative; there is a sequence of alternating guesses and feedbacks of information which suggest modifications. If all goes well, the process will converge, though usually only after infinite time. Computational time is the time of the dynamics of market adjustment and stability analysis in standard economic theory, if we view the markets as computational devices for achieving an optimum.[4]

The third kind of time is cumulative time, due to the growing knowledge of the laws of nature, not only in economics proper but also in the technol-

---

3. The proximate decision problem should be formulated by replacing Q^* by a plausible guess, say $\bar{Q}$, on the right-hand side of (3-5), which is then reduced to a simple maximization problem. The result of the operation would yield a new value for $Q^*(x_0)$, at least for the particular value of x_0 at the start, and so in the future we would be able to use a somewhat improved guess $\bar{Q}$ at the same time; if a is sufficiently small (if the effect is discounted sufficiently sharply), the effect of an incorrect guess can be made small.

4. The concept of the competitive market as a computational device which solves a system of equations by successive approximations is implicit in virtually all economic thinking from Adam Smith on. It is given very explicit formulation by L. Walras (1954, pp. 162–163, 169, and elsewhere); for a very forcible statement, see V. Pareto (1927, pp. 233–234): "Si on pouvait vraiment connaître toutes ces équations, le seul moyen accessible aux forces humaines pour les résoudre, ce serait d'observer la solution pratique que donne le marché" ("If all these equations could be truly known, the only humanly feasible method of solving them would be to observe the solution given by the practice of the market"). Strong emphasis was placed on this viewpoint for a socialist economy by O. Lange (1938, pp. 70–82).

ogy of production and presumably in consumer and worker psychology. A statistician may view cumulative time as increase in sample size, a psychologist as successive steps in learning, an anthropologist as cultural evolution. The concept of cumulative time has played little formal role in economics, though references to the growth of knowledge as the greatest source of wealth are to be found among the less orthodox economists.[5] Some empirical studies have laid great stress on the cumulation of information as the main source of economic growth.[6] Of course, these studies refer to technological knowledge; I would like to believe that such cumulation can be as characteristic of economic as of physical knowledge.

Corresponding to the three types of time are three types of information, to which we may give the corresponding names. Indeed, if I understand some scientific philosophers correctly, the accumulation of information and the passage of time are really the same thing.[7] To avoid misunderstanding, let me say that the three types of information are not necessarily exclusive; the same information may serve two or three of the functions of sequential, computational, or cumulative information.

Let us discuss each of these functions of data in turn. For definiteness in the discussion, we assume that the objective function of the economy depends on present and future national incomes and their distributions by size.

Sequential Information

In the area of sequential information, what we want is a snapshot of the economy sufficiently detailed to make reasonably good forecasts of the effects of alternative policies in the short run. I do not think it difficult to see that this modest aim is far from achieved at the present time [1957]. Let me just enumerate a few items which are either not measured at all on an annual basis or are measured with admittedly wide margins of error: stocks of inventories classified by commodities, stock of fixed capital by product (a measure independent of reported depreciation rates), interindustry flows, geographic differences in cost of living, size distribution of income, personal savings, classification of government expenditures by commodities. This list

---

5. See, for example, Veblen (1919).
6. See Abramovitz (1956); Schultz (n.d.).
7. For example, Grünbaum (1955).

is not the result of any systematic survey, but just a number of items in which I have encountered deficiencies in my own work. Even in areas where figures are available, closer examination shows that the coverage is far from adequate.[8]

The experience of other countries is a good deal worse than ours. An especially striking case is the British, especially since they were attempting to do so much more detailed planning and thus had a much greater need for economic information. It was startling to find in a nation attempting to plan in an inflationary situation and particularly to direct the allocation of resources between consumption and investment that there were no surveys of consumption and investment intentions and that savings was estimated solely as a residual.[9]

I think it certainly reasonable to assume that the expenditure on sequential information is probably far below the optimal level as determined by its marginal social productivity. I would like to make clear that I mean no criticism of the statistical agencies of the United States government; my impression is that the ingenuity and thoroughness of the American statistical work is considerably above that of any other country. I am contending that much greater expenditure on economic statistics is called for than the $10–20 million currently allocated [1957] for this purpose.

Computational Information

Because of the impossibility of giving explicit solutions to any computational problem above the trivial level, we need a system of signals for correcting mistakes. We may have to assume that the government will guess at a policy, for example, a rediscount rate or a level of public works expenditure, and watch some observed variable for suggestions for change. Standard economic analysis regards the market as performing this function; prices react to the cue of an inequality between supply and demand. Similarly, we might expect the government's monetary or fiscal policy to react to movements of the general price level or of the level of employment. In an economy which seeks to allocate investment directly, it would perhaps

---

8. The remarkably complete and honest account of the sources of our national income accounts in U.S. Department of Commerce (1954), pt. 3, shows the inadequacies of coverage in most areas. See, for example, the discussion of statistics on new construction.

9. For a recognition of the role of inadequate information in British planning, see Marris (1954, pp. 10–12); for some constructive suggestions, see Marris, pp. 32–38.

be inequalities in the marginal productivity of capital which would constitute the signals.

One implication derived from computing experience is the value of speed in responses. The British Chancellor of the Exchequer once remarked that trying to deal with foreign currency reserve depletion with existing information was like trying to catch a railroad train with last year's schedules. Speed is of course something which can be purchased, partly by greater expenditures and partly by loss of accuracy, as in the substitution of sample surveys for complete enumerations. (However, to get a good historical series for other purposes, particularly cumulative information, it is necessary to supplement surveys periodically with complete enumerations to serve as benchmarks.)

I believe that new types of information will be needed to really carry through the computational processes. One could in principle wait to see the effect of a change in the rediscount rate on the price level, but there is apt to be a long delay, and in any case the economic system is a fairly uncontrolled matrix for experiments. It will be necessary to increase the intensity of observation. Along the lines of the investment surveys of the Securities and Exchange Commission, it may well be possible to find out by direct interrogation to what extent investment and consumption projects have been curtailed by the interest rate changes. I have no doubt that our survey techniques for examining these problems are still crude; I do doubt that they will be improved without putting them into practice.

Cumulative Information

In the area of cumulative information especially, it is the role and duty of the economist to suggest what information is relevant and needed. Too much energy has gone into squeezing the last bit of juice out of old data collected for different purposes relative to the design of new types of data. Of course, any extension of information anywhere, for sequential or computational purposes, will be useful for increasing the understanding of economic principles. But a few additional suggestions are in order. For one thing, it will be well worthwhile to start new time series even though it may be many years before enough observations accumulate to make analysis worthwhile. There is room for projects of this type which will not pay off for many years, just as there is for great dams.

But the paucity of time-series information at the moment does compel us to look to cross-section studies of one type or another. Two examples of types of studies that have been made but not yet on a sufficient scale are engineering studies to get at the structure of production[10] and panel studies of income (that is, repeated observations on the same individuals' income over time) and associated variables to arrive at a better understanding of the dynamics of income distribution.[11] Perhaps, too, the time is ripe for controlled experimentation on economic motivation and behavior, along the lines fruitfully developed by social psychologists.

Discretion versus Automatism

The preceding remarks cast some light on the dispute between discretionary policies and automatic rules. An automatic rule which does not include among its variables all the relevant information available is clearly not optimal.[12] On the other hand, the specification of such a rule in the presence of a considerable body of information quickly becomes impractical. The determination of the optimal automatic rule involves solving a sequential decision problem, which is ordinarily not possible. We act by solving or approximating the solution of a proximate decision problem. The choices of both the proximate problem and the computing methods are acts of judgment, which can improve with time and experience. Thus there seem to be strong grounds for defending discretionary procedures under conditions of uncertainty.

Now the defender of automatic rules will probably grant the inefficiency of any practical automatic rule relative to an ideal but will argue that the loss is outweighed by the subjectivity and unpredictability of administrators' discretion. A greatly increased body of information should, however, circumvent this point, for I assume that the scope of discretion will be greatly reduced by increased knowledge, even if the policies implied by the information cannot be easily specified beforehand by a formula.[13]

---

10. A remarkable early study of this type was done for air transportation by L. Bréguet, as reported by E. H. Phelps Brown (1936, pp. 249–259). More recently there has been an increasing number of such studies, partly growing out of linear programming and other forms of activity analysis, including those of A. P. Carter (Grosse) (1953) on the cotton textile industry, H. B. Chenery (1953) on gas transmission, A. R. Ferguson (1953) on air transportation, A. Charnes, W. W. Cooper, and B. Mellon (1952) and A. S. Manne (1956) on various aspects of petroleum, and unpublished work by H. Markowitz (1954) on metalworking. See also a general review of some of this work in H. Markowitz (n.d.).

11. See M. Friedman and S. Kuznets (1945), Solow (1951), and Summers (n.d.).

12. The optimal policy $y^*(x)$ in note 3 would be an automatic rule, if it could be found.

13. See Savage (1954, p. 156) for the remark that additional observations are among the devices for reducing interpersonal differences in judgment.

Conclusion

In view of the magnitude of an economic system, it would take only a very small percentage of improvement in economic stability or growth to make almost any conceivable data collection worthwhile. The situation is analogous to reported results of the use of linear programming in industry; the gains are small in proportion to previous profit levels but still very much larger than the costs of the programming. No country is adequate in respect to its data. In particular the underdeveloped countries, with their ambitious programs, might well ponder whether or not the marginal productivity of investment in better economic statistics is perhaps not higher than almost any conceivable alternative; they have more need and fewer data.

References

Abramovitz, Moses. "Resource and Output Trends in the United States Since 1870," *American Economic Review, Papers and Proceedings of the American Economic Association,* 46:5–23 (May, 1956).

Arrow, Kenneth J., Theodore Harris, and Jacob Marschak. "Optimal Inventory Policy," *Econometrica,* 19:250–272 (July, 1951).

Bellman, Richard. *An Introduction to the Theory of Dynamic Programming.* Santa Monica, California: The RAND Corporation, 1953.

Carter (Grosse), Anne P. "The Technological Structure of the Cotton Textile Industry," in W. W. Leontief (ed.), *Studies in the Structure of the American Economy,* pp. 360–420. New York: Oxford University Press, 1953.

Charnes, A., W. W. Cooper, and B. Mellon. "Blending Aviation Gasolines—A Study in Programming Interdependent Activities in an Integrated Oil Company," *Econometrica,* 20:135–159 (1952).

Chenery, Hollis B. "Process and Production Functions from Engineering Data," in W. W. Leontief, *American Economy,* pp. 297–325.

Dvoretzky, A., J. Kiefer, and J. Wolfowitz. "The Inventory Problem," *Econometrica,* 20:187–222, 450–466 (1952).

Ferguson, Allen R. "Commercial Air Transportation in the United States," in W. W. Leontief, *American Economy,* pp. 421–447.

Friedman, Milton, and Simon Kuznets. *Income from Independent Professional Practice.* New York: National Bureau of Economic Research, 1945.

Grünbaum, Adolf. "Time and Entropy," *American Scientist,* 43:550–572 (1955).

Hart, Albert G. *Anticipations, Uncertainty, and Dynamic Planning.* New York: Augustus M. Kelley (reprinted), 1951.

Hart, Albert G. "Risk, Uncertainty, and the Unprofitability of Compounding Probabilities," in O. Lange, F. McIntyre, and T. O. Yntema (eds.), *Studies in Mathematical Economics and Econometrics,* pp. 110–118. Chicago: University of Chicago Press, 1942.

Hicks, J. R. *Value and Capital,* 2nd ed. Oxford: Clarendon Press, 1946.

Karlin, Samuel. "The Structure of Dynamic Programming Models," *Naval Research Logistics Quarterly,* 2:285–294 (1955).

Lange, Oskar, and Fred M. Taylor. *On the Economic Theory of Socialism,* ed. B. Lippincott. Minneapolis: University of Minnesota Press, 1938.

Manne, Alan S. *Scheduling of Petroleum Refinery Operations.* Cambridge, Massachusetts: Harvard University Press, 1956.

Markowitz, Harry. "Process Analysis of U.S. Technology" (abstract), *Econometrica,* 22:515 (1954).

Markowitz, Harry. "Industry-Wide, Multi-Industry, and Economy-Wide Process Analysis," chap. 5 in T. Barna (ed.), *The Structural Interdependence of the Economy.* New York and Milan: John Wiley and Sons and A. Giuffré (n.d.).

Marris, Robin. *The Machinery of Economic Policy.* London: Fabian Research Bureau, no. 168, 1954.

Massé, Pierre B. D. *Les réserves et la régulation de l'avenir dans la vie économique.* Paris: Harmann et Cie., 1946.

Pareto, Vilfredo. *Manuel d'économie politique,* 2nd ed. Paris: Marcel Giard, 1927.

Phelps Brown, E. H. "Cost Categories and the Total Cost-Function," *Econometrica,* 4:242–263 (1936).

Savage, Leonard J. *The Foundations of Statistics.* New York and London: John Wiley and Sons and Chapman Hall, 1954.

Schultz, Theodore W. *The Economic Test in Latin America.* Ithaca, New York: Bulletin 35, New York State School of Industrial and Labor Relations, Cornell University (n.d.).

Simon, Herbert A. "Dynamic Programming under Uncertainty with a Quadratic Criterion Function," *Econometrica,* 24:74–81 (January, 1956).

Solow, Robert. *On the Dynamics of the Income Distribution.* Unpublished doctoral dissertation, Harvard University, 1951.

Summers, Robert. *An Econometric Investigation of the Size Distribution of Lifetime Average Annual Income.* Stanford, California: Technical Report no. 31, Contract N6onr-25133 (NR-047-004). Department of Economics, Stanford University (n.d.).

Theil, Henri. "Econometric Models and Welfare Maximisation," *Weltwirtschaftliches Archiv,* 72:60–83 (1954, no. 1).

Tinbergen, Jan. *On the Theory of Economic Policy,* Amsterdam: North-Holland, 1952.

U.S. Department of Commerce. *National Income: 1954 Edition, A Supplement to the Survey of Current Business.* Washington, D.C.: Government Printing Office, 1954.

Veblen, Thorstein. "On the Nature of Capital," in *The Place of Science in Modern Civilization and Other Essays,* pp. 324–386. New York: B. W. Huebsch, 1919.

Wald, Abraham. *Statistical Decision Functions.* New York and London: John Wiley and Sons and Chapman and Hall, 1950.

Walras, Léon. *Elements of Pure Economics,* trans. W. Jaffé. London: George Allen and Unwin, 1954.

4 Decision Theory and Operations Research

Decision theory, as it has grown up in recent years, is a formalization of the problems involved in making optimal choices. In a certain sense—a very abstract sense, to be sure—it incorporates operations research, theoretical economics, and wide areas of statistics, among others. The formal structure of a decision problem in any area can be put into four parts: (1) the choice of an *objective function* defining the relative desirability of different outcomes; (2) specification of the *policy alternatives* which are available to the agent, or decision maker; (3) specification of the *model,* that is, empirical relations that link the objective function, or the variables that enter into it, with the policy alternatives and possibly other variables; and (4) *computational methods* for choosing among the policy alternatives that one which performs best as measured by the objective function. In the last part, the objective function is maximized subject to the constraints imposed by the model. It is for this reason that decision theory is mathematically, to a great extent, a branch of the theory of constrained maxima.

Strictly speaking, decision theory really is concerned only with the fourth part of the division given above, that is, the determination of the computational methods for optimization. Given the determination of the other three factors—the objective function, the range of policy alternatives, and the model—the ideal picture is that someone, presumably the firm that hires the operations researcher, hands him, on a silver platter, an objective function. By talking to the engineers, or by looking into a few scientific laws,

Reprinted from *Operations Research,* 5 (1957):765–774.

he determines the policy alternatives available and also the model. From there on, the thing is now formalized as a mathematical problem, which may, indeed, involve considerable ingenuity in solving.

It is interesting to note the asymmetry of this formulation. Everyone expects that the solution of a decision-theoretical problem will in many cases be quite complex. This journal and many others, as well as many books, attest to the mathematical difficulties in the solution of optimization problems. But the other parts of an operations-research problem or of decision problems in general are somehow available. In particular, the objective function is taken by decision theorists to be an easily ascertainable datum.

Now I am sure the practicing operations researcher will immediately deny the picture I have drawn. For him, all four parts of the problem have to be treated. In some cases, indeed, one or the other may be quite simple. It is even possible, and true in many cases, that it is the computation of a solution that is the easy part of the problem. The point, however, is that in fact — as opposed to textbooks — the four parts of the problem constitute an interrelated whole, and they modify each other in many ways. Certainly the availability and knowledge of computational methods have a strong influence on the rest of the problem. We frequently choose our models, our objective functions, and even our ranges of policy alternatives so as to be analytically manageable. There is no point in posing a problem for which we cannot find the solution, so we tend to modify our formulation of the problem in order to make it practical.

The influence of mutual adaptation of the parts works in other directions, of course. The formulation of the policy alternatives will certainly affect the variables which enter into our objective function. We will tend to ascribe definite values to the policy alternatives or to variables closely related to them, even though we really do not have very definite values to ascribe. Again, the model, which is built up out of our empirical knowledge of the situation, will constrain sharply the choice of policy alternatives. A policy alternative whose empirical relation to performance characteristics is unknown is obviously not of much use.

Articulation of a decision model, therefore, is relative to the knowledge about computing methods, to knowledge about the solution of the mathematical problems imposed by decision theory, to the knowledge about the subject matter displayed in the model, to the understanding of the objectives of the agent as revealed in the objective function, and to the imagination and knowledge required to specify the range of policy alternatives. There is, therefore, no sense in which we can speak of a decision problem as having been finally solved. The very solution of a particular decision model will change the state of knowledge available, and thus enable us to look at the original problem, or related problems, in a new light. Indeed, I suspect in a great many applications the principal virtue of operations research has been to force a rethinking of the situation, and the gain may well have been due as much or more to the new knowledge unearthed by the forced new analysis as to the formal apparatus of the optimization process.

These remarks should not be surprising. After all, they are all true of scientific problems, with which operations research is so closely connected. No problem in science, in a sense, is ever completely solved.

I would like to put forth the thesis that the open, tentative character of operations research, and of all scientific analysis, can be itself discussed in terms of decision theory. More specifically, I believe that the notions of decision analysis in sequential situations, sometimes called dynamic programming, can, if properly understood, be very revealing of the tentative and approximate nature of any particular solution to an operations-research problem. This shows that, on the one hand, solutions to particular problems are less definitive than their formal statement suggests, and, on the other, formal oversimplified models which are not yet capable of being quantified may nevertheless be of great practical value.

From a broadly philosophical point of view, one obvious fact about all forms of research, or indeed about all forms of human activity, is that they take place in time. Events and learning processes are sequential, in this sense. Now, one characteristic ordinarily (not invariably) associated with the passage of time is accumulation of information. That which is a random variable or in some other way is unknown at time t_0 may well be a known fact at a later time, t_1.

This property has been widely made use of in certain decision-theoretic problems. Although it is difficult to pin the genesis of any broad concept down to a single person, I think the name of Abraham Wald must be mentioned prominently. His sequential analysis of statistical data contained the essence of the notion of sequential decision making for the accumulation of information.[1]

---

1. See A. Wald (1950), especially theorem 4.2 on p. 105. An independent formulation much closer to the usual applications in business is that of Pierre Massé (1946), which was inspired chiefly by hydroelectric problems. Applications to the theory of inventory holding were given by Arrow, Harris, and Marschak (1951) and Dvoretzky, Kiefer, and Wolfowitz (1952). Richard Bellman was the first to see the generality of the procedure and to give it the name of *dynamic programming;* see, among many other publications, Bellman (1953). An elegant formulation is that of Samuel Karlin (1955).

Let us first take another example, that of inventory control. In a simple situation, as is by now well known, we may suppose there is a firm selling a single product at regular intervals. The demand is assumed to be a random variable, ξ, with known distribution, the same in every period. At the beginning of each period the firm must make a decision to order some quantity of the goods, possibly 0, for which it pays a cost, which is some function, $c(X)$, of the amount X ordered. At the end of the period the inventory left over is equal to the stock on hand at the beginning of the period, plus the amount ordered, minus the amount demanded during the period, unless this quantity is negative, in which case the inventory becomes 0. If Y_t is the amount of inventory at the beginning of the peak period, we may define the following two variables:

(4-1) $\qquad Z_t = X_t + Y_t - \xi_t,$

(4-2) $\qquad Y_{t+1} = \max (Z_t, 0).$

If Z_t is negative, there is presumably some penalty which in general will depend on Z_t and will vanish when Z_t is greater than or equal to 0. If Z_t is positive, then Y_{t+1} will be positive, and there is a storage cost attached to the holding. In general, then, we may say there is a penalty or storage cost that may be assimilated to a single function of Z_t designated by $f(Z_t)$. If we agree that all units are measured in value terms, the profit made in time period t is given by

(4-3) $\qquad P_t = \xi_t - c(X_t) - f(Z_t).$

At the initial period when the decision problem is posed, the decision made will affect the values of P_t over long, perhaps indefinite, periods in the future. For an objective function, we might consider some combination of all these values of P_t. But presumably the further ones in time are to play a lesser role. This may be accomplished by discounting them, that is, by multiplying by some number that decreases geometrically into the future. Thus we will let the discounted stream of profits P be given by

(4-4) $\qquad P = \sum_{t=0}^{t=\infty} \alpha^t P_t,$

where α is a number between 0 and 1. Of course, we cannot in fact determine the value of P, since it depends, among other things, on future demands, ξ_t, which are random variables. Hence our policy is presumably chosen to maximize the mathematical expectation of P.

Now the significant point for the solution of this problem is that the decision to order X_t is, under the assumptions of the problem, not needed to be made until time t. At time t, the decision maker has available as information all events of the first $t - 1$ periods. Actually, as can be seen from the structure of the problem, all that is really relevant to a choice of X_t is the value of the stock of inventory on hand, Y_t. Therefore, at the initial period, the problem is not to choose a number X_t for each t, but rather a sequence of functions, $X_t = \phi(Y_t)$. (Because of the especially simple structure of this problem, the function ϕ can easily be seen to be the same for all values of t.)

Not only can the decision about X_t be postponed until more information is acquired — that is, until the value of Y_t is actually known — but this fact is known at the initial period and is taken into account in determining the optimal decision function. Consider now the situation at time 0, the initial period. The only decision that has to be made immediately is a choice of X_0. Let us see how we might look at this.

We can write (4-4) in the following form, where we make use of (4-3) for the case $t = 0$.

$$(4\text{-}5) \qquad P = \xi_0 - c(X_0) - f(Z_0) + \alpha \sum_{t=1}^{t=\infty} \alpha^{t-1} P_t.$$

The last term of (4-5) depends on the choice of the function ϕ, the stock of inventory at time 1, namely Y_1, and on the random demands occurring in the periods beginning with the first. Given strategy ϕ, the expectation of the last term will therefore be a function of Y_1, say $Q(Y_1)$. Hence we can write:

$$(4\text{-}6) \qquad E(P) = E(\xi_0) - c(X_0) - E[f(Z_0)] + E[Q(Y_1)].$$

If we recall that Z_0 is a random variable whose distribution depends on X_0, (and of course Y_0, which is presumed to be known), and that Y_1 is similarly a random variable whose distribution depends on X_0, we see that (4-6) is simply a function of X_0 and that the infinite-dimensional problem has been reduced to a one-dimensional one. Of course, there is a catch in this. The function $Q(Y_1)$ cannot be specified without knowing the strategy to be applied in the future, that is, the ordering decision as a function of the stock on hand for each of the future time periods.

I am suggesting the following. Formula (4-6) displays the fact that the choice of X_0, the decision to be made here and now, depends on certain factors: the cost directly associated with acquiring X_0; the expected costs of either penalty, if the demand exceeds supply, or storage, in the contrary case; and a term that reflects the value of the stock on hand at the end of the period for future operations. It may well be possible to estimate the last term in some manner based on good judgment and past experience that will enable us to consider the inventory problem as a one-dimensional or one-time-period problem.

I further suggest that this picture is a paradigm of most operations-research problems. The consequences of most decisions go beyond the small problem we generally isolate for the purpose of analysis. To pursue all these consequences would be an impossible undertaking in general. But we can think of the problem in the small, provided that our objective function properly takes account of the ulterior consequences of our action. For most purposes, a rough allowance suffices. I think one could easily get a qualitative picture of the value to be placed on the stock of inventory on hand at the end of the period and put down an approximation that reflects the value with sufficient accuracy as far as the purpose at hand is concerned. Naturally, better results will be obtained by broadening and deepening the problem, by extending it in our inventory example to more time periods. But there is always a point where we must stop.

What are the consequences of this viewpoint for the formulation of decision problems in operations research? As far as the objective function is concerned, the important point is that some of the outcomes of the particular situation will have consequences in other subsequent operations. Without trying to trace out the consequences in any detail, it is still vital to set the valuations upon these outcomes if one is to arrive at a just appreciation of the particular problem at hand. How do we make this allowance, or set this valuation? It must always depend, to some extent, of course, on sheer judgment. In fact, the valuation is distinctly a creative act. But, like all creative acts, it can be helped. I think that here lies one of the great values of theoretical model building, that is to say, model building going beyond the computational possibilities of the moment or the data availabilities. In the first place, an articulated model that cannot be solved will frequently enable us to see connections, to realize implications, and to specify which of the outcomes of the present situation will have an influence on the future. Second, simplified theoretical models—that is to say, models too simple to be considered as solutions of realistic problems—will still enable us, when solved, to have a qualitative appreciation of the influence of our variables on the future. In addition to the effect on the objective function, we observe that even the short-run decision problem is changed, as time goes on, by change in the information available. In the inventory problem, this is represented solely by change in the one variable Y_t, the initial conditions. In general situations, of course, it is more complex.

This first model does not illustrate all the relevant points. In particular, the effect of growth in the amount of initial information is not represented. I therefore would like to modify the first problem somewhat. Suppose that all the assumptions of the problem are retained except the one that the distribution of demands is known. We continue to assume, however, that the unknown distribution is the same from time to time and that the successive demands are stochastically independent. A possible but not optimal procedure is certainly the following.

At the *t*th trial, we form an estimate of the probability distribution of demand, based on the observations of the preceding trials. The form of this estimate depends, of course, on what assumptions we are willing to make a priori about the nature of the demand function. If it is assumed to belong to a known family, characterized by a few parameters, then we can form estimates of the parameters. If we wish to make no assumptions at all about the shape of the distribution, then the best estimate of the demand function would be the sample frequency distribution in the preceding trials.

Thus at the *t*th trial, we have an estimate of the frequency distributions of demands. We may then solve the problem at the *t*th trial, supposing that the true frequency distribution is the estimated one. At the $(t + 1)$st trial we have a new estimate of the frequency distribution, since there has been one more observation, and we solve the problem again.

The point to be illustrated here is that the model may change over time because of the accumulation of information. Therefore, there is nothing inconsistent about solving the operations-research problem again, even though we have solved it, in a sense, correctly the first time. However, it should also be noted that an optimal procedure would have to take into account the fact that we are going to revise our estimate of the frequency distribution in the future. Hence there probably would be a greater hedge against uncertainty, in the form of higher inventory levels, in the earlier periods when our information is less certain.[2]

The example also illustrates, although somewhat dimly, still another point. In order to form our sample of frequency distribution, we have to keep records of past demands. If we suppose that the keeping of records involves some cost, we have actually introduced a new dimension to the range of policy alternatives. At each stage the alternatives must be not only how much to order, but also whether or not to record. This simple example illustrates the possibility of keeping information that the firm has at one

---

2. After the original publication of this paper, the optimal inventory policy for unknown demands was found by Scarf (1959).

time but does not ordinarily retain because it does not fit into the conventional accounting procedures. That is, it points up the possibility that accounting and other record-making procedures should be revised and augmented so as to serve not only the functions of control but those of forming a better basis for forecasting and, more generally, for improving the model that must be used for operations-research purposes.

Record keeping is a special case of a more general type of policy alternative, namely, the acquisition of information as a deliberate policy rather than as a by-product of other activities. Let me modify the example once again. Going back to the original example, suppose it is possible to ask some or all of the potential customers what their demands will be in the next period. We may assume that the responses are not perfect forecasts, but that the conditional distribution of the demand, given the responses, will have a considerably smaller variance than the unconditional distribution of demand. That is, we can observe a variable η — the responses to the questionnaires — and use a conditional distribution $f(\xi/\eta)$. There is, of course, a cost attached to this questionnaire. We thus have an additional variable in our policy alternatives; that is, not only must we choose a value for X, but we must also decide whether or not to observe η. Now the observation of η has no direct utility at all. Yet by improving the accuracy of prediction, it must be taken into account as a possible policy alternative, and in a one-period approximation to the long-term decision problem, we must perforce attach some value to the collection of the information η. That is to say, if we compress the problem to a one-period one, as is indicated above, we must give in the objective function some valuation to the collection of η. This valuation itself will change with experience, if it is not possible to estimate it correctly the first time.

I suspect this corresponds to a common observation among operations researchers. In many cases, the improvement in performance attendant upon operations research is caused not so much by the formal optimization procedure but by the fact that it calls attention to the proper data to be collected. It stresses the information upon which any rational decision must be made, and by so doing improves the value of the decision as much as or more than the exact attainment of the optimum solution of the problem, once properly formulated. Again, this is a justification for theoretical oversimplified models to analyze situations that we cannot reach quantitatively. Such theoretical models enable us to perceive the value of certain types of information, and thus enable us to specify the short-period objective function more accurately.

I would like to turn, for a few minutes, to computation. Computing again, as a practical art, has the same open, tentative character that we have assigned specific operations-research problems. Beyond the simplest cases, any computing procedure is a procedure of successive approximation. With computing machines of finite size, with human brains of limited capacity, the mere statement that we must achieve an optimum is not a sufficient guide. In fact, in a sense, the problem of optimal decision making could be regarded as completed once we formulate the problem and issue the injunction: "Find the maximum." From a certain point of view, provided certain existence and uniqueness conditions are met, this is a solution to the original problem. The only objection to it is that it is in many cases a useless solution, and most of decision theory is, in fact, concerned with the question of getting simple, manageable expressions for the solutions to various specific problems. Now, a solution in closed form is a nice thing to have, although sometimes it is not very useful. But what is more important is that this is not the most common situation. For the most part, we have to expect that our solutions can only be obtained by methods of successive approximations of one kind or another. The classic method of finding a maximum is the gradient method, or really, the gradient family of methods. That is, in the case of an unconstrained maximum, we seek to climb uphill. Now, as I remarked earlier, the typical maximization problem in operations research is a problem of a constrained maximum. It is possible in many cases to extend the classic gradient method to the problem of constrained maxima by making use of equivalence of constrained maxima and games (Arrow and Hurwicz, 1957).

The point to be stressed is that with the gradient method or any other method of successive approximations, we never, strictly speaking, achieve the solutions. We only stop when we have decided that the path is stable enough to warrant cessation. Further, as the problem becomes more and more complicated, the possibility of achieving even this level of approximation decreases. One can always think of realistic problems that are beyond the capacity of any given set of computing machines. This is not to minimize the tremendous developments that the last few years have seen. Problems that could not have been regarded as within the realm of practical solution now fall into this realm. All this seems to do, of course, is to whet our appetite for still bigger problems.

There are several approaches to the computational problem. One is to examine closely the special features of the particular problem and try to devise computational methods that will exploit those special features and thus be efficient. (From a theoretical viewpoint, the discovery of new computational methods is also a decision-theoretical problem, and yet it is not one that has been much handled or well handled. It really becomes a creative act, within the present realm of our experience.) The simplex and other methods in linear programming and the method of functional equations in dynamic programming are examples of this procedure. As we get to more and more specific problems, we find certainly more and more toeholds for computational methods. But usually there are severe limitations to their applicability.

A second technique has been to treat not the original problem but a simpler problem that can be managed. It is hoped that enough of the features of the original problem will remain so that the solution is useful. This method is, in fact, universal. I doubt if there is any real problem that anybody has handled which does not involve a suppression of at least some complications. Again, the question of simplification is a creative act.

Still a third technique is to abandon the search for the optimum and seek instead to find satisfactory procedures. That is, we guess at a procedure and then seek to determine, by real or simulated experience, what its operating characteristics are. If they strike us as being good enough, we use them. Otherwise, we search for more and better methods. In a sense, this last procedure, which ties in closely with what psychologists call the achievement of a level of aspiration, is a dynamic counterpart to the seeking of an optimal method. In fact, it is a method of successive approximations applied to the choice of a computing method. Once a satisfactory method has been found, there is always a tendency to try to improve it. Presumably this process will continue until it converges to the optimum. Like all methods of successive approximations, the convergence will take infinitely long, if indeed it converges at all.

To sum up, at any stage in our operations research, we deal with problems more limited than those we know are real — more limited in time if not in other ways. Our problem must be stated as if it were closed, so that it can be solved, and yet its elements must contain within themselves the possibility of fitting into a larger model. The objective function must reflect the fact that the problem will have implications for the future. Among other things, we must assign valuation to information-gathering and recording activities in our short-run or proximate objective function. We must assign values to the physical outcome of the current decision situation which somehow reflect our estimates, however formed, of their implications for the future. We must, in short, build the possibility of learning into our decision models.

Moreover, even then, we frequently cannot solve our decision problems in the sense of genuinely achieving an optimum with a small expenditure of computing effort. So we are approximating in many different directions. This kind of view of the world may seem somewhat disturbing to some. One likes the idea that there is a finite solution to problems — that they all can be solved with expenditure of sufficient mental energy. But the whole history of mathematics and science is a disproof of any such simple notion. And personally, I now find it rather attractive that the world is an open one, and that there always will be new problems to solve. At no stage will we be able to rest content. As Goethe says: "Whoever strives, him can we save."

References

Kenneth J. Arrow, Theodore Harris, and Jacob Marschak, "Optimal Inventory Policy," *Econometrica,* 19, 250–272 (1951).

Kenneth J. Arrow and Leonid Hurwicz, "Gradient Methods for Constrained Maxima," *Operations Research,* 5, 258–265 (1957).

Richard Bellman, *An Introduction to the Theory of Dynamic Programming,* The Rand Corporation, Santa Monica, California, 1953.

Aryeh Dvoretzky, J. Kiefer, and Jacob Wolfowitz, "The Inventory Problem," *Econometrica,* 20, 187–222, 450–466 (1952).

Samuel Karlin, "The Structure of Dynamic Programming Models," *Naval Res. Log. Quart.,* 2, 285–294 (1955).

Pierre B. D. Massé, *Les réserves et la régulation de l'avenir dans la vie économique,* Hermann and Cie, Paris, 1946.

Herbert Scarf, "Bayes Solutions of the Statistical Inventory Problem," *Annals of Mathematical Statistics,* 30, 490–508 (1959).

Abraham Wald, *Statistical Decision Problems,* Wiley, New York, and Chapman and Hall, London, 1950.

5   Decision Theory and the Choice of a Level of Significance for the *t*-Test

From the viewpoint of decision theory, the choice of a fixed level of significance for tests of statistical hypotheses, regardless of the sample size and of the costs associated with erroneous decisions, was clearly absurd. Yet statistical practice continued and still continues to be dominated by some arbitrary conventions. There is, of course, one strong practical reason, objectivity; it ensures the public that the levels of significance are not being manipulated to persuade readers to a preassigned conclusion. I faced this issue as a pedagogue, since I frequently taught elementary and beginning mathematical statistics in the first twelve years or so of my academic career. This paper, written as part of a festschrift honoring my mentor, Harold Hotelling, was an attempt to provide a reasonably objective procedure that would reflect our changing knowledge as sample size grew and provide a signal to indicate that the inferences themselves were more or less reliable. The paper seems to have had no effect, though it is somewhat gratifying to find one recent sequel in the literature (Shervish, 1983).

It is very remarkable that the rapid development of decision theory has had so little effect on statistical practice. Ever since the classic work of

Neyman and Pearson (1933) it has been apparent that, in the choice of a test for a hypothesis, the power of the test should play a role coordinate with the level of significance. Yet to this day the choice of a critical level for a test statistic is made in practice by an arbitrary conventional choice of the probability of a Type I error; hardly if ever is there explicit justification of the choice made by comparison with the power curve. Twenty-five years after his original paper on the subject, Neyman (1958) again felt impelled to call attention to the disregard of the power concept in choosing a level of significance and a sample size in the testing of hypotheses.

It is true that the original Neyman-Pearson formulation, while making clear the importance of considering the two types of errors, gave no basis for balancing them. The problem is compounded for most practical cases, such as in tests for the mean of a normal distribution, by the multiplicity of the alternative hypotheses. To the single probability of a Type I error must be compared a whole power function. Each test thus defines a pair consisting of a number (the level of significance) and a function (the power function); a preference ordering of the resulting space is by no means easy to define. It is not surprising that attention was largely concentrated on comparisons among tests with the same level of significance, so that only an ordering of power functions was needed, though even this was not a trivial matter when the alternative hypothesis was composite.

A decisive conceptual step forward was the introduction of the weight function by Wald (1950). In the case of testing a hypothesis about the mean of a normal distribution, Wald's theory may be sketched as follows. Let μ be the true mean, $\tilde{\mu}$ the hypothetical mean, a the action of accepting the null hypothesis, r the action of rejecting. Let $w_a(\mu)$ be the loss incurred by accepting the null hypothesis when the true value of the mean is μ, and $w_r(\mu)$ the loss incurred by rejecting the null hypothesis when the true value of the mean is μ. It is assumed that the loss is zero if the action most appropriate to the true value of the mean is taken, so that we may assume that

(5-1) $w_a(\mu) \geqq 0,$ $w_r(\mu) \geqq 0,$ at least one equals zero.

This assumes that the statistician is charged only with that portion of the loss which results from not knowing the true value of μ, a point especially stressed by L. J. Savage (1954, pp. 163–164, 169–171).

Let T be the rejection region in sample space, and $P(T|\mu)$ the probability of rejection if the true value of the mean is μ; we suppose for the moment that this is the only unknown parameter. Then $1 - P(T|\mu)$ is the probability of acceptance. The expected loss or *risk, R(μ)*, is then given by

(5-2) $R(\mu) = w_a(\mu)[1 - P(T|\mu)] + w_r(\mu)P(T|\mu).$

Before simplifying and specializing, let us ask how useful is this formalism. It brings out explicitly the importance of the costs of different types of errors. For the statistician or his client to use this procedure, there are still two difficult questions to be answered. The first is the choice of the weight functions, $w_a(\mu)$ and $w_r(\mu)$. Knowledge of these implies considerable sophistication with respect to the implications of incorrect decisions. The second is the preference ordering among risk functions, $R(\mu)$. For the latter purpose, Wald proposed the minimax principle; for each test, consider the greatest possible risk corresponding to some value of the parameter μ, that is, $\max_\mu R(\mu)$, and then choose that test for which this maximum risk is a minimum. Since the original formulation of the minimax principle, there has been considerable critical analysis of this and alternative principles for ordering risk functions (such as subjective a priori probabilities) as tested against intuitively plausible conditions. Perhaps the most nearly definitive treatment is that of Milnor (1954), who showed in effect that *every* proposed ordering principle contradicts at least one reasonable axiom.

In this chapter I propose to use the minimax principle and to specialize the weight functions so that the value information demanded for their application is reduced to a reasonable minimum. Only tests for the mean of a normal population (with known or unknown variance) are considered. Instead of the present procedure, in which the test is determined by fixing a *statistical* level of significance, the proposed approach is to require fixing a difference in the parameter space which is significant in the more literal sense of the word, that is, a difference which is meaningful from the viewpoint of the losses associated with incorrect choices. The details of the tests for the one-sided and two-sided cases with known and unknown variances are given, along with some computational approximations for large samples.

Economically Significant Differences and the Equal-Probability Test

It is necessary to have some information on the relative values of different errors in order to find an optimal test, but we wish to require as little as possible. Let us permit ourselves the following single question: For what value of the unknown mean do we consider the corresponding Type II error to be just as costly as a Type I error? We will call the difference between this value of the mean and the hypothetical value an *economically significant difference,* denoted by δ_0. Then the test proposed here has the requirement that the probability of a Type II error, when the difference between the true and hypothetical means is the economically significant difference, shall equal the probability of a Type I error. Such a test will be termed an *equal-probability test.*

In this section the concepts will be developed for the case of one-sided alternatives to a hypothesis about the mean of a normal distribution with known variance. To begin with, assume that the hypothetical mean is 0, the known variance is 1, and the sample size is 1. The minimax test will be briefly recapitulated and shown to include the equal-probability test as a special case.

If x is the observation, then the optimal test will, of course, have the form of accepting when $x \leq x_c$ and rejecting otherwise, for some *critical test-value* x_c. The cost of rejecting the null hypothesis will be assumed to fall toward zero as μ increases from zero, while the cost of accepting becomes greater as μ increases. In view of Eq. (5-1), we may write

(5-3) $w_r(\mu) = 0$ for $\mu > \mu_0$, $w_a(\mu) = 0$ for $\mu < \mu_1$,

where

(5-4) $0 < \mu_0 < \mu_1$.

Under these conditions it has been shown (Allen, 1953; Karlin, 1957, p. 307) that the minimax critical test-value x_c is determined by the equation

(5-5) $\displaystyle\max_{\mu \leq \mu_0} w_r(\mu)P(x \geq x_c|\mu) = \max_{\mu \geq \mu_1} w_a(\mu)P(x \leq x_c|\mu)$.

By suitable choice of the units of measurement of losses, we can assume without loss of generality that

(5-6) $w_r(0) = 1$,

which is the cost of a Type I error. It is reasonable to assume that $w_r(\mu)$ falls off very rapidly for $\mu > 0$. Indeed, from a decision-theoretic viewpoint, there is no special parameter value which can be designated as the hypothetical value of the mean; all the information is already contained in the two weight functions. We may assume that the class of problems usually referred to as testing of hypotheses is characterized by the rapid fall of the function $w_r(\mu)$ beyond the value usually referred to as the hypothetical mean. To a first approximation, then, we may suppose that $w_r(\mu) = 0$ for $\mu > 0$, or

(5-7) $\mu_0 = 0$.

There is great variety in the possible shapes of the function $w_a(\mu)$. As already remarked, it ought to be monotone increasing; from general theoretical principles it ought to be bounded.[1] From the definition of the economically significant difference δ_0 and from the normalization (5-6),

(5-8) $w_a(\delta_0) = 1.$

The simplest function satisfying these conditions is the step-function

(5-9) $w_a(\mu) = \begin{cases} 0, & \text{for } \mu < \delta_0. \\ 1, & \text{for } \mu \geq \delta_0. \end{cases}$

One can, of course, argue that this class of functions is too simple; however, for practical purposes it is very useful to work with a one-parameter family of functions so that the particular weight function to be used in any given case can be determined by a single piece of information, such as a knowledge of δ_0.

If we assume the values given in Eqs. (5-7) and (5-9), then, for the normal distribution (and a great many others), Eq. (5-5) reduces to

(5-10) $P(x \geq x_c | \mu = 0) = P(x \leq x_c | \mu = \delta_0),$

that is, the equal-probability test.[2]

In the case of the normal distribution, (5-10) leads immediately to the simple characterization

(5-11) $x_c = \delta_0/2.$

To examine the implications of this critical test-value as opposed to those implied by a conventional level of significance, let us first consider what values of δ_0 are reasonable. The most convenient way of judging this is to assume that we seek to characterize the distribution so as to make predictions about future values of the random variable. Suppose, for example, that we are interested in knowing the probability that $x \geq 0$ (as in comparing a new proposed treatment with an existing one). Under the null hypothesis, the probability is, of course, 0.50. For values of $\mu = 0.25, 0.50, 1.00, 2.00,$ and 3.00, the probability that $x \geq 0$ becomes 0.60, 0.69, 0.84, 0.98, and 1.00

---

1. Otherwise a form of the St. Petersburg paradox will occur; this was first observed by Menger (1933), who, however, drew other inferences. See also Blackwell and Girshick (1954, pp. 104–111); and Arrow (1958).

2. A more general class of tests which includes the equal-probability test has been suggested by Lehmann (1958, p. 1171).

(to two decimal places), respectively. Even the smallest of these figures is considerably different from 0.50, the probability under the null hypothesis. It would appear that the Type II error corresponding to $\mu = 1.00$ would in almost any circumstances be more costly than the corresponding Type I error, so that δ_0 would be less than 1 and frequently less than 0.50.

Suppose, then, to illustrate the equal-probability test, we assume that $\delta_0 = 0.50$. Then the critical value x_c is 0.25, which corresponds to a level of significance in the classical sense of 0.40. This may seem outrageously high when compared with the usual level of 0.05 or less. But consider a Type II error corresponding to $\mu = 0.5$. Under the equal-probability test, the probability of this error is again 0.40, and under the classical test with a 0.05 significance level, 0.87! A dim realization of the very low power of the classical test for small samples is in the minds of those scientific workers who, after reporting the absence of significant differences, add that the difference would have been significant if the sample size had been larger.

This simple example also shows that the equal-probability test will increase the real usefulness of the significance level, for it will now represent the probabilities of two errors whose meaning is easily understood, so that the statistician and the reader can immediately form a judgment about the reliability of the whole statistical procedure. Present practice does not provide any such figure, other than the uncertain information implied by the sample size.[3]

The formulation of the test for samples of any size and (known) standard deviation of any magnitude proceeds along obvious lines. It is worth noting, however, that the intuitive considerations on reasonable magnitudes of δ_0 remain valid if the difference of the means is measured in standard deviation units, not absolute units. From this point on, we will assume that *the economically significant difference is always measured in standard deviation units.* Let

$$(5\text{-}12) \qquad z = \sqrt{N}(\bar{x} - \tilde{\mu})/\sigma,$$

where N is the sample size, $\bar{x}$ the sample arithmetic mean, $\tilde{\mu}$ the hypothetical mean, and σ the standard deviation of the underlying population. Then, of course, z has a normal distribution with unit variance and a mean which is zero under the null hypothesis. If δ_0 is the economically significant differ-

---

3. Publication of the power of the test for at least one alternative hypothesis would be helpful even with the constant-level-of-significance test.

ence for x, $\sqrt{N}\,\delta_0$ is the economically significant difference for z, and the critical test-value is

$$(5\text{-}13) \qquad z_c = \sqrt{N}\,\delta_0/2,$$

the null hypothesis being accepted for values of z smaller than z_c and rejected for larger ones. To illustrate, again with $\delta_0 = 0.50$ and $\sigma = 1$ for a sample size of 9, the test with a 0.05 level of significance has a 0.56 probability of a Type II error at $\mu = 0.5$, while the equal-probability test has a level of significance (and a probability of Type II error at $\mu = 0.5$) of 0.23. The equal-probability and 0.05-level-of-significance tests coincide for a sample size of 43. For larger sample sizes, the constant-level-of-significance test provides excessive protection against Type II errors. With the same example, for a sample of 100, the 0.05-level-of-significance test gives a virtually zero probability of Type II error at $\mu = 0.5$, while the equal-probability test gives a probability of either error of less than 0.01. The slight loss of protection against Type II errors seems to be far more than made up by the great reduction in the probability of Type I errors.

Indeed, as N approaches infinity, the inadequacy of the constant-level-of-significance test becomes more glaring. The probabilities of all kinds of errors approach zero in the equal-probability test, while in the constant-level-of-significance test the probability of a Type I error is maintained constant; all the gain in information due to larger sample size is taken out in the form of increased power. There is no logical foundation for this behavior.

Two-Sided Test with Known Variance

In the two-sided case, the functions $w_a(\mu)$ and $w_r(\mu)$ are symmetric functions of μ about $\mu = \tilde{\mu}$ (the hypothetical mean). If we proceed as before, we assume that

$$(5\text{-}14) \qquad w_r(\mu) = \begin{cases} 1, & \text{if } \mu = \tilde{\mu}, \\ 0, & \text{if } \mu \neq \tilde{\mu}, \end{cases}$$

$$w_a(\mu) = \begin{cases} 1, & \text{if } |\mu - \tilde{\mu}|/\sigma \geq \delta_0, \\ 0, & \text{if } |\mu - \tilde{\mu}|/\sigma < \delta_0. \end{cases}$$

The analog of (5-10) is

$$(5\text{-}15) \qquad P(|z| \geq z_c | \mu = \tilde{\mu}) = P(|z| \leq z_c | \mu = \tilde{\mu} + \delta_0\sigma).$$

Since z is normally distributed with mean $\sqrt{N}(\mu - \tilde{\mu})/\sigma$ and unit variance,

Eq. (5-15) is equivalent to

(5-16) $2 - 2\Phi(z_c) = \Phi(z_c - \sqrt{N}\,\delta_0) - \Phi(-z_c - \sqrt{N}\,\delta_0),$

which defines a relation between the critical test value z_c and the quantity $\sqrt{N}\,\delta_0$; here, $\Phi(x)$ is the cumulative normal distribution. The null hypothesis is rejected when $|z| \geq z_c$ and accepted otherwise.

The Case of Unknown Variance

In the one-sided case, the previous considerations lead to the formula

(5-17) $P(t \geq t_c | \mu = \tilde{\mu}) = P(t \leq t_c | \mu = \tilde{\mu} + \delta_0\sigma),$

where $t = \sqrt{N}(\bar{x} - \tilde{\mu})/s$, and s is the sample standard deviation. The statistic t has the cumulative noncentral t-distribution with parameter $\lambda = (\mu - \tilde{\mu})/\sigma_{\bar{x}}$, equal to 0, $\sqrt{N}\,\delta_0$, in evaluating the left-hand and right-hand sides of (5-17), respectively; when $\lambda = 0$, the distribution is, of course, Student's distribution. The probabilities also depend on the number of degrees of freedom ($N - 1$ in the problem being studied), though this dependence is not indicated in the notation. Equation (5-17) can be solved by successive approximation with the aid of a table of the noncentral t-distribution (Resnikoff and Lieberman, 1957).

For samples of size greater than 30, it appears that $t_c = \sqrt{N}\,\delta_0/2$, the formula for the normal case, will be a good approximation. To see this, we use the remark of Wallis (1947, pp. 57–59) that $\bar{x} + ks$ is approximately normally distributed with mean $\mu + k\sigma$ and standard deviation $\sigma\sqrt{(2 + k^2)/2N}$. (Wallis gives this formula as $\sigma\sqrt{(1/N) + k^2/2(N-1)}$, but for N of any significant magnitude, the two should essentially coincide.) Then, if $t_0 = t_c/\sqrt{N}$ and $\psi(x) = 1 - \Phi(x) = \Phi(-x)$, we obtain

(5-18) $\begin{aligned} P(t \leq t_c | \mu = \tilde{\mu} + \delta_0\sigma) &= P(\bar{x} - \tilde{\mu} - t_0 s \leq 0 | \mu = \tilde{\mu} + \delta_0\sigma) \\ &= \Phi[(t_0 - \delta_0)/\sqrt{(2 + t_0^2)/2N}\,] \\ &= \psi[(\delta_0 - t_0)/\sqrt{(2 + t_0^2)/2N}]. \end{aligned}$

Let p be the common value of the two sides of (5-17), and let k_p be the normal deviate exceeded with probability p. Then, from (5-18), we get

(5-19) $(\delta_0 - t_0)/\sqrt{(2 + t_0^2)/2N} = k_p.$

Squaring both sides and simplifying yields

(5-20) $(1 - k_p^2/2N)t_0^2 - 2\delta_0 t_0 + (\delta_0^2 - k_p^2/N) = 0.$

It is also true that $P(t \leq t_c | \mu = \tilde{\mu}) = 1 - p$. In Eq. (5-20), set $\delta_0 = 0$, and replace k_p by $k_{1-p} = -k_p$:

(5-21) $(1 - k_p^2/2N)t_0^2 - k_p^2/N = 0$.

If we subtract (5-21) from (5-20), we find that $t_0 = \delta_0/2$, or $t_c = \sqrt{N}\,\delta_0/2$.
For the two-sided case, the critical test-value t_c is the solution of

(5-22) $P(|t| \geq t_c|\mu = \tilde{\mu}) = P(|t| \leq t_c|\mu = \tilde{\mu} + \delta_0\sigma)$,

which can in principle be solved with the aid of noncentral t-tables. For
sample size greater than 30, Wallis's procedure sketched above can be
applied to yield another approximation. We can write

$$(5\text{-}23)\quad P(|t| \leq t_c|\mu = \tilde{\mu} + \delta_0\sigma) = P(\bar{x} - \tilde{\mu} - t_0 s \leq 0|\mu = \tilde{\mu} + \delta_0\sigma)$$
$$- P(\bar{x} - \tilde{\mu} + t_0 s \leq 0|\mu = \tilde{\mu} + \delta_0\sigma)$$
$$= \psi[(\delta_0 - t_0)/\sqrt{(2 + t_0^2)/2N}\,]$$
$$- \psi[(\delta_0 + t_0)/\sqrt{(2 + t_0^2)/2N}\,]$$

with the aid of (5-20). Let c_2 and c_1 be the two expressions in brackets in
(5-23), respectively, and let $2p$ be the common value of the two sides of
(5-22). Then

$$(5\text{-}24)\quad 2p = P(|t| \geq t_c|\mu = \tilde{\mu}) = 2P(t \geq t_c|\mu = \tilde{\mu})$$
$$= 2P(\bar{x} - \tilde{\mu} - t_0 s \geq 0|\mu = \tilde{\mu})$$
$$= 2\psi[t_0/\sqrt{(2 + t_0^2)/2N}\,],$$

so that

(5-25) $t_0/\sqrt{(2 + t_0^2)2N} = k_p$.

If we solve for t_0 from (5-25) and substitute into c_1 and c_2, we find that

(5-26) $c_1 = k_p + \delta_0\sqrt{(2N - k_p^2)/2}$, $c_2 = -k_p + \delta_0\sqrt{(2N - k_p^2)/2}$.

Thus p has to satisfy the equation, from (5-23),

(5-27) $\psi(c_2) - \psi(c_1) = 2p$,

which can be solved by successive approximations using only normal tables.
Once $2p$ is found, t_c can be found from the relation $P(|t| \geq t_c|\mu = \tilde{\mu}) = 2p$.

Tests of Regression Coefficients

Write a regression relation as

(5-28) $\tilde{Y}_X = \mu_Y + \beta(X - \bar{X})$,

where $\tilde{Y}_X$ is the conditional mean of Y given X, and $\overline{X}$ is the sample mean. If β_0 is a hypothetical value for the regression coefficient, then the null hypothesis asserts that the conditional mean is

$$(5\text{-}29) \qquad \tilde{Y}_{0X} = \mu_Y + \beta_0(X - \overline{X}).$$

If the null hypothesis is false, an error is made concerning the conditional mean:

$$(5\text{-}30) \qquad \tilde{Y}_X - \tilde{Y}_{0X} = (\beta - \beta_0)(X - \overline{X}).$$

It is this difference which is analogous to the error in the hypothetical mean in the univariate case if we know in advance for what value of X we are going to use the regression relation. More generally, we may imagine planning to use the regression relation for many different values of X. Let μ_X be the mean of these future values of X and let σ_X^2 be their variance. Then the standard error in the conditional mean is

$$(5\text{-}31) \qquad L = |\beta - \beta_0|[\sigma_X^2 + (\mu_X - \overline{X})^2]^{1/2}.$$

As before, the economic significance of this loss will be judged relative to the standard deviation, in this case, the conditional standard deviation of Y given X, $\sigma_{Y \cdot X}$, which, in usual regression theory, we assume to be independent of X. Then the *economically significant difference* δ_0 will be a value of $L/\sigma_{Y \cdot X}$ such that the cost of a Type II error will equal that of a Type I error.

The test of significance is based, of course, on the statistic

$$(5\text{-}32) \qquad t = (b - \beta_0)/s_b,$$

where b and s_b are the usual estimates of β and σ_b, respectively. The statistic t has, in general, the noncentral t-distribution with parameter

$$(5\text{-}33) \qquad \lambda = (\beta - \beta_0)/\sigma_b.$$

If we find the value of $\beta > \beta_0$ for which $L/\sigma_{Y \cdot X} = \delta_0$ and then substitute into Eq. (5-33), we find

$$(5\text{-}34) \qquad \lambda_0 = \{\delta_0/[\sigma_X^2 + (\mu_X - X)^2]^{1/2}\}(\sigma_{Y \cdot X}/\sigma_b).$$

Notice that the ratio $\sigma_{Y \cdot X}/\sigma_b$ is equal to $\Sigma(X - \overline{X})^2$, the summation being over sample values, and thus does not involve any unknown parameters.

In the one-sided case, the equal-probability test requires choosing t_c so that

$$(5\text{-}35) \qquad P(t \geq t_c | \lambda = 0) = P(t \leq t_c | \lambda = \lambda_0),$$

and in the two-sided case, so that

(5-36) $P(|t| \geq t_c | \lambda = 0) = P(|t| \leq t_c | \lambda = \lambda_0)$.

The approximations of the previous section can be used, with $\sqrt{N} \, \delta_0$ replaced by λ_0.

References

Allen, S. G., Jr. A class of minimax tests for one-sided composite hypotheses. *Ann. Math. Stat.,* 1953, vol. 24, 295–298.

Arrow, K. J. Bernoulli utility indicators for distributions over arbitrary spaces. Technical Report no. 57, ONR Contract N6onr 25133. Stanford, Calif: Department of Economics, Stanford University, July 30, 1958.

Blackwell, D., and Girshick, M. A. *Theory of Games and Statistical Decisions.* New York: Wiley, 1954.

Karlin, S. Pólya-type distributions, II. *Ann. Math. Stat.,* 1957, vol. 28, 281–308.

Lehmann, E. Significance level and power. *Ann. Math. Stat.,* 1958, vol. 29, 1167–76.

Menger, K. Das Unsicherheitsmoment in der Wertlehre. *Z. Nationalökonomie,* 1933, vol. 4, 459–485.

Milnor, J. Games against nature. Chap. 4 in R. M. Thrall, C. H. Coombs, and R. L. Davis (eds.), *Decision Processes.* New York: Wiley, 1954.

Neyman, J. The use of the concept of power in agricultural experimentation. *J. Indian Soc. Agric. Stat.,* 1958, vol. 9, 9–17.

Neyman, J., and Pearson, E. S. On the problem of the most efficient tests of statistical hypotheses. *Phil. Trans. Roy. Soc. (London),* Ser. A, 1933, vol. 231, 289–337.

Resnikoff, G. J., and Lieberman, G. J. *Tables of the Non-Central t-Distribution.* Stanford, Calif.: Stanford University Press, 1957.

Savage, L. J. *The Foundations of Statistics.* New York: Wiley, 1954.

Shervish, M. 1983. User-oriented inference. *J. Am. Stat. Assoc.,* 1983, vol. 78, 611–615.

Wald, A. *Statistical Decision Functions.* New York: Wiley, 1950.

Wallis, W. A. Use of variables in acceptance inspection for percent defective. Chap. 1 in C. Eisenhart, M. Hastay, and W. A. Wallis (eds.), *Selected Techniques of Statistical Analysis.* New York: McGraw-Hill, 1947.

6   Insurance, Risk, and Resource Allocation

In writing on the economics of medical care (Arrow, 1963; to appear in a later volume of these Collected Papers), I began to perceive the importance of difference in information among different parties in a market relation. The original examples were medical insurance, where the insurance company cannot monitor adequately the need for medical care, and the relations between physician and patient. As it happens, I had had a brief quasi-involvement with the actuarial profession and noticed the connections with some concepts that insurance practice had dealt with. Looking for a job to earn some money during the summer of 1940, I had by chance found one as an actuarial clerk with a small insurance company. My job was routine calculation of premiums, but I learned a good deal about the concepts used. While a graduate student having no clear prospects that could meet my depression-born needs for security, I took the precaution of taking the examinations of the Actuarial Society of America. (I eventually passed three, after some failures, and was offered a job; but when Tjalling Koopmans, who had worked for an insurance company, assured me that "there was no music in it," I went to the Cowles Commission instead.) Much of the material to be learned was extremely detailed algebra, but I did encounter some interesting concepts such

Reprinted from K. J. Arrow, *Aspects of the Theory of Risk-Bearing* (Helsinki: Yrjö Jahnssonin säätio, 1965), lecture 3.

as *moral hazard* and *adverse selection.* They came to my mind again in the study of medical economics, and I began to see a more general pattern applicable elsewhere in economic behavior.

As mentioned in the headnote to Chapter 9, Volume 3, I was invited to give the Ÿrjö Jahnsson lectures in December 1983 and chose the economics of uncertainty as the theme. In the third of these lectures I laid out the basic problems for economic analysis suggested by differential information, though it remained for others to make a positive contribution to their analysis. It is this lecture that follows. It originally appeared in the published version of the Yrjö Jahnsson lectures and was later reprinted as chapter 5 in a volume of essays on risk-bearing (Arrow, 1971).

Insurance is an item of considerable importance in the economies of advanced nations, yet it is fair to say that economic theorists have had little to say about it, and insurance theory has developed with virtually no reference to the basic economic concepts of utility and productivity. Insurance is not a material good; although it is usually classified as a service, its value to the buyer is clearly different in kind from the satisfaction of consumers' desires for medical treatment or transportation. Indeed, unlike goods and services, transactions involving insurance are an exchange of money for money, not money for something which directly meets needs. The closest analogue in ordinary economic theory to an insurance policy is a bond or note, an exchange of money now for money later. But an insurance is a more subtle kind of contract; it is an exchange of money now for money payable contingent on the occurrence of certain events.

I wish to explore, in a tentative way, the lessons that economic theory on the one hand and insurance theory and practice on the other can bring to each other. It will be seen that the shifting of risks, the very essence of insurance, occurs in many forms in the economic system, but always with some limits. The economic system is hobbled by these limits; it is desirable to extend the scope of risk shifting, and indeed from time to time new economic institutions arise with precisely this aim in view. But an examination of insurance itself shows that there are strong reasons for its being limited to such a relatively narrow field. By understanding the restrictions on insurability of risks, we can understand better the reasons why the economic system in general is so limited in its risk-bearing ability, and therefore we will be in a better position to expand that ability.

Although our economics textbooks have remarkably little to say about the matter, nothing is more obvious than the universality of risks in the economic system. Machines break down from time to time; the coordination of complex production processes can never be perfect; despite the decreasing importance of agriculture, the uncertainties of the elements still play an important role; the search for mineral deposits is notoriously chancy; the demand for a product may change unpredictably in relatively short time spans, due to changing tastes or the development of substitutes; in a capitalist society, the success of new businesses and the movements of the stock market cannot be foreseen; and above all, technological progress and the development of new knowledge are by their very nature leaps into the unknown.

In any economic system, capitalist or socialist, there is a responsible agent on whom the burden of any given risk falls in the first instance. In a capitalist world, with which I shall be mostly concerned, the owner of a business typically is supposed to assume all the risks of uncertainty, paying out the unexpected losses and enjoying the unexpected gains. But society has long recognized the need for permitting him to shed some of the risks. A man's capacity for running a business well need not be accompanied by a desire or ability for bearing the accompanying risks, and a series of institutions for shifting risks has evolved.

Insurance itself is an early and important example of such an institution. The risks of business losses due to maritime disaster or fire were at an early stage shifted from the business firm to specialized insurance companies. But other institutions for risk shifting have emerged. The most important is the market for common stocks. By this means, the owner of a business could divest himself of some of the risks, permitting others to share in the benefits and losses. Since each individual could now own a diversified portfolio of common stocks, each with a different set of risks attached, he could derive the benefits of a reduced aggregate risk through pooling; thus, the stock market permits a reduction in the social amount of risk bearing.

To my knowledge, there are no other major institutions in which the shifting of risks through a market appears in such an explicit form as in insurance and common stocks. Nevertheless, the universal presence of risk is necessarily felt, even though only implicitly, in any contracts requiring performance in the future. A case in which the risk elements still show fairly clearly is that of contracting for military procurement. If the government were to purchase in accordance with the usual procedure of the market, it would settle, by bargaining or bidding, on a fixed price which would be paid to the producer for each unit delivered. Indeed, this procedure is followed for products of a routine nature, such as clothing or office supplies or even arms and ammunition of types that have been in production for a long time. But in purchasing very large and expensive items which have not been produced in large quantities previously, most especially airplanes, the contract used is of the so-called cost-plus variety. The government agrees beforehand to reimburse the producer for all his costs, whatever they may be, plus a fixed agreed profit.

The reason for this alternative mode of payment is, of course, that the producer finds himself very uncertain about costs and is unwilling to bear the risks. One can, for analytic purposes, regard a cost-plus contract as being made up of two contracts, one a fixed-price contract of the usual commercial type, and one an insurance contract by which the government agrees to reimburse the manufacturer for his unexpected costs. Thus the change from one contract to another can be regarded as a shifting of cost uncertainties from its normal locus in the producing firm to the purchaser, in this case, the government. We notice that private purchasers do not offer similar contracts to their suppliers, even in analogous cases; for example, airlines do not offer cost-plus contracts to aircraft manufacturing companies. The explanation for the range of use of cost-plus contracts is the same as that for the existence of insurance companies; it is profitable for all concerned that risks be shifted to the agency best able to bear them through its wealth and its ability to pool risks. The government, above all other economic agencies, fits this description.

Risks enter necessarily into all contracts into the future, but only as one element among others. Any bond has, after all, the risk of default, and the rate of interest is in fact greater on bonds judged risky by the market than for government bonds; the interest rate differential is in effect a premium paid by the borrower for insurance against default, the lender being at the same time the insurer. Futures contracts in commodities and in foreign exchange are well known to supply insurance against price movements among their other social functions.

At this point it might be useful to ask more specifically, What is the social usefulness of markets for shifting risks? Of course, there is always the simple justification for any contract freely arrived at between two individuals; if both of them choose to enter the contract, then both of them must be better off. Society, after all, is just a convenient label for the totality of individuals, and if the two contracting parties are better off, then so is society, unless other individuals are injured in some way. If I dislike an uncertainty and if I can find someone else or some organization to whom the cost of bearing the uncertainty is less than it is to me, then there will be some trade possible, by which the other party assumes the risk, I pay a fixed premium, and both of us are better off.

But the mere trading of risks, taken as given, is only part of the story, and in many respects the less interesting part. The possibility of shifting risks, of insurance in the broadest sense, permits individuals to engage in risky activities which they would not otherwise undertake. I may well hesitate to erect a building out of my own resources if I have to stand the risk of its burning down; but I would build if the building can be insured against fire. The shifting of risks through the stock market permits an adventurous industrialist to engage in productive activities, even though he is individually unable to bear the accompanying risks of failure. Of course, under these circumstances, some projects will be undertaken which will turn out to be mistakes; that is what is meant by risk. But at any moment society is faced with a set of possible new projects which are on the average profitable, though one cannot know for sure which particular projects will succeed and which will fail. If risks cannot be shifted, then very possibly none of the projects will be undertaken; if they can be, then each individual investor, by diversification, can be fairly sure of a positive outcome, and society will be better off by the increased production.

A particularly important class of projects that society may consider are research activities. By definition, research is a venture into the unknown, such as geographic exploration was in the time of Columbus. The outcome of any research project is necessarily uncertain, and the most important results are likely to come from projects whose degree of uncertainty to begin with was greatest. The shifting of risks is thus most needed for what is very likely the most profitable of activities from society's point of view.

Suppose that we could introduce into the economic system any institutions we wished for shifting risks instead of being confined to those developed historically. In view of the preceding discussion, it is not hard to see what an ideal arrangement would consist of. We would want to find a market in which we could insure freely against any economically relevant event. That is, an individual should be able to bet, at fixed odds, any amount he wishes on the occurrence of any event which will affect his welfare in any way. The odds — or, in a different and more respectable language, the premium on the insurance — should be determined, as with any other price, so that supply and demand are equal.

Under such a system productive activity and risk bearing can be divorced, each being carried out by the one or ones best qualified. It must be pointed out, though, that the range of insurance policies required by this ideal system is indeed very wide. An entrepreneur would wish to be insured against shifts in demand for his product as well as against unexpected difficulties in production. He or the investor in his enterprises might even wish to insure against his failure to make an appropriate judgment in some future situation.

The devices actually available for risk shifting, common stocks and forward contracts, are far from meeting the ideal standards suggested above. The entrepreneur can shift his risks through floating common stocks, but only in an undiscriminating way. Suppose he is quite certain about the production costs of a new product but uncertain about the market. He would like insurance only about sales, but the issue of common shares means that he has to share the fruits of his special knowledge of production methods, about which he is not uncertain, in order to be protected against selling risks. He may therefore be motivated not to enter into production at all.

Another example of the inadequacy of the stock market can be given. Suppose that all firms tend to be profitable or unprofitable together as a result, for example, of shifts in foreign demand. The investors would like to find insurance against a generally unfavorable development, but they cannot find it by any amount of diversification. There may indeed be individuals or organizations who would be willing, at a price, to pay compensation for the occurrence of the unfavorable event, but the stock market does not provide any opportunity for a mutually advantageous insurance transaction to occur.

It would prolong the analysis too much to go into other types of risk shifting, such as forward contracts. In each case, one can see that not all the risks which it would be desirable to shift can be shifted through the market.

The incomplete shifting of risks gives rise to problems which have been recognized by society and solved in different ways. Let me start with one example different in character from those presented before. An individual who needs the services of a physician is uncertain of the quality of medical care he will get. He is further unable to buy insurance against poor quality of care. Society has met this problem by insisting on the licensing of physicians; the uncertainty is reduced by a special process of information gathering and, at the same time, restriction of entry. It is not left to the market to discriminate among different qualities of physicians.

A second solution to problems created by the inability to shift risks is represented by bankruptcy and limited liability laws. The law in effect requires creditors to assume some of the risks of the debtor; it does not leave him free to negotiate a risk-free investment, and it provides for an inalienable limitation of risks to the debtor. The law thus steps in and forces a risk shifting not created in the marketplace.

Yet another step in surmounting market limitations to the shifting of risks is expansion of the scope of direct authority. In all countries we have seen the development of large, integrated business organizations. Within these organizations there are economic problems of allocation and distribution, and in particular there are risk elements, most especially in the production and delivery of component parts and semifinished goods which go into assembly or other additional processing. But the price system, which the economist tends to regard as essential to the rational allocation of resources, is not used within a business organization at all. There are, of course, many reasons for the superior survival value of the large organization, but one of the most important, surely, is its ability to bear risks in individual parts of its total activity.

To illustrate, consider the activity of supplying engines to an automobile assembly line. The engines could in principle be produced by a company different from that assembling the automobiles; indeed, just such a separation does occur in aircraft manufacturing. However, relatively minor variations in the rate at which engines are delivered may cause very considerable losses to the automobile assembly plant, which might find the resulting risks too great to bear. An ideal market for risks, of the type sketched earlier, would create appropriate incentives to the supplier to regularize his delivery, for example by building up inventories. The way this works is that the assembly plant would be willing to pay large premiums for insurance against delivery delays; the supplier would find it profitable to sell such insurance and then take steps to minimize his payments of claims. In addition, it may be profitable for third parties to sell such insurance if they have a greater capability for pooling risks.

This ideal market could be approximated by an agreement between the two parties whereby the supplier pays penalties for poor timing of his deliveries. But such arrangements quickly become too complex for practical application. Instead, we have a tendency toward vertical integration. The supplier of engines and the assembly plant are placed under single management. The overall efficiency of the two units is now achieved by authoritarian rather than market relations; the engine supply is regularized, insofar as possible, by direct orders to do so rather than by price incentives.

Thus, in one way or another, the failures of the market to achieve adequate risk shifting lead to compensatory alterations in social institutions, licensing, bankruptcy and limited liability, and large business organizations. But all of these institutions are steps away from the free working of the price system, which, with the defects that have been noted, has also many virtues which do not need to be expanded on here. Especially, we expect all these institutions to decrease the flexibility and responsiveness of the system to change and innovation. What we observe is that the failure of the price system to handle risk bearing adequately leads to a diminished use of prices even in contexts where they would be most useful in bringing about a careful and flexible confrontation of needs and resources.

Let us now ask why the economic system has not developed a more completely adequate set of markets for risk bearing. To gain insight, we return to the workings of the insurance sector, where risk-bearing markets appear in their purest form. As suggested at the beginning of this chapter, we start from the observation that the operations of insurance are limited in many ways; the reasons for these limitations are the primary reasons for the limited markets for risk bearing in general.

In the first place, insurance is limited as to scope. Many (indeed most) risks are classified as "uninsurable." (This concept is not absolute; the risks that are regarded as insurable vary somewhat from company to company, and there are special groups, such as Lloyd's of London, which will, for suitable prices, insure many risks that ordinary insurance companies will not.)

In the second place, insurance is frequently limited as to amount. Thus, an insurance against fire or similar property loss is invariably limited to the amount of actual loss. This seems so reasonable that one may be surprised at my bringing it up; but in fact the matter is not so simple. If the fire or other loss is a purely random affair, the company is engaging in a bet; if it finds the odds satisfactory, there is no reason why it should not take as much of the bet as the insured wants, provided any individual policy is still relatively small compared to the total resources of the company.

In the case of fire insurance, it might perhaps be held that a rational insurer would never want to insure for more than the value of the loss; but it is easy to find similar types of insurance, most especially private medical insurance, where the limitation on the total amount for which the company is liable is in fact very undesirable for the insured. Indeed, it is precisely the rare case of extraordinarily high medical expenses that one would most want to be insured against.

A third limitation of insurance from the economic viewpoint is its resort to direct controls over the insured. He must submit to a medical examination, in the case of life insurance; his premises must be inspected and he must agree to certain precautions, in the case of fire insurance.

The reasons for these limits have been discussed, of course, in the standard insurance literature, and it would be tedious, though not unprofitable from our general point of view, to examine them in detail. But the factor known as the "moral hazard" is perhaps the most important: *The insurance policy might itself change incentives and therefore the probabilities upon which the insurance company has relied.* Thus, a fire insurance policy for more than the value of the premises might be an inducement to arson or at least to carelessness.

Once stated, it is clear that this principle explains the limitations of both insurance in particular and risk shifting through the market in general. The problem is that the insurer, or more broadly, the risk bearer cannot completely define his risks; in most circumstances he only observes a result which is a mixture of the unavoidable risk, against which he is willing to insure, and human decision. If the motives of the insured for decision are to reduce loss, then the insurance company has little problem. But the insurance policy may, as we have seen, lead to a motive for increased loss, and then the insurer or risk bearer is bearing socially unnecessary costs. Either he will refrain from insuring or he will resort to direct inspection and control, to make as certain as he can that the insured is minimizing all losses under the latter's control.

The case of cost-plus contracts, discussed earlier as a risk-shifting device, has indeed attracted much attention. The supplier is relieved of all risks attached to costs; by the same token, he has no incentive to keep costs to a minimum. If life is made more comfortable by not paying strict attention to economy, it is to be expected that costs will show a tendency to rise above the necessary level. Indeed, it is widely charged that this is precisely what does occur. It is now easy to see why insurance against failure of businesses or of research projects has not arisen; the incentive to succeed may be too greatly reduced.

I have now first sketched an ideal method of shifting risks and then argued that the moral hazard, as well as other factors not discussed, will prevent the method from being realized in practice. Can we say nothing further? I think we can go back to insurance practice once more for a general principle, that of "coinsurance." When told that two ideals are in conflict, the economist's typical reaction is, or should be, that some middle way can be found which will best compromise the two goals. If a complete absence of risk shifting is bad because it inhibits the undertaking of risky enterprises, and if total risk shifting is bad because it reduces the incentives for their success, then it is reasonable to suggest that partial risk shifting might be best. This is precisely what is meant by coinsurance; the insurer pays some stated proportion of the loss. Devices can undoubtedly be found whereby part but not all of the risks on new businesses or on research projects will be borne by others, reducing as far as possible the obstacles to risk taking without diluting too greatly the necessary motivation for efficiency.

References

Arrow, K. J. 1963. "Uncertainty and the Welfare Economics of Medical Care," *American Economic Review,* 53:941–973.
Arrow, K. J. 1971. *Essays in the Theory of Risk-Bearing.* Chicago: Markham, and Amsterdam: North-Holland.

7 Statistical Requirements for Greek Economic Planning

I had known Andreas Papandreou when he was chairman of the Department of Economics at the University of California, Berkeley, for a few years around 1960. He went on leave in 1962 to head the Ford Foundation–financed Center for Economic Research in Athens. As he explained at a farewell party, he felt an obligation, as an American of Greek origin, to use his abilities as an economist to help his native country.

I spent the academic year 1963–64 as an Overseas Fellow at Churchill College in Cambridge, England. During the fall my friend and then colleague at Stanford, Hollis Chenery, came through, and upon hearing that I had no particular plans for the summer of 1964, promptly suggested that I visit the Center for Economic Research. He himself visited Papandreou shortly thereafter, and he invited me. The idea of a summer in Greece was attractive to my family as well as to me, and I accepted. By this time, however, Andreas's father, George Papandreou, had become prime minister, and

Reprinted from *Statistical Requirements for Greek Economic Planning,* Center of Planning and Economic Research, Lecture Series no. 18 (Athens, 1965). I wish to express my gratitude for the invaluable work of my research assistant, T. Velissaropoulos, and for the penetrating criticisms of Pan A. Yotopoulos. I also wish to acknowledge benefit from reading the excellent and stimulating memorandum prepared by T. Balogh for the National Statistical Service, "Suggestions on a Closer Linkage of Statistics-Economics Research and Planning for an Integration of Greece with EEC," dated September 1962. Balogh's memorandum was primarily concerned with recommendations for research, and only to a limited extent with statistics in the strict sense.

shortly thereafter Andreas renounced his American citizenship and became a member of his father's government. By the time I arrived in Greece, there was new leadership at the center.

Nevertheless, the atmosphere was very stimulating. There were a number of visitors and a number of bright young Greek economists. There was, to be sure, the background of a complex political situation, internally and with the United States, which was to erupt a few years later. In addition, there were the distractions of Greek tourism and daily life. I decided that this was a time to do something more practical and specific to the environment. To this end, I followed the precepts I had laid down in my paper on statistics and economic policy (Chapter 3 of this volume) and suggested the collection of additional economic data with a view to improving the decision-making processes of the government.

Decision making, economic or other, always involves predictions of the future. The purpose of adopting a new policy is to cause the future to be different, and presumably better, than it otherwise would have been; to make an intelligent choice, then, it is essential to predict, within the smallest possible margins of uncertainty, the difference which the policy will make to the future evolution of the economic system.

But knowledge of the future is only derivable from that of the past and present. Moreover, the knowledge we need for prediction is not merely knowledge of isolated facts, important as these are, but even more of regularities and relations among economic magnitudes. In economic analysis, these have typically been derived either from cross-section or from time-series analyses. The former requires detailed knowledge of individual units in the present, the latter more aggregated knowledge not only of the present but also of a period in the past sufficiently long that stable relations may have a chance to be revealed and tested. Both forms of analysis are useful, but there are some important questions, such as the rate of technological advance, which can only be settled by time-series analysis. Now the attempt to estimate series of economic magnitudes for the past, though not necessarily impossible, is difficult, costly, and likely to lead to estimates with high and frequently unknown limits of uncertainty. On the other hand, a series begun now will, in ten years' time, be a series of adequate length for sophisticated time-series analysis. It is not now possible to have an adequately measured past; but by enlarging the scope of collection of statistical data, such a past will become available in the not-too-distant future.

It is true, then, that a major part of the value of increased data collection will not accrue for some period of time. But of course the same can be said of many capital-intensive projects, such as irrigation, and yet they may well be excellent investments. In the case of data collection, it should be observed first that there will clearly be an immediate value to the data for the derivation of predictable relations by cross-section analysis, and second, that the value of relations derived from time series, when there is sufficient accumulation of data, is incomparably greater than any conceivable cost.[1]

Facts and regular relations perceived from them do not of themselves determine policy. But in their presence many conceivable alternatives become obviously infeasible or nonoptimal, and argument necessarily takes place in a more relevant and fruitful context. This has been most conspicuously shown by discussions of contracyclical policy in the United States and western Europe since 1945. The development of highly reliable and ramified national income and unemployment statistics has made it impossible to question the reality even of recessions that would have been completely disregarded sixty years ago. Further, the presence of continued series has made it possible to meet, by simple reference to historical experience, arguments such as the following: Tax cuts are useless for achieving full employment since individuals will save the entire amount of the cut. The value to the economy of such economic intelligence, measured in terms of national income, must be many thousands of times the cost.

In brief, then, I am arguing that increased knowledge of economic facts is likely to be as productive an investment as any economy is likely to have available. I would hold that this proposition is true even for the United States, which already has a rich and highly sophisticated and reliable statistical system. The proposition is a fortiori true for developing countries; on the one hand, their economies are undergoing radical structural alterations and therefore require for their understanding more thorough observation; on the other hand, such countries are very apt to be underdeveloped statistically as well.

Greece, indeed, appears (to this very casual observer's eye) to be unusually capable of handling an increased collection of data. The Statistical Service

---

1. It should be noted that the data requirements for cross-section analyses which are to be repeated regularly are the same as those for time-series analyses. Thus the individual input and output entries in a Census of Manufactures can be used for estimating production functions on a cross-section basis, at least if certain conditions are fulfilled; the aggregate inputs and outputs obtained by summarizing successive censuses (and the intervening sample surveys) can be used for time-series estimates of production functions. But the data actually collected are the same.

appears, from its product, to have adequate statistically trained personnel to move further in the direction of thorough coverage of economic intelligence.

In the next section I will discuss briefly some general principles which should guide decisions on the range of economic data to be collected. Following that, a set of assumptions will be made about the general nature of Greek economic policy. As will be brought out, the statistical requirements for economic decision making depend on the range of economic instruments the government allows itself. The fourth section will present some general recommendations about the collection of economic statistics. The last three sections will present recommendations for the collection of specific economic magnitudes in the fields of investment and capital, labor, and foreign trade, respectively.

Principles for the Selection of Economic Data

It is useful, and conformable to a growing usage, to differentiate between *planning* and economic *decision making.* Planning is the drawing up of long-term plans covering the economy as a whole. It tends to be general and aggregative; it does not imply specific economic decisions but only strategies and broad lines of policy. Plans (of which the French is probably the most developed example) really tend to be projections over a period of four to five years, alternative projections being made for different sets of assumptions about broad economic magnitudes such as the savings ratio, the proportions of gross national product originating in manufacturing and other equally broad sectors, or the desired rate of growth.

Specific economic decisions are, or should be, taken in the context of the plan. A specific decision might be an investment, a change in tariff structure, or the establishment of new sources of credit; in any case, it is an action, not merely a general intention to perform a class of actions. Economic decisions may be made in various places: they may be public (governmental) or private (household or firm). It is worth noting here that information is needed for both kinds of decisions and, what may be less obvious, that publicly collected and distributed information can be highly useful for private decision making. (The converse, of course, is also true; after all, government statistics are to a large extent a summarization of private information.) Indeed, the plan itself serves as information to private firms, since it gives a broad picture of the evolution of the economy in the near future. The individual firm can therefore economize on the use of its resources for forecasting by accepting the government's projections and concentrating on the variables more individual to the firm.

For planning or for predicting the consequences of an individual decision, it is necessary to have a system of relations for projecting into the future. The relations used may be simply assumptions of constant ratios (for example, capital-output, savings-income) or they may be more complex production and consumption functions, but in any case they have to be given some numerical content based on past observations. Thus the *estimation* of economic relations is a prime use for economic data.

In any realistic projection some, at least, of the relations must be dynamic, that is, involving economic variables of different date. If nothing else, we find that capital, the accumulated stock of productive equipment, necessarily enters into any growth model in some form or other, and the definitional relation that capital this year equals capital last year, plus net investment, is certainly dynamic. It is now being realized that perhaps equally important are relations involving the accumulation of human capital through education, industrial experience, and migration.

To solve a dynamic system, it is necessary to have *initial values* for at least some of the variables. We will need to have as a datum this year's capital in order to use our system of relations to determine simultaneously next year's capital and investment. Next year's capital, once projected, serves in turn as an initial value for projections to the year after that, and so forth. Thus, once the current-year initial values are known, the dynamic relations can be used to project as far into the future as desired.

This account might give the misleading impression that once we have estimated the relations and measured the initial values, the future is determined and no more data need be collected. Of course, this is false because the relations do not hold exactly, but only with error (and also because the variables are measured only with error). This has the following interesting implications for the use of data in forecasting. (1) Since the projected initial values for the second year are bound to be incorrect, a new projection for the entire relevant future (say five years) should be made each year using the initial values actually observed instead of those projected the previous year. (2) The relations themselves, having been estimated with error, should be reestimated on the basis of the additional data each year, or at any rate, frequently. (3) The actual values each year should be compared with the projections from previous years, to serve as a check on the accuracy of the relations used and to identify as precisely as possible the sources of errors.

So far the emphasis has been on the collection of data for variables used in projections. In a growth context these variables tend to be real magnitudes —investment, capital, labor force. But economic theory has historically stressed the role of prices (in this context, relative prices) as *signals* for the allocation of resources. Speaking in the crudest way, if the same commodity has two different prices in two parts of the market, there is evidence of resource misallocation. In this context the term "prices" must be interpreted to include wages and rates of return on capital in different industries.

Prices have many limitations as indicators of resource allocation, especially in the field of economic growth. But these well-advertised deficiencies should not blind us to their great value when used with appropriate caution. The recording of these signals can be most valuable in calling the attention of the government to blockages in resource allocation and to appropriate policies for their removal. Thus, wide discrepancies in the rate of return between industries suggest, at the very minimum, study to find the cause and possibly indicate the desirability of improved credit facilities, better information to potential investors, the breaking up of a monopoly situation, or even direct government investment. Similarly, wide discrepancies in wages for comparable skills in different sectors suggest imperfections in the labor market, and wide wage discrepancies between occupations for which the training costs differ only slightly may suggest the high social return to investment in training facilities or the breaking up of a monopoly situation.

The public diffusion of information about prices, wages, and especially rates of return will also improve the quality of private decision making. Realization of previously unnoticed profit opportunities will cause capital to flow into more profitable, and therefore more productive, channels. Similarly, labor may gravitate more quickly to high-wage sectors or occupations if the wage differences become sufficiently publicized.

But, as already indicated, prices are far from infallible as a guide to resource allocation. Modern welfare economics suggests that *shadow* or accounting *prices* be calculated and that decisions be based on them. Productive activities should then be chosen so as to maximize shadow profits, which are profits computed according to shadow prices. The differences between shadow and actual prices represent corrections for imperfections in the market mechanism. The calculation of shadow profits is identical with what is usually termed *benefit-cost analysis.*

The computation of shadow prices cannot, at least at this time, be regarded as data collection in the ordinary sense of the term; it is rather part of the research activities which must be associated with government economic decision making. But at least some of the data needed for determination of shadow prices should be collected regularly as part of the general statistical program of the government. Doubtless, some part of the data will have to be collected ad hoc for each particular benefit-cost analysis.

To sum up, then, data are required for (1) the estimation of economic relations, (2) initial values and continued series for revision and verification of projections, (3) price signals, including wages and rates of return, to indicate inefficiencies in the economic system, and (4) raw material for the computation of shadow prices.

The Instruments of Government Policy

As has already been stressed, information is needed for decisions, whether made by the government or by private enterprises. Nevertheless, the exact nature of the data requirements does depend on the role the government has assigned to itself. In a highly centralized economy, where the government has made itself responsible for the bulk of production decisions, it would have to have a correspondingly vast accumulation of detailed data. On the other hand, in an economy where the government leaves the bulk of detailed decisions to private enterprise, it may also assume that the individual firms will collect the data peculiar to their specialized needs and, indeed, that they can do so much more efficiently than the government could. The informational role of the government is then to collect the data useful for its own decision making and those common to the needs of many individual firms. The latter are classic examples of public goods, since the use of data by one firm does not exhaust it for another.

The range of data useful for the government's own decision making depends on the range of decision areas to which it has restricted itself or, in Tinbergen's terms, to the *instruments* of government policy. No official list appears to be available, but the following seems to summarize the instruments available for economic growth.[2]

1. Development corporations for lending and buying equities, to better tap the investment market.
2. Credit policy, particularly setting of priorities in bank loans.
3. Improvement of the private capital market.

---

2. The list is largely derived from the article by A. G. Papandreou, "New Government Vows Sustained Growth Drive," in *Journal of Commerce,* International Edition, August 3, 1964, section 3, pp. 1A, 21A, with some additions based on interviews.

4. Creation of industrial zones or estates which will provide electricity, buildings, and, possibly, machinery to industrial tenants.
5. Feasibility studies for particular kinds of industrial development.
6. Tax policy to encourage fixed investment.
7. Increased education.

Taken together, these items point to a relatively restrained role for the Greek government in economic decision making. The first three instruments are primarily devoted to overcoming imperfections in the capital market. The fourth also has this aim, but in addition permits the exploitation of certain external economies. The fifth instrument is, in fact, the creation of certain kinds of information, specifically benefit-cost analyses. The sixth, if it is to serve the desired purpose, again must be based on the idea of overcoming market imperfections, or on shadow profit computations. The seventh is based on the general hypothesis, derived from a great deal of research in various countries, that the shadow rates of return in education are apt to be very high. For detailed guidance on specific directions for the expansion of education, more specific analyses are still needed.

For this list, it is clear that the role of what I have called signals can be very great. In the following recommendations I have gone somewhat beyond the implications of the list by suggesting that signals as to misallocation of labor, particularly skilled labor, should be collected regularly, as well as those indicating misallocation of capital.

Though signals have a high priority in data collection with this set of instruments, the data needed for the estimation of economic relations and for initial values cannot be neglected. The evolution of an economic plan is also one of the government's aims (I have not classified the plan itself as an instrument, but one could make a case for so doing), and the plan will supply the background information essential to private decision making and to individual benefit-cost analyses by the government. The profits, real or shadow, from any long-lived investment require for their estimation a forecast of the general economic environment which affects both demand and the supply of complementary factors. So, along with the signals, priority must be given to the variables which enter into the general macroeconomic system of dynamic relations.

General Recommendations on the Collection of Data

It will be convenient to group in this section several recommendations which apply to broad categories of data rather than to the collection of specific kinds.

Complete Sector Coverage

With regard to all the data whose collection is recommended in the following section, as well as similar kinds of data now collected, it is strongly recommended that they be collected from *all* sectors of the economy. The tendency now is to collect such data primarily for manufacturing. But it is equally important to have information on agriculture, services (especially the distributive services), and construction. This is in no way a denial that manufacturing must grow more rapidly than other sectors, but its growth will depend in part on the (relative) withdrawal of resources from other sectors. Hence, data which will cast light on efficiency changes in nonmanufacturing sectors are just as important for policy formation as data for manufacturing itself. In addition, of course, it is not always to be presupposed that manufacturing is the sole road to increased wealth, and opportunities for investment in particular branches of nonmanufacturing sectors should not be overlooked dogmatically.

Publicity of Methodology

One procedural matter should be given a good deal of stress. It is very important for the proper working of a statistical system that the maximum publicity be given to its methods of procedure and calculation. Thus, the consumer of the statistics will be properly apprised of its value to him, and the producer will be subject to more scrutiny. This should not be thought of as a disadvantage to the latter; it enables him to benefit from the comments of others, and if deficiencies exist which are the result of inadequate resources, it enables him to make a better case for more funds.

In particular, it does not appear that there exists, for general circulation, an adequate statement of the procedure and sources used in deriving the Greek national income accounts and, specifically, of the price deflators used in arriving at real national income figures. Since these numbers are of crucial importance, both in estimating economic relations and, perhaps more important, in checking ex post on the performance of the economy, they deserve the most complete explanation of methodology and sources possible.

Presentation of Comparative Experience

One major source of information about economic relations appropriate to Greece is the experience of other more or less comparable countries. Such comparisons are in fact made all the time, implicitly or explicitly, in current studies of economic development. It would be useful and probably not too expensive to keep routinely comparable series on key indicators of economic growth and accompanying structural changes. These might include real national income and its components, distribution of employment and domestic products originating by sectors (on a two-digit basis if possible), rates of return, capital-output and labor-output ratios by sector (two-digit or even three-digit if possible), real wages (preferably differentiated by occupation and sector), savings ratios, consumption patterns, and exports and imports (on a sector basis if possible). Of course, a number of the items mentioned will not be currently available, but the list does express comparative data which it would be useful to have.

Thought would have to be given to the choice of countries, and much would depend on the availability of statistics as well as the comparability of the countries. They should not all be similar to the Greek economy in level and structure; it would be well to include, for comparative purposes, some economies with considerably different per-capita income levels, both higher and lower. Suitable countries which come immediately to mind are Belgium, France or West Germany, Italy, Spain, Turkey, Israel, Japan, Egypt, Mexico, and Ghana.

There would be some work involved in making the series comparable, and a fairly good knowledge of the statistical systems of the individual countries would have to be acquired. (The figures obtained should therefore have a higher degree of comparability than those compiled in the United Nations.) Possibly some cooperative statistical arrangements among several countries could reduce the burden, but it is better to start the collection of comparative series now than to wait for the negotiation of agreements.

It would be best to publish the comparative statistics separately rather than to introduce them into the *National Accounts of Greece* or the *Statistical Yearbook.* The status of the data is different, since they are drawn from foreign sources, and the format will necessarily be affected by the availability of foreign data, which should not affect the complete presentation of domestic data in the usual statistical compilations.

Coordination between Statistical and Planning Agencies

In view of the increasing development of the planning and research activities in the Center of Planning and Economic Research and in the Ministry of Coordination, the using agencies should have a stronger say in the determination of the data to be collected and the methodology of its collection. A

Coordinating Committee for Economic Statistics should be created, with representatives of the Center and the Ministry as well as the National Statistical Service, the National Accounts Division, the new Industrial Development Bank, the Bank of Greece, the Agricultural Bank, and, probably, one or two more ministries which produce or consume statistics. This should provide a channel for communicating need and feasibility in the statistical field. In this way, the statistical services will find it easier to provide the data of greatest use.

Specific Recommendations: Investment, Capital, and Rates of Return

Investment

It is desirable to have an annual table showing for each sector of the economy its purchases from each capital goods sector. Both purchasing and selling sectors should be at the two-digit level.[3] Imported capital goods should be classified with the sector that would have produced them if they had been produced domestically, but the published figures should retain the distinction between imported and domestically produced goods. Since most machinery is currently imported, these data should be relatively easy to collect.

For a time series it is most important to have the quantity flows from capital goods sectors to purchasing sectors. Hence, it will be necessary to form price indices for each flow (or at least for every producing sector) to deflate the value series.

It is important to include in the flow table the purchases of capital goods by the government and by paragovernmental organizations, such as municipalities, public enterprises, and the church.

In addition to fixed investment, figures on inventory accumulation are needed. It would be desirable to have figures on the inventory accumulation of the products of each two-digit sector and of its raw materials classified by sector of origin.

Capital Stock

There is no need to enlarge on the importance to economic growth of the capital stock and its distribution by sectors. Unfortunately, it is also true that

---

3. Such a table now exists, but on a more highly aggregated level than that recommended; see Statistical Service, *1961 Industrial Survey and Survey on Gross Investments* for 1958–60, pp. 25–30 and 54–58.

the measurement of capital is far more difficult, both conceptually and practically, than the measurement of flows. Nevertheless, experience abroad suggests ever more plainly that the task is not beyond the bounds of practicality, and its value in analysis and policy guidance cannot be overestimated. A set of interrelated recommendations is presented here.

(1) Quantity. The simplest requirement is for the book value of the assets, brought to a real basis. It should be presented in two ways, both depreciated and undepreciated. The former measures the productive capacity of the country in a relatively long-run sense, allowing for future replacement needs. The depreciation figures should probably, as in other countries, be taken from standards set by the Statistical Service, not from those used by individual firms which reflect various pressures from tax laws and from the marketplace. The undepreciated stock of capital goods in existence probably better reflects immediate productive capacity. The capital figures should be presented on a two-digit sector basis, if not on an even more refined basis.[4]

Several sources will probably have to be used conjointly to get a reliable capital stock series. The balance sheets of corporations are the main starting point, but in view of probable wide variations in meaning and interpretation, they need to be supplemented. The Census of Manufactures and the annual Industrial Surveys could be used, with suitable questionnaires, to have the firms themselves adjust their balance sheets to common definitions.

An alternative method, which should be used at any rate as a check, is the perpetual inventory method, used by Goldsmith in developing his time series of United States wealth[5] and in current studies by the Office of Business Economics of the U.S. Department of Commerce. This method is based essentially on applying a table of assumed lifetimes of different types of capital goods to historical records of their domestic output and imports. It avoids the vagaries of financial considerations in the construction of balance sheets but may suffer from considerable arbitrariness in the assumption of fixed lifetimes for capital goods.

---

4. A table such as that recommended here appears in Statistical Service, *Results of the Industrial Survey of the Year 1958,* pp. 20–21, but with too limited sectoral coverage and apparently without any revaluation of reported assets or depreciation.

5. R. W. Goldsmith, *A Study of Saving in the United States* (Princeton, N.J.: Princeton University Press, 1956).

The best method of all is a true inventory of the stock of capital goods. This is not impractical, especially if done on a sample basis. It has in fact already been carried out by Japan, for the year 1955 (and also by the Soviet Union in 1959).

As a final remark, it may be worth noting that land is part of the capital stock and should be given explicit treatment. This will require, in effect, a classification of land according to category of use. (A cadaster is not necessary for this purpose, though it may well be desirable on other grounds; a sample survey is sufficient.)

(2) Age. It would be valuable, in an analysis of production functions, to indicate the age distribution of capital goods separately by some detailed classification, or at least by machines and buildings. At a minimum, the mean age (weighted by undepreciated value) should be found. This should be carried out for each two-digit sector.

(3) Power. The present series on amount of power installed should be continued with broader sectoral coverage. A number of studies suggest that power is a useful surrogate variable for capital plus technological progress, and power per worker or per unit output may be a very useful indicator of technological level.

(4) Multiple shift use. This is frequently regarded as an easy way of increasing productivity in a capital-poor country. Good data on its prevalence would be a first step toward consideration of policy.

Rate of Return

The rate of return is the ratio of profits to net worth. If book value can be obtained, net worth should not be too hard to estimate. The estimation of profits will be difficult for several reasons, one being the prevalence of small firms in which salaries and payout of profits may be difficult to distinguish, and another the difficulties with depreciation. Nevertheless, this figure is of such key importance, as has been stressed earlier, that strong efforts should be devoted to its estimation.

The Relation between Savings and Investment

Since it is commonly agreed that the imperfection of the capital market is one of the chief problems of the Greek economy, it is important to have a fairly precise picture of the channels by which savings become investment. For this purpose what is needed is a complete flow-of-funds analysis for savings. One would like to know the volume of business savings and how it is allocated among reinvestment in the business, lending for use elsewhere, and accumulation of bank deposits and currency; the allocation of personal savings among currency, deposits, other financial intermediaries, bonds, equities, and direct investment; the distribution of types of lending by banks and financial intermediaries; and the disposition of savings through the government and the foreign sector.

Specific Recommendations: Labor

The literature on economic development has tended to stress problems in the allocation of capital and to neglect those in that of labor. There may be some justification for this in dealing with countries with massive unemployment, but Greece is reaching a state where labor scarcity is real. In any case, it is increasingly recognized that the skill levels of the working force may be of critical importance for growth: undifferentiated numbers of workers are not adequate data for planning.

Wages

Annual wages for manufacturing workers are currently reported, but the coverage should be extended to other sectors of the economy. Further, the wage levels should be differentiated by occupation (taken as some indication of skill level) within each sector. In other words, there should be a two-way classification of wage rates, by sector and occupation. If at all possible (or as a substitute for the occupational classification), wages should also be differentiated by educational level. The latter data will arise more naturally from a population census than from an industrial survey.

Skills

The employees in each sector should be classified by occupation and educational level, using a three-way classification. The distribution of skills in the population as a whole and its annual change as a result of education and training (on or off the job) should also be presented.

Employment and Unemployment

The present employment coverage should be extended to all sectors of the economy. A glaring gap is the omission of data on unemployment to be derived from a survey of the labor force. If possible, such a survey should also try to obtain some further characteristics of the unemployed, particularly their skills and educational attainments. In rural areas, the labor force survey should measure seasonal unemployment in order to cast some light on the possibilities for complementary seasonal industries and on the true labor return to farmers.

Specific Recommendations: Foreign Trade

Price and Quantity Indices

Export and import price indices seem to be weak in all countries. For some reason of convenience, they are not constructed according to usual price index methods but according to unit value. That is, volume is measured by weight, then prices obtained by dividing value by volume. Obviously, a procedure which equates a ton of sand to a ton of silk is not very reliable. A study by R. G. Lipsey for the National Bureau of Economic Research has shown that there are considerable differences between the movements of unit value indices and price indices constructed according to more standard rules (that is, Laspeyres indices) for the United States. I recommend, therefore, the appropriate change both for imports and for exports.

Exports to Specific Countries

Since export markets will play an increasingly important role in Greek economic growth with its participation in the European Economic Community, it is important to collect data which will best measure the competitive position of Greece in its foreign markets. Currently, exports to specific countries are reported in a very satisfactory degree of sector detail. However, they need to be put on a real basis (deflated by appropriate price indices, as suggested above) to form a useful time series, in conjunction with an index of price movements (which may have to be different for different importing countries). To gauge the Greek competitive position more accurately, there should also be given for each importing country and each sector that part of the total import market and of the total market, import and domestic, which Greek exports represent.

There is no implication that the list of recommended items for collection is in any way complete. In the first place, the emphasis has been placed on real resource allocation problems; monetary questions have been almost completely neglected, although I do not claim that monetary policy may not have a significant effect on economic growth. In the second place, regional problems have been omitted, especially since regional statistics are already under study elsewhere. Finally, even within these limitations there are many more types of data which would be of the greatest use to the planner. But there will be time enough to consider the collection of additional statistics when the considerable program suggested here has been carried out.

8 The Economics of Moral Hazard: Further Comment

A paper by Mark Pauly (1968) has enriched our understanding of the phenomenon of so-called moral hazard and has convincingly shown that the optimality of complete insurance is no longer valid when the method of insurance influences the demand for the services provided by the insurance policy. This point is worth making strongly. In the theory of optimal allocation of resources under risk bearing it can be shown that competitive insurance markets will yield optimal allocation when the events insured are not controllable by individual behavior. If the amount of insurance payment is in any way dependent on a decision of the insured as well as on a state of nature, then the effect is very much the same as that of any excise tax, and optimality will not be achieved either by the competitive system or by an attempt on the part of the government to simulate a perfectly competitive system. For some earlier, less detailed discussions of this point see Chapter 6 of this volume and Arrow (1963, pp. 961–962).

In this chapter I should like to stress a point which Pauly overlooks in his exclusive emphasis on market incentives. Pauly has a very interesting sentence: "The above analysis shows, however, that the response of seeking more medical care with insurance than in its absence is a result not of moral perfidy, but of rational economic behavior."[1] We may certainly agree that the seeking of more medical care with insurance is a rational action on the part of individuals if no further constraints are imposed; it does not follow

Reprinted from *American Economic Review*, 58 (1968):537–539.

1. Pauly (1968), p. 535.

that no constraints ought to be imposed, or indeed that in certain contexts individuals should not impose constraints on themselves. Pauly's wording suggests that "rational economic behavior" and "moral perfidy" are mutually exclusive categories. No doubt Judas Iscariot turned a tidy profit from one of his transactions, but the usual judgment of his behavior is not necessarily wrong.

The underlying point is that if individuals are free to spend as they will with the assurance that the insurance company will pay, the resulting resource allocation will certainly not be socially optimal. This makes perfectly reasonable the idea that an insurance company can improve the allocation of resources to all concerned by a policy which rations the amount of medical services it will support under the insurance policy. This rationing may in fact occur in several different ways: (1) there might be a detailed examination by the insurance company of individual cost items, allowing those that are regarded "normal" and disallowing others, where normality means roughly what would have been bought in the absence of insurance; (2) the company may rely on the professional ethics of physicians not to prescribe frivolously expensive treatment costs, at least where the gain is primarily in comfort and luxury rather than in health improvement proper; (3) the company may even—and this is not as absurd as Pauly seems to think—rely on the willingness of the individual to behave in accordance with some commonly accepted norms.

The last point is perhaps not so important in the specific medical context, but the author had clearly broader implications in mind and so do I. Because of the moral hazard, complete reliance on economic incentives does not lead to an optimal allocation of resources in general. In most societies alternative relationships are built up which to some extent serve to permit cooperation and risk sharing. The principal-agent relation is very pervasive in all economies and especially in modern ones; by definition the agent has been selected for his specialized knowledge, and therefore the principal can never hope to check completely the agent's performance. One cannot, therefore, easily take out insurance against the failure of the agent to perform well. One of the characteristics of a successful economic system is that the relations of trust and confidence between principal and agent are sufficiently strong that the agent will not cheat even though it may be "rational economic behavior" to do so. The lack of such confidence has certainly been adduced by many writers as one cause of economic backwardness.

The lesson of Pauly's paper is that the price system is intrinsically limited in scope by our inability to make factual distinctions needed for optimal pricing under uncertainty. Nonmarket controls, whether internalized as moral principles or externally imposed, are to some extent essential for efficiency.

References

Arrow, K. J., *Aspects of the Theory of Risk-Bearing.* Helsinki: Yrjö Johanssonin Säätio, 1965, lecture 3. Reprinted as Chapter 6 of this volume.

Arrow, K. J., "Uncertainty and the Welfare Economics of Medical Care," *American Economic Review,* vol. 53, December, 1963, pp. 941–973.

Pauly, M. V., "The Economics of Moral Hazard," *American Economic Review,* vol. 58, 1968, pp. 531–537.

9   The Value of and Demand for Information

A Model of Behavior under Uncertainty

In what follows it is assumed that the only actions available are bets on the occurrence of states of nature. This case may be more interesting than appears at first sight since, in the general competitive equilibrium of a pure exchange economy under uncertainty, only these bets need take place, all other random investments being expressible in terms of the basic bets. Let X_i be the odds on the occurrence of state of nature i; that is, an individual who bets on state i receives X_i for each dollar bet if state i occurs and nothing otherwise. The number of states of nature, S, is assumed to be finite.

The individual is supposed to have fixed total resources, to which we assign the value 1. Let a_i be the amount bet by the individual on the occurrence of state i. For the most part we assume that all resources are invested.

$$(9\text{-}1) \qquad \sum_i a_i = 1.$$

The individual is assumed, as usual, to maximize the expected value of a utility function with diminishing marginal utility:

$$(9\text{-}2) \qquad \sum_i p_i U(a_i X_i),$$

where p_i is the (subjective) probability of state i, and $U(y)$ is the utility of

---

Reprinted from *Decision and Organization,* ed. C. B. McGuire and R. Radner (Amsterdam: North-Holland, 1971), pp. 131–139.

income y. From the usual Kuhn-Tucker conditions, the optimum a_i is characterized by (9-1) and the relations

(9-3) $\qquad p_i X_i U'(a_i X_i) = \lambda \quad$ for $a_i > 0$,

$\qquad\qquad p_i X_i U'(0) \quad \leq \lambda \quad$ for $a_i = 0$,

for some λ (a Lagrange multiplier).

For later reference, consider the special case where U is the (natural) logarithm. Since $U'(0) = +\infty$, the second line of (9-3) cannot hold. The expected utility, (9-2), becomes

$$\sum_i p_i \log a_i + \sum_i p_i \log X_i.$$

Since the second term is independent of a_i, maximization of (9-2) is equivalent to maximization of the first term, which does not involve the X_i's. In fact, for the logarithmic utility function, $a_i = p_i$. The optimal policy does not involve the odds, and the optimal value is

(9-4) $\qquad \sum_i p_i \log p_i + \sum_i p_i \log X_i.$

As a slight digression, suppose for the moment that the individual is not required to invest all his wealth, so that (9-1) is replaced by

(9-5) $\qquad \sum_i a_i \leq 1.$

The individual's wealth if state i occurs is then

$$a_i X_i + 1 - \sum_i a_i.$$

It may be asked under what conditions the constraint (9-5) is binding; that is, when will the individual bet all his money? *If $U'(0) = +\infty$, then the individual will invest all his money if and only if there exists a system of bets such that the individual cannot lose.* The last statement, symbolically, means the existence of $\bar{a}_i$ $(i = 1, \ldots, S)$, such that

$$\bar{a}_i \geq 0, \qquad \sum_i \bar{a}_i = 1, \qquad \bar{a}_i X_i \geq 1 \quad \text{for all } i,$$

which is equivalent to the condition

(9-6) $\qquad \sum_i (1/X_i) \leq 1.$

Proof. Let

$$b = 1 - \sum_j a_j;$$

then we seek to maximize

$$\sum_i p_i U(a_i X_i + b),$$

subject to the constraints

$$\sum_i a_i + b = 1, \qquad a_i \geqq 0, \qquad b \geqq 0.$$

Necessary conditions for an optimum are

(9-7) $p_i X_i U'(a_i X_i + b) \leqq \lambda,$

(9-8) $p_i X_i U'(a_i X_i + b) = \lambda \quad \text{if } a_i > 0,$

(9-9) $\sum_i p_i U'(a_i X_i + b) \leqq \lambda.$

Suppose that (9-7)–(9-9) hold with $b = 0$ (all resources invested). If, for some i, $a_i = 0$, then, since $U'(0) = +\infty$, (9-7) could not hold. Hence, $a_i > 0$, all i, and (9-8) holds for all i. If both sides of (9-8) are divided by X_i and then summed over i, it follows from (9-9) that

$$\lambda \sum_i (1/X_i) \leqq \lambda,$$

and, since $\lambda > 0$ by (9-8), (9-6) holds.

For the converse, consider any system of bets, a_i, b for which $b > 0$. Let $a_i' = a_i + b\bar{a}_i$, $b' = 0$. Then

$$a_i' X_i + b' = a_i X_i + b\bar{a}_i X_i \geqq a_i X_i + b,$$

and then, trivially,

$$\sum_i p_i U(a_i' X_i + b') \geqq \sum_i p_i U(a_i X_i + b),$$

while also

$$\sum_i a_i' + b' = \sum_i a_i + b \sum_i \bar{a}_i = \sum_i a_i + b = 1,$$
$$a_i' \geqq 0, \qquad b' \geqq 0.$$

Hence, under the hypothesis, for any system of bets in which not all money is invested, there is another at least as good for which all money is invested.

Note 1. The existence of a sure system of bets is sufficient for an individual to invest all his money even if $U'(0) < +\infty$, but it is not necessary, as can easily be seen if U is linear, $p_j X_j > 1$, some j, in which case it is optimal to invest all in that i for which $p_i X_i$ is a maximum even if there is no sure system.

Note 2. The optimal set of bets need not be a sure set, as the logarithmic case shows: as seen earlier, the optimal policy requires $a_i = p_i$, independent of the X_i's, so we certainly can have $p_i X_i < 1$ for some i, even if there exists a sure bet.

Amount and Value of Information

The *amount of information* about the state of the world is given, according to Shannon, by

$$(9\text{-}10) \qquad H = -\sum_i p_i \log p_i.$$

The most interesting economic interpretation of this quantity is given by the proposition that a communications channel with capacity H could convey a message giving the state of the world with arbitrarily small error. If we assume that the cost of a channel is proportional to its capacity, we find, as Marschak has pointed out (1959, p. 81), that the amount of information is a measure of the supply price, not of the demand.

An attempt to interpret H as the *value* (in the demand sense) *of information* was begun by Kelly (1956) and completed by Bellman and Kalaba (1957) and by Marschak (1959, pp. 92–95). The value of a given channel is defined as the difference between the maximum utilities achievable with and without the channel. In the case of a logarithmic utility function, this does indeed lead to H, although of course the definition yields different results in general. If a channel of capacity H is installed, then the individual knows the state of the world and bets everything on it; his return is X_i, which has a utility of $\log X_i$. Hence, his expected return is

$$\sum_i p_i \log X_i.$$

If we compare this with (9-4), the maximum utility achievable without information, we see indeed that the value of information is precisely H.

In this case, the value of information is independent of the rewards. It can be shown that this is the only such case; *if the value of information is independent of the rewards, then the utility function must be logarithmic.*

Proof. Choose a to maximize (9-2) subject to (9-1); the maximum value of (9-2) is the utility received without information. If the channel is installed, the expected return, by the argument just applied to the logarithmic case, is

$$\sum_i p_i U(X_i),$$

and the value of information, V, is

(9-11) $V = -\sum_i p_i U(a_i X_i) + \sum_i p_i U(X_i).$

The hypothesis is that V is independent of the X_i's. Differentiate (9-11) partially with respect to X_j, and equate the derivative to 0.

(9-12) $p_j a_j U'(a_j X_j) + \sum_i p_i X_i U'(a_i X_i)(\partial a_i / \partial X_j) = p_j U'(X_j).$

From (9-1),

(9-13) $\sum_i (\partial a_i / \partial X_j) = 0.$

If the strict inequality holds in (9-3), then $a_i = 0$ and would remain 0 for small variations in X_j, so that $\partial a_i / \partial X_j = 0$ in that case. Hence, whether the equality or the inequality holds in (9-3), we have

$$p_i X_i U'(a_i X_i)(\partial a_i / \partial X_j) = \lambda(\partial a_i / \partial X_j).$$

Sum over i, use (9-13), substitute into (9-12), and divide through by p_j.

(9-14) $a_j U'(a_j X_j) = U'(X_j).$

If $U'(0)$ is finite, then, from (9-14), $a_j > 0$; if $U'(0)$ is infinite, then, from (9-3), $a_j > 0$; hence $a_j > 0$ in any case, and the equality holds in (9-3). Then eliminate $U'(a_j X_j)$ from (9-3) and (9-14):

(9-15) $\lambda a_j = p_j X_j U'(X_j).$

Sum over j; from (9-1),

(9-16) $\lambda = \sum_j p_j X_j U'(X_j).$

Suppose now that the function $U(X)$ were such that, for some $X = X^0$,

$d[XU'(X)]/dX \neq 0$. From (9-16), $\partial\lambda/\partial X_i \neq 0$ for $X_i = X^0$ and then, from (9-15),

(9-17) $\partial a_j/\partial X_i \neq 0$ for $i \neq j$, $X_i = X^0$.

Multiply through in (9-14) by X_j, and let $j = 2$:

(9-18) $a_2 X_2 U'(a_2 X_2) = X_2 U'(X_2)$.

Let $z = a_2 X_2$, R be the range of z when X_1 is held fixed at X^0 and X_2, ..., X_n vary freely. By assumption, the right-hand side is not identically constant; the left-hand side is thus also not constant, so R must contain more than one point and is a nondegenerate, possibly infinite, interval. Differentiate (9-18) with respct to X_1:

(9-19) $\left.\dfrac{d[zU'(z)]}{dz}\right|_{z=a_2 X_2} X_2(\partial a_2/\partial X_1) = 0$.

From (9-17) and (9-19) we see that, for $X_2 > 0$, $d[zU'(z)]/dz = 0$ for all z in R, and therefore, for some K, $zU''(z) = K$ for all $z \in R$. But since X_2 can be chosen arbitrarily, (9-18) states that $XU'(X) = K$ for all $X > 0$, so that $U(X)$ is indeed logarithmic.

So far, channels have been noiseless, and their choice has been an all-or-none proposition. Discrete choices are never convenient for economic analysis. A continuous version of channel choice makes use of Shannon's *rate of transmission.* Suppose the channel conveys a message $j = 1, \ldots, M$, which has some joint distribution with the state of the world. Specifically, let q_{ji} be the probability that message j will be transmitted if the state of the world is in fact i, while p_i is, as before, the probability of state i. Then $q_{ji} p_i$ is the joint probability that the world is in state i and that the message transmitted is j. The receiver of the message is interested in a different set of probabilities, namely, the conditional probability, p_{ij}, that the state of the world is i if the message transmitted is j, and q_j, the unconditional probability that the message transmitted is j. The two sets of probabilities are linked by the relations

$q_{ji} p_i = p_{ij} q_j$.

When message j arrives, the conditional information about the state of the world which has not yet been acquired is

$$H(i/j) = -\sum_i p_{ij} \log p_{ij},$$

which is the same as (9-10) for a given message j. Since the message is itself a random variable, the quantity of relevance to the user is the mathematical expectation of $H(i/j)$, where j is the random variable, that is,

$$E_j[H(i/j)] = \sum_j H(i/j)q_j.$$

If $H(i)$ is the amount of information in a noiseless channel, then the rate of transmission $R(i,j)$ is defined as

$$H(i) - E_j[H(i/j)].$$

$R(i,j)$ is symmetric in i and j.

If a noisy channel with rate of transmission R is installed and a message j is received, the individual will optimize as in the previous section, but he will use the conditional probabilities of states. An easy calculation then shows that *the value of information in the channel* (the expected gain in maximum obtainable utility due to the messages) *is precisely the rate of transmission,* again independent of the odds, *when the utility function is logarithmic.*

The Demand for Information

Marschak (1959, p. 80) refers to the value of information as the demand price. That is, a channel will be worth acquiring if the value exceeds the cost. This cannot be the case. Indeed, as we have just seen, if the utility function is logarithmic and there are constant costs in channel capacity, both the value of information and its cost are proportional to the amount of information; the individual will then either buy an infinite channel or no channel at all or will be indifferent among all channel capacities. This hardly seems reasonable.

Marschak compares the utility of income with the cost. Obviously, there is a dimensional problem here; costs are measured in terms of dollars or resources, not in terms of utilities. In effect, if Y is income and C costs, Marschak is maximizing a function of the general form $U(Y) - C$, or, more precisely, the expected value of such a function. From the viewpoint of the individual, it is net income, $Y - C$, that he winds up with, and to which utility should be attached. The same difficulty appears in attempts, such as those of Savage (1954, p. 214) and of Raiffa and Schlaifer (1961, chap. 4), to provide a rigorous basis for sampling theory;[1] it also appears in Eckstein's

---

1. Raiffa and Schlaifer recognize the special assumptions made and seek to justify them (1961, pp. 79–81).

treatment of the economics of flood control (1961, pp. 471–474, especially eq. 5.5). A fully correct formulation is given by La Valle (1968).

Let, then, C be the cost of channel capacity per unit. Then the individual must choose a channel with messages j and a policy $a_i(j)$ stating the allocation as a function of the message so as to maximize

$$\sum_j q_j \sum_i p_{ij} U[a_i(j)X_i - CR],$$

where R is the rate of transmission of the channel.

Consider again the special case where U is logarithmic. First, optimize on the policy. It can easily be seen that

$$a_i(j) = p_{ij}\left[1 - CR \sum_k (1/X_k)\right] + (CR/X_i),$$

so that the maximum value of utility becomes, after substituting the definition of R,

$$\sum_i p_i \log p_i + \sum_i p_i \log X_i + R + \log\left[1 - CR \sum_k (1/X_k)\right],$$

which then has to be optimized with respect to R, yielding

$$R = -1 + \left[1/C \sum_k (1/X_k)\right].$$

There is an alternative approach which yields the same solution, properly interpreted. Suppose the cost of the channel is subtracted from the initial resources rather than from the final outcome. Then the maximand is

$$\sum_j q_j \sum_i p_{ij} \log [a_i(j)X_i],$$

with the constraint

$$\sum_i a_i(j) = 1 - CR.$$

The optimum policy then is obviously

$$a_i(j) = p_{ij}(1 - CR),$$

and the maximum value of utility is

$$\sum_i p_i \log p_i + \sum_i p_i \log X_i + R + \log (1 - CR).$$

The optimum value of R is then

$$R = -1 + (1/C).$$

The apparent discrepancy is the same as the problem discussed at the beginning of the chapter. There are really two unconnected kinds of money, initial and final; only if the resource constraint takes the form (9-5) is there a possibility of arbitraging between them. If

$$\sum_k (1/X_k) = 1,$$

there is a system of bets which will exactly break even for certain. This condition, used in Volume 2, Chapter 3, Eq. (3-5), ensures the identity of the two solutions in this case. It could be thought of as a simple numéraire condition.

The simplicity of the solution in the logarithmic case will not generalize. For one thing, the increased value to the channel will not depend solely on its transmission rate. Two channels with the same rate may nevertheless yield different increments in utility.

References

Bellman, R., and R. Kalaba, "Dynamic Programming and Statistical Communication Theory," *Proceedings of the National Academy of Sciences,* vol. 43, 1957, pp. 749–751.

Eckstein, O., "A Survey of the Theory of Public Expenditure Criteria," *Public Finances: Needs, Sources, and Utilization,* a report of the National Bureau of Economic Research. Princeton, N.J.: Princeton University Press, 1961, pp. 439–494.

Kelly, J. L., Jr., "A New Interpretation of Information Rate," *Bell System Technical Journal,* vol. 35, 1956, pp. 917–926.

La Valle, I., "On Cash Equivalents and Information Evaluation under Uncertainty, Part I: Basic Theory," *Journal of the American Statistical Association,* vol. 63, 1968, pp. 252–276.

Marschak, J., "Remarks on the Economics of Information," in *Contributions to Scientific Research in Management.* Los Angeles: Western Data Processing Center, University of California, 1959, pp. 79–98.

Raiffa, H., and R. Schlaifer, *Applied Statistical Decision Theory.* Boston: Harvard University Business School, 1961.

Savage, L. J., *The Foundations of Statistics.* New York and London: Wiley and Chapman and Hall, 1954.

10   Higher Education as a Filter

This chapter sketches a model of the economic role of higher education rather different from the current human capital orthodoxy. It is designed to formalize views expressed by some sociologists (for example, Berg, 1970) that the diploma serves primarily as an (imperfect) measure of performance ability rather than as evidence of acquired skills. I think the model is capable of illuminating certain aspects of the economic returns to higher education and gives an interpretation alternative to the conventional one.

The model certainly abstracts from aspects which have been much considered. I am not apologetic for this abstraction, but I am for the fact that the model is still so primitive in form and in particular for the fact that it seems so difficult to test. I hope to work further on it and to encourage others to do the same.

The conventional view among economists is that education adds to an individual's productivity and therefore increases the market value of his labor. From the viewpoint of formal theory, it does not matter how the student's productivity is increased, but implicitly it is assumed that the student receives cognitive skills through his education. Educators, on the other hand, have long felt that the activity of education is a process of socialization, with the latent content of the process—the acquisition of skills such as the carrying out of assigned tasks, getting along with others, regularity, punctuality, and the like—being at least as important as the

Reprinted from *Journal of Public Economics,* 2 (1973): 193–216.

manifest objectives of conveying information. This last doctrine has been revived by radical economists, though with a negative rather than a positive valuation. But from the viewpoint of economic theory, the socialization hypothesis is just as much a human capital theory as the cognitive skill acquisition hypothesis. Both hypotheses imply that education supplies skills that lead to higher productivity.

I would like to present a very different view. Higher education, in this model, contributes in no way to superior economic performance; it increases neither cognition nor socialization. Instead, higher education serves as a screening device in that it sorts out individuals of differing abilities, thereby conveying information to the purchasers of labor.

(Perhaps I should make clear that I personally do not believe that higher education performs only a screening purpose. Clearly professional schools impart real skills valued in the market, and so do undergraduate courses in the sciences. The case is considerably less clear with regard to the bulk of liberal arts courses. But in any case I think it better to make a dramatic and one-sided presentation of the screening model in order to develop it than to produce a premature synthesis. It should also be understood that I am speaking only about the contribution of higher education to production; the consumption aspects are real and important, but they are irrelevant to the points being made here.)

The screening or *filter* theory of higher education, as I shall call it, is distinct from the productivity-adding human capital theory but is not in total contradiction to it. From the viewpoint of an employer, an individual certified to be more valuable is more valuable, to an extent which depends on the nature of the production function. Therefore, the filtering role of education is a productivity-adding role from the private viewpoint; but as we shall see, the social productivity of higher education is more problematic.

The filter theory of education is part of a larger view about the nature of the economic system and its equilibrium. It is based on the assumption that economic agents have highly imperfect information. In particular, the purchaser of a worker's services has a very poor idea of his productivity. In this model, I assume instead that the buyer has very good statistical information but nothing more. That is, I assume that there are certain pieces of information about the worker, specifically whether or not he has a college diploma, which the employer can acquire costlessly. He knows, from general information or previous experience, the statistical distribution of productivities given the information he has, but has no way of distinguishing the productivities of individuals about whom he has the same information.

It will probably be argued that this description is valid enough at the time of hiring, but that after a period of time the employer will know his workers and their productivities on an individual basis. No doubt there is something to this viewpoint, but not as much as may be thought. After all, what is needed for allocative efficiency is the marginal productivity of each individual. But in a complex production process, the employer has simply no way of determining this. All he can do is act like an ideal econometrician, relating his output to the numbers of different kinds of workers (and other inputs, from which I am abstracting in this chapter). Here two workers are of the same kind if the employer's information about them is the same.

The general point that information in the real world is much more limited than that assumed in our usual equilibrium models has a long history among critics of the mainstream of economic thought. In recent years it has been especially stressed by Herbert A. Simon and his followers. The particular emphasis on lack of information concerning the productivity of workers has been argued by me in the context of racial discrimination in employment (Arrow, 1972a, b) and, in a more general way, by A. Michael Spence (Spence, 1973). The hypothesis that the actors in an uncertain world have a correct perception of the probability distribution of that uncertainty is a fairly standard one. In particular, this can be applied to lack of information about endogenous economic variables, such as prices or productivities; it becomes a condition of equilibrium that the distribution, when believed, helps generate such behavior as to maintain the distribution.

The Basic Model

We shall assume that each individual has three characteristics: his record before entering college, the probability of his getting through higher education, and his productivity. These have a joint distribution and presumably are positively correlated. The producers know about an individual only whether or not he is graduated from college.

The colleges serve really as a double filter, once in selecting entrants and once in passing or failing students. In admitting students, the colleges aim to maximize the expected number of graduates. Let

y = record before college,

z = productivity,

$f(y,z)$ = joint density of the two variables.

For applicants with a record y, the college is only interested in the conditional probability of their graduating. Hence it can be assumed without loss of generality that y is the probability of graduating conditional on the precollege record, for the conditional probability of success is the only aspect of the precollege record relevant to admission and to the model as a whole. If the capacity of the college is limited, then choice of admission procedures to maximize the expected number of graduates implies choice of a cutoff number, y_0, such that an applicant is admitted if and only if

(10-1) $y \geq y_0$.

Let

N_e = proportion of population admitted to college,

N_g = proportion graduating.

Since y has been transformed to be a probability, it varies from 0 to 1. The variable z is only constrained to be a nonnegative variable and therefore may range from 0 to $+\infty$. From the definitions let

$$g(y) = \int_0^{+\infty} f(y,z)\,dz$$

be the marginal density of y. From the definitions,

(10-2) $N_e = \int_{y_0}^1 \int_0^{+\infty} f(y,z)\,dz\,dy = \int_{y_0}^1 g(y)\,dy = P(y \geq y_0)$,

(10-3) $N_g = \int_{y_0}^1 \int_0^{+\infty} yf(y,z)\,dz\,dy = \int_{y_0}^1 yg(y)\,dy$

$\qquad\qquad = E(y|y \geq y_0)P(y \geq y_0) = \bar{y}_e P(y \geq y_0)$,

where

(10-4) $\bar{y}_e = E(y|y \geq y_0)$

is the probability of graduation of a random college entrant.

A detailed interpretation of productivity has not yet been given; in what follows, two alternative interpretations will be used. However, under either interpretation we will regard total output of the appropriate commodity to be the sum of the productivities of individuals. Then the average productivity of all individuals is

(10-5) $\bar{z} = \int_0^1 \int_0^{+\infty} zf(y,z)\,dz\,dy = E(z)$, and the total product of college graduates (per unit of total labor force) is

$$(10\text{-}6) \quad Z_g = \int_{y_0}^1 \int_0^{+\infty} zyf(y,z) \, dz \, dy = \int_{y_0}^1 yE(z|y)g(y) \, dy$$
$$= E(zy|y \geq y_0)P(y \geq y_0).$$

Under what conditions does college filtering convey any information? From (10-6) and (10-3), the expected productivity of a college graduate is

$$(10\text{-}7) \quad \bar{z}_g = Z_g/N_g = E(zy|y \geq y_0)/E(y|y \geq y_0).$$

College graduation has some (positive) information content if the productivity of a randomly chosen college graduate exceeds that of a randomly chosen member of the population, that is, if

$$(10\text{-}8) \quad \bar{z}_g > E(z).$$

The existence of the admission procedure suggests the following additional question; is it the admission or the college itself that performs the screening function? This is, after all, an important policy question, since admission procedures are much cheaper; for a first approximation we may suppose them free. Then admission procedures convey information if

$$(10\text{-}9) \quad E(z|y \geq y_0) > E(z),$$

and college itself has additional informational content over simple admission if

$$(10\text{-}10) \quad \bar{z}_g > E(z|y \geq y_0).$$

Since

$$(10\text{-}11) \quad E(z) = E(z|y \geq y_0)P(y \geq y_0) + E(z|y < y_0)P(y < y_0),$$
$$E(z|y \geq y_0) - E(z) = P(y < y_0)[E(z|y \geq y_0) - E(z|y < y_0)],$$

that is, if the expected productivity of those admitted is greater than that of those rejected, then the admission procedure has predictive value.

$$(10\text{-}12) \quad \bar{z}_g - E(z|y \geq y_0) = \frac{E(zy|y \geq y_0) - E(z|y \geq y_0)E(y|y \geq y_0)}{E(y|y \geq y_0)}$$

$$= \frac{\sigma_{yz|y \geq y_0}}{E(y|y \geq y_0)},$$

where use is made of (10-7), and $\sigma_{yz|y \geq y_0}$ means the conditional covariance of y and z, given admission to college. Thus college education conveys information about productivity beyond admission if there is a positive correlation between productivity and probability of college success among those admitted.

It is easy to see that both (10-9) and (10-10) hold if we make the following assumption.

POSITIVE SCREENING ASSUMPTION. *$E(z|y)$ is an increasing function of y.*

Under this assumption, it is obviously true that

$$E(z|y \geq y_0) > E(z|y_0) > E(z|y < y_0),$$

so that, from (10-11), (10-9) holds.

Also, under any condition on the range of y, the covariance of y and z is the same as that between y and $E(z|y)$, by the definitions. But the covariance between any random variable, over any range, and an increasing function of it is certainly positive, so that, from (10-12), (10-10) is certainly true.

The productivity advantage of college graduates over the average member of the population can be found by adding (10-11) and (10-12).

The Social Value of College Screening: The One-Factor Case

But even if college does have a positive informational value, it by no means follows that it is socially worthwhile. The filter model thus leads to a very different conclusion from the human capital model; for, as we will now see, there can easily be a divergence between social and private demands for information.

Consider the simplest model of production; all individuals are perfect substitutes in production with ratios given by their productivities. Then there is no social value to information about productivity. The total output of society will be $E(z) = \bar{z}$ (normalized on the labor force); the more productive individuals will produce more whether or not anyone knows who they are. (I am abstracting from incentive questions here.) There will, however, be a private value to a college diploma for those most likely to get it, if we assume a competitive world. For then, the wage of an individual will be the expected value of his product conditional on the information available to the employer. Let us assume that the individual has no better information about his prospects of going through college than the college has. Suppose further that anyone can go to college if he pays its cost, c. (Since education is also a consumers' good, the cost, c, is to be interpreted here empirically as the cost over and above its consumption value.) Suppose no one is going to college initially. Then a few individuals go to college; if they have selected themselves properly, then the expected value of their productivity, conditional on graduation, is greater than the overall average, $\bar{z}$. Clearly, if it is sufficiently greater and if the probability of passing is high enough, then it pays to incur the costs. But these costs are simply a social waste.

In fact, a detailed examination shows that, under certain informational assumptions, everybody would gain by prohibiting college (the following argument is really a special case of Spence's). Let us study the equilibrium. Some go to college, and some don't. The employers know the expected productivities of college graduates and of others (I assume here that employers do not distinguish between college failures and those who do not enter; such a distinction could easily be introduced if deemed realistic). Assume further that potential entrants know the overall probability of graduation among those who enter but not the probability conditional on their own record. The colleges do know these conditional probabilities. As before, there is a critical level, y_0, such that individuals are admitted to college if and only if $y \geqq y_0$ (the critical level here is determined by demand for college entrance, not, as before, by capacity restrictions). The employers then pay to college graduates $\bar{z}_g = \bar{z}_g(y_0)$, as defined in (10-7). Let $\bar{z}_n(y_0)$ be the expected productivity of the nongraduates. Then

$$(10\text{-}13) \qquad \bar{z} = \bar{z}_g(y_0)N_g + \bar{z}_n(y_0)(1 - N_g);$$

N_g, as defined in (10-3), is, of course, also a function of y_0.

If an individual goes to college, he graduates with probability $\bar{y}_e$, and fails with probability $1 - \bar{y}_e$. He incurs a cost of c in any case, so that his expected return from college is

$$\bar{z}_g(\bar{y}_e) + \bar{z}_n(1 - \bar{y}_e) - c.$$

If he does not go to college, his return is $\bar{z}_n$ with certainty. In the absence of risk aversion, equilibrium requires that the two returns be equal; for if the expected return from going to college were the greater, individuals with records slightly less than y_0 would find it profitable to go to college.

$$\bar{z}_g\bar{y}_e + \bar{z}_n(1 - \bar{y}_e) - c = \bar{z}_n,$$

or, after simplification,

$$(10\text{-}14) \qquad \bar{y}_e(\bar{z}_g - \bar{z}_n) = c,$$

which immediately shows that $\bar{z}_g > \bar{z}_n$. But then, from (10-13), $\bar{z}_n < \bar{z}$. Therefore, the income of a nongraduate is lower than it was before; but since the expected income of college entrants equals that of nongraduates, the college entrants do not benefit either, at least not ex ante.

Hence, we have the remarkable possibility that if college is a filter, its abolition may help everyone. Not only is there no efficiency gain, but college has also created an inequality in ex post income where none existed before.

We are accustomed in theory to argue that information may be underproduced because its social value is greater than its private. But the opposite possibility has also been shown by Hirshleifer (1971) in a very important article. Information not used in production may merely convey a competitive advantage.

Of course, our conclusion depended on free entry to college. If college entrance is limited in some manner, then the equality in (10-14) becomes an inequality, and the college entrants may gain on average. The nonentrants certainly lose in any case, and further, it would have paid them to bribe the entrants not to enter. The effects on equality are even worse in this case.

William Brainard has pointed out to me that the strong result found so far depends on the assumption that the potential entrant does not know the probability of graduation conditional on his own record but only the probability conditional on the fact of entrance. If the stronger informational condition holds, the expected return from college for an individual whose precollege record is y is

$$(10\text{-}15) \qquad \bar{z}_g y + \bar{z}_n (1 - y) - c = (\bar{z}_g - \bar{z}_n) y + \bar{z}_n - c,$$

and therefore equilibrium is obtained by setting this return equal to $\bar{z}_n$ for the *marginal* man, for whom $y = y_0$. Therefore, (10-14) is replaced by

$$(10\text{-}16) \qquad y_0(\bar{z}_g - \bar{z}_n) = c.$$

It remains true that $\bar{z}_g > \bar{z}_n$ and therefore $\bar{z} > \bar{z}_n$, so that the nongraduates are worse off than they would be in the absence of college education. However, individuals with sufficiently good records, that is, sufficiently high values of y, may have expected returns (10-15) which are at least equal to $\bar{z}$, the expected return in the absence of college filtering. If y_1 is the smallest such value of y,

$$(\bar{z}_g - \bar{z}_n)y_1 + \bar{z}_n = \bar{z} + c.$$

If (10-13) is subtracted from this equation, we see that

$$(\bar{z}_g - \bar{z}_n)(y_1 - N_g) = c,$$

and dividing through by (10-16) yields

$$y_1 = N_g + y_0.$$

If there are no values of y above y_1, then it remains true that everybody gains by changing from competitive equilibrium to the abolition of college. However, in any case, the fundamental point remains unaltered; there is a net gain in social output by abolishing college, and everybody could be made better off by doing so and redistributing income suitably.

(This statement may appear hard to reconcile with our usual expectation that college education is insufficient. Of course, I am abstracting from credit rationing, which has been the most powerful force working in the opposite direction. My guess is that we are moving into a period where public subsidies to higher education plus improved credit facilities are making effective credit restriction on higher education a thing of the past.)

The Social Value of Screening: Two-Factor Model

To understand better the social role of education as a filter, one must consider more complicated production functions in which there are complementary kinds of labor. Then education has a positive value in sorting out types of workers. For simplicity, suppose there are two kinds of labor. Everyone is capable of supplying one unit of type 1 labor, and this fact is known to all. However, there is also needed type 2 labor, of which different individuals can supply different amounts. In this model z will be interpreted as the supply of type 2 labor, measured in efficiency-units. To emphasize the complementarity of the different types of labor, we will assume that production requires fixed proportions of the two types of labor (remembering always that type 2 labor is measured in efficiency-units). By proper choice of units, we can require without loss of generality that one unit of each type of labor is needed to produce one unit of product.

In this model, filtering is no longer useless. Suppose there are two classes of people, say A and B, with expected productivities $\bar{z}_A$ and $\bar{z}_B$, respectively, $\bar{z}_A > \bar{z}_B$ (remember that "productivity" here means supply of efficiency-units of type 2 labor). Then clearly it can never be optimal to have simultaneously individuals of class A performing type 1 labor and individuals of class B performing type 2 labor. For suppose this happened. Efficiency also requires that the sum of the z's of those in type 2 labor equal the number in type 1 labor. Then remove some class A individuals from type 1 labor and replace them with an equal number of class B individuals from type 2 labor, making all selections at random. The number of type 1 laborers is unchanged, and the expected number of efficiency-units of type 2 labor is increased. Output does not yet increase, since the number of type 1 laborers is a bottleneck. But then we can transfer individuals from type 2 to type 1 labor; by increasing the number of type 1 laborers, total output is increased, provided not so many are transferred that the supply of type 2 labor is reduced below that of type 1 labor.

Thus total output is increased by successful filtering, provided, of course, that the cost of the filter is not too high. We can easily calculate the gain in output due to filtering at zero cost. Let N_A and N_B be the proportions of individuals of the two classes, $N_A + N_B = 1$. Then

$$\bar{z} = N_A\bar{z}_A + N_B\bar{z}_B.$$

If the filter is not used, a fraction N_1 of the entire population is assigned to type 1 labor and the rest to type 2 labor. Since the assignment is random, the total supply of type 2 labor in efficiency-units is $(1 - N_1)\bar{z}$. Efficiency requires that

$$(1 - N_1)\bar{z} = N_1,$$

and the output is the common value of the two sides, so that

(10-17) $N_1 = \bar{z}/(1 + \bar{z}) =$ output without filtering.

Now suppose for the moment that the filter is used naively, that is, all individuals of class A are assigned to type 2 jobs and only such. The supply of type 2 labor is then $N_A\bar{z}_A$, that of type 1 labor, N_B. Of course, these two need not be equal; if they are not, the allocation is inefficient. Suppose first that $N_B < N_A\bar{z}_A$. Then clearly some class A labor will have to be assigned to type 1 jobs. That is, $N_1 > N_B$. Clearly, efficiency requires

$$(1 - N_1)\bar{z}_A = N_1,$$

so that

(10-18) $N_1 = \bar{z}_A/(1 + \bar{z}_A) =$ output with filtering and excess of class A labor.

The increase in output due to filtering is, then,

$$\frac{\bar{z}_A}{1 + \bar{z}_A} - \frac{\bar{z}}{1 + \bar{z}} = \frac{\bar{z}_A - \bar{z}}{\bar{z}(1 + \bar{z}_A)} \frac{\bar{z}}{1 + \bar{z}},$$

the first factor showing the proportionate increase in output.

If there is a deficiency of class A labor for the type 2 jobs, $N_B > N_A\bar{z}_A$, optimal allocation requires that all the class A labor be assigned to those jobs plus enough of the class B labor so that the supplies of the two types of labor are equal.

$$N_A \bar{z}_A + (N_B - N_1)\bar{z}_B = N_1,$$

so that

(10-19) $\quad N_1 = \bar{z}/(1 + \bar{z}_B) = $ output with filtering and a deficiency of class A labor,

and the increase in output is

$$\frac{\bar{z}}{1 + \bar{z}_B} - \frac{\bar{z}}{1 + \bar{z}} = \frac{\bar{z} - \bar{z}_B}{1 + \bar{z}_B} \frac{\bar{z}}{1 + \bar{z}}.$$

Now let us identify these general classes A and B with graduates and nongraduates, respectively. Then it has been shown that college education pays if it is free (in which case everyone goes to college and the screening is solely through passing or failing), and, by continuity, some college education pays if c is sufficiently small. Suppose at the optimum $N_g \bar{z}_g > 1 - N_g$. Then the output is given by (10-18) but from this must be subtracted the cost of education. If c is measured in terms of output, the cost is $cP(y \geq y_0)$, where y_0 is the cutoff record for admission. Hence, the net output of society for a given y_0 is

$$[\bar{z}_g/(1 + \bar{z}_g)] - cP(y \geq y_0).$$

But an increase in y_0 can be shown to increase $\bar{z}_g$ and therefore will increase $\bar{z}_g/(1 + \bar{z}_g)$, and it will also decrease $P(y \geq y_0)$; hence such an allocation cannot be optimum, a contradiction.

To see that an increase in y_0 will increase $\bar{z}_g$, first differentiate the definition (10-7) logarithmically with respect to y_0.

$$\frac{1}{\bar{z}_g} \frac{d\bar{z}_g}{dy_0} = \frac{1}{Z_g} \frac{dZ_g}{dy_0} - \frac{1}{N_g} \frac{dN_g}{dy_0}$$

$$= \frac{-y_0 E(z|y_0)g(y_0)}{Z_g} + \frac{y_0 g(y_0)}{N_g} \quad \text{[from (10-3) and (10-6)]}$$

$$= [y_0 g(y_0)/Z_g][\bar{z}_g - E(z|y_0)],$$

which is positive if $\bar{z}_g > E(z|y_0)$; but since every graduate has a record at least equal to y_0, the last inequality follows from the positive screening assumption.

It has therefore been shown that the optimal amount of college education will be such that

(10-20) $N_g \bar{z}_g \leq 1 - N_g$.

It is interesting to note that the cost c does not enter into this condition, so it is valid even if $c = 0$. Even if education is free, it is socially optimal to restrict it so as to improve its screening function.

Since (10-20) holds, the net output of society is given by (10-19), and the optimal amount of higher education is obtained by choosing y_0 to maximize

(10-21) $[\bar{z}/(1 + \bar{z}_n)] - cP(y \geq y_0) = F(y_0, c) = H(y_0) - cP(y \geq y_0)$,

subject to (10-20).

The full statement of the derivative conditions implied by this maximization can be easily written down, but they do not appear simple enough for useful interpretation. However, some implications are useful to draw, in particular conditions under which the constraint (10-20) is binding. When this holds, the filter is working most smoothly, in that every graduate goes into type 2 jobs and every nongraduate into type 1 jobs. In this case, we will say that the filter is *complete*.

First note that the function

$$G(y_0) = N_g \bar{z}_g + N_g = Z_g + N_g$$
$$= \int_0^{+\infty} \int_{y_0}^1 y(1 + z) f(y,z) \, dy \, dz,$$

from (10-3) and (10-6), is clearly a strictly decreasing function of y_0 in any region of positive density. Hence, the equation

(10-22) $G(y_0^*) = 1$

has a unique solution, and the inequality (10-20) can be written $G(y_0) \leq 1$, or

(10-23) $y_0 \geq y_0^*$.

The variables $\bar{z}_g$ and $\bar{z}_n$ are functions of y_0; their values when $y_0 = y_0^*$ will be denoted by $\bar{z}_g^*$ and $\bar{z}_n^*$, respectively. The starred magnitudes characterize the complete filter.

Next we note that the value of y_0 which maximizes (10-21) subject to (10-20) or, equivalently, (10-23) must be a monotone increasing function of c. Actually, this conclusion must be stated more precisely, since nothing has been said which implies that the maximum must be unique. Suppose $c_1 < c_2$. Then we show that every maximal value of y_0 for $c = c_2$ exceeds every maximal value for $c = c_1$, except that if y_0^* is the unique maximal value of y_0 for $c = c_1$, then it can happen that y_0^* is also a maximal value for $c = c_2$.

To see this, let y_0^1 be any maximal value for $c = c_1$ and y_0^2 for $c = c_2$. From (10-21),

$$F(y_0,c_1) + (c_1 - c_2)P(y \ge y_0) = F(y_0,c_2).$$

By definition of a maximum,

$$F(y_0^1,c_1) \ge F(y_0^2,c_1).$$

Add

$$(c_1 - c_2)P(y \ge y_0^1)$$
$$= (c_1 - c_2)P(y \ge y_0^2) + (c_1 - c_2)[P(y \ge y_0^1) - P(y \ge y_0^2)]$$

to this inequality.

$$F(y_0^1,c_2) \ge F(y_0^2,c_2) + (c_1 - c_2)[P(y \ge y_0^1) - P(y \ge y_0^2)]$$
$$\ge F(y_0^1,c_2) + (c_1 - c_2)[P(y \ge y_0^1) - P(y \ge y_0^2)],$$

from the fact that y_0^2 maximizes $F(y_0,c_2)$ in the range (10-23). Hence,

$$(c_1 - c_2)[P(y \ge y_0^1) - P(y \ge y_0^2)] \le 0,$$

or, since $c_1 < c_2$,

$$P(y \ge y_0^1) \ge P(y \ge y_0^2),$$

which is possible only if $y_0^2 \ge y_0^1$. That is, if the cost of education rises, any optimal cutoff level for entrance must be at least as high as it was before the raise.

But when can the equality $y_0^1 = y_0^2$ hold? This means that y_0^1 is optimal for $c = c_1$ and for $c = c_2$. Suppose $y_0^1 > y_0^*$. Then the constraint (10-23) is not effective, so that $\partial F/\partial y_0 = 0$ at $y = y_0^1$ for both values of c. But

$$dP(y \ge y_0)/dy_0 = -g(y_0),$$

and, from (10-21),

$$\frac{\partial F}{\partial y_0} = H'(y_0) + cg(y_0),$$

so that if y_0^1 is optimal for two different levels of c and $y_0^1 > y_0^*$, we would have

$$H'(y_0^1) + c_1 g(y_0^1) = 0, \qquad H'(y_0^1) + c_2 g(y_0^1) = 0.$$

This is impossible if $g(y_0) > 0$, which we can assume. Hence, the equality $y_0^1 = y_0^2$ can hold only if $y_0^1 = y_0^*$.

To complete the argument, suppose that at $c = c_1$, y_0^* is optimal, but there is also another optimal value, say $y_0 = y_0'$. But then, as already shown, $y_0^2 \geq y_0' > y_0^*$ for any value of y_0 optimal for $c = c_2$. Hence, there can be a common optimal value for $c = c_1$ and $c = c_2$ only if y_0^* is the unique optimal cutoff point for the lower cost.

We can then conclude that the complete filter is optimal, if ever, only for an interval of c-values starting at $c = 0$. If, for any c, y_0^* is not the unique optimal value, then it is not optimal for any larger values of c.

It is, of course, clear that y_0^* cannot be optimal for all c. For consider what happens when y_0 is raised to its upper limit, 1; this means approaching the no-filter situation, in which there is no higher education. In that case, $\bar{z}_n \to \bar{z}$, while $P(y \geq y_0)$ approaches zero; hence, the net output tends to $\bar{z}/(1 + \bar{z})$, as already seen in (10-17). On the other hand, if the complete filter were used for all values of c, it can be seen from (10-21) that the net output would eventually fall below this level (and indeed would eventually become negative and therefore infeasible). Clearly, the complete filter cannot be optimal if it is inferior to no filter. Hence the c-interval in which the complete filter is optimal, if it exists, is bounded above.

It remains to see if there is any interval of costs of education for which the complete filter is optimal. Actually, this interval can be shown to exist only under an additional, though natural, assumption. Note that $F(y_0,0) = H(y_0)$. If it is true that $H'(y_0) < 0$ for all y_0, then the only optimal cutoff for free education would clearly be to make y_0 as small as possible, that is, to let $y_0 = y_0^*$. What happens for c slightly greater than 0? I shall show that there must be an interval of c-values in which y_0^* is the unique optimum.

For suppose not; then we can find a sequence $\{c^v\}$ of c-values, arbitrarily small, such that for $c = c^v$, there is an optimal value $y_0 = y_0^v > y_0^*$. By definition of an optimum,

$$F(y_0^v, c^v) \geq F(y_0^*, c^v), \quad \text{each } v.$$

Either the sequence $\{y_0^v\}$ has a limit point $y_0^{**} > y_0^*$ or else $y_0^v \to y_0^*$. In the first case, by continuity, we would have $F(y_0^{**},0) \geq F(y_0^*,0)$, in contradiction to the fact that y_0^* is the unique optimum when $c = 0$. Hence,

$$(10\text{-}24) \qquad \frac{F(y_0^v, c^v) - F(y_0^*, c^v)}{y_0^v - y_0^*} \geq 0, \qquad y_0^v \to y_0^*.$$

From (10-21),

$$\frac{F(y_0^v,c^v) - F(y_0^*,c^v)}{y_0^v - y_0^*} = \frac{H(y_0^v) - H(y_0^*)}{y_0^v - y_0^*}$$

$$- c^v \frac{P(y \geqq y_0^v) - P(y \geqq y_0^*)}{y_0^v - y_0^*}.$$

From the definition of a derivative and other remarks made above, we know that, as v approaches $+\infty$,

$$\frac{H(y_0^v) - H(y_0^*)}{y_0^v - y_0^*} \rightarrow H'(y_0^*), \qquad c^v \rightarrow 0,$$

$$\frac{P(y \geqq y_0^v) - P(y \geqq y_0^*)}{y_0^v - y_0^*} \rightarrow -g(y_0^*);$$

hence,

$$\frac{F(y_0^v,c^v) - F(y_0^*,c^v)}{y_0^v - y_0^*} \rightarrow H'(y_0^*),$$

and, from (10-24), $H'(y_0^*) \geqq 0$, in contradiction to the assumption that $H'(y_0) < 0$ for all y_0.

Thus, the condition $H'(y_0) < 0$ implies the existence of a cost $c = c_1 > 0$ such that the complete filter is optimal for $0 \leqq c \leqq c_1$ and not for higher values of c. It remains only to restate the condition, $H'(y_0) < 0$. Clearly, from (10-21), this holds if and only if $d\bar{z}_n/dy_0 > 0$. As already seen in (10-13), $N_g\bar{z}_g + (1 - N_g)\bar{z}_n = \bar{z}$, and this for all y_0. From (10-7) and (10-6), $N_g\bar{z}_g = Z_g$, and

$$\frac{dZ_g}{dy_0} = -y_0 \int_0^{+\infty} zf(y_0,z)\, dz.$$

If we differentiate (10-13) with respect to y_0, we find, after some transposition, that

$$(1 - N_g)\left(\frac{d\bar{z}_n}{dy_0}\right) = \bar{z}_n\left(\frac{dN_g}{dy_0}\right) - \left(\frac{dz_g}{dy_0}\right)$$

$$= y_0 \int_0^{+\infty} zf(y_0,z)\, dz - y_0\bar{z}_n \int_0^{+\infty} f(y_0,z)\, dz$$

$$= y_0 \int_0^{+\infty} f(y_0,z)\, dz[E(z|y_0) - \bar{z}_n],$$

with the aid of (10-3). Hence, $H'(y_0) < 0$ if and only if

(10-25) $E(z|y_0) > \bar{z}_n$.

This asserts that, for any given cutoff admission criterion, the average productivity of those marginally admitted exceeds the average productivity of nongraduates. Notice that this assumption is somewhat strong, for the nongraduates include those with preadmission records predicting a probability of graduation greater than y_0. Indeed, (10-25) can hardly hold for $y_0 = 0$; for in that case, $\bar{z}_n$ is the average productivity of all those who failed when everyone is permitted to go to college, while $E(z|y_0)$ is the average productivity of the subgroup whose failure was perfectly predictable. By the same token, we would certainly expect (10-25) to hold when $y_0 = 1$. In this case, there is no filter at all, that is, no higher education, so that $\bar{z}_n = \bar{z}$; we would certainly expect that the expected productivity of those who, on the basis of their precollege records, would be certain to pass if admitted would be higher than the average in the population. We can therefore assume that (10-25) holds for y_0 sufficiently high; in particular, we assume that it holds for $y_0 \geqq y_0^*$, which is all that is needed.

We can thus conclude the following. If (10-25) holds for cutoff points y_0 at least equal to that for the complete filter, then there is a cost, $c_1 > 0$, such that the complete filter is uniquely optimal for education costs $0 \leqq c \leqq c_1$ and not for higher cost levels. If (10-25) does not hold, then the same may be true, or else it may be that the complete filter is never optimal. In any case, for cost levels for which the complete filter is not optimal, the cutoff point increases with educational costs, and the number of graduates is less than the number of type 2 jobs. For sufficiently high costs, the abolition of higher education is optimal.

Competitive Equilibrium with Screening: The Two-Factor Model

As in the one-factor model, it is important to ask to what extent the competitive market achieves an optimal or satisfactory level of education. It remains true that there is a divergence between private and social benefits in filtering, but, as has been shown, it is no longer true that the socially optimal level of college education is zero.

The following will now be shown: If the complete filter is optimal, then it is achieved by the competitive market in which college education is supplied to everyone willing to pay for its cost. The complete filter remains the competitive allocation for higher cost levels, even up to levels such that everyone is worse off than they would be under no filtering. For still higher cost levels, the competitive equilibrium is no longer the complete filter but rather one in which the number of graduates is less than the number of type 2 jobs; it remains true that, under the same informational assumptions made earlier, everyone is worse off under the equilibrium allocation than they would be under no filtering.

In the two-factor model, let w_1 be the price per unit of type 1 labor, w_2 the price per efficiency-unit of type 2 labor. Obviously, there will be at least one graduate working at type 2 labor; since the wages per man of graduates must be the same in all uses, a graduate must earn $w_2 \bar{z}_g$ per man. Similarly, a nongraduate must earn w_1 per man. At equilibrium, the expected wage of an entrant, minus the cost of education, must equal the wage of a nongraduate.

$$\bar{y}_e(w_2\bar{z}_g) + (1 - \bar{y}_e)w_1 - c = w_1,$$

or, analogously to (10-14),

(10-26) $\quad \bar{y}_e(w_2\bar{z}_g - w_1) = c.$

Since one unit of type 1 labor and one efficiency-unit of type 2 labor together produce one unit of product, exhaustion of the product implies

(10-27) $\quad w_1 + w_2 = 1.$

From (10-26), it follows immediately that $w_2\bar{z}_g > w_1$ if $c > 0$. This statement in turn implies that no graduate is working at a type 1 job, for, since all graduates are indifferent in the marketplace, all can earn $w_2\bar{z}_g$ and therefore none will work for w_1 at a type 1 job. The total supply of type 2 labor by all graduates therefore does not exceed the number of units of type 2 labor used in the economy at equilibrium.

(10-28) $\quad N_g\bar{z}_g \leqq 1 - N_g,$

a condition which also holds at the optimal allocation, according to (10-20). If the equality held, then no nongraduate would prefer to work in a type 2 job. Since his income in such a job would be $w_2\bar{z}_n$, we must have, in this case, $w_1 \geqq w_2\bar{z}_n$. On the other hand, if the inequality holds in (10-28), some nongraduates are working in type 2 jobs, so that $w_2\bar{z}_n = w_1$. Thus, one of the two following situations must hold at equilibrium:

(10-29) $\quad N_g\bar{z}_g = 1 - N_g \quad$ and $\quad w_1 \geqq w_2\bar{z}_n;$

(10-30) $\quad N_g\bar{z}_g < 1 - N_g \quad$ and $\quad w_1 = w_2\bar{z}_n.$

As will now be shown, which one of these holds will depend on the parameters of the problem — in particular, given other parameters, on the education cost c.

As we know from (10-22)–(10-23), when (10-29) holds, $y_0 = y_0^*$. Let $\bar{y}_e^*$ be the corresponding value of $\bar{y}_e$, the probability of graduation conditional on admission. If (10-29) holds, then solve for w_1 and w_2 from (10-26) and (10-27):

$$(10\text{-}31) \quad w_1 = \frac{[\bar{z}_g^* - (c/\bar{y}_e^*)]}{(1 + \bar{z}_g^*)},$$

$$(10\text{-}32) \quad w_2 = \frac{[1 + (c/\bar{y}_e^*)]}{(1 + \bar{z}_g^*)}.$$

From (10-29), these are the equilibrium wages, and the complete filter is the equilibrium allocation, provided that $w_1 \geqq w_2 \bar{z}_n^*$. From (10-31)–(10-32), this condition can be written

$$(10\text{-}33) \quad c \leqq \frac{\bar{y}_e^*(\bar{z}_g^* - \bar{z}_n^*)}{(1 + \bar{z}_n^*)} = c_2.$$

Thus, for c in this range, the complete filter is competitive equilibrium.

Recall that, as in the one-factor model, the equilibrium condition for choosing entrance to college implies that the ex ante expected income (net of educational costs) is the same for all, and therefore equal to w_1. We can then compare w_1 with the expected output in the absence of a filter, $\bar{z}/(1 + \bar{z})$ from (10-17). Since w_1 is linear in c, from (10-31), we need make the comparisons only for c approaching 0 and $c = c_2$, as far as equilibria satisfying (10-29) are concerned.

First note that from (10-26) and either (10-29) or (10-30),

$$w_2 \bar{z}_g > w_1 \geqq w_2 \bar{z}_n,$$

so that

$$(10\text{-}34) \quad \bar{z}_g > \bar{z} > \bar{z}_n$$

in any equilibrium. Then, for c approaching 0,

$$w_1 \to \frac{\bar{z}_g^*}{(1 + \bar{z}_g^*)} > \frac{\bar{z}}{(1 + \bar{z})};$$

as might be expected, when c is small, the competitive equilibrium is better than no filter. On the other hand, when $c = c_2$, we find, on substitution from (10-33) into (10-31) and some simplification, that

$$w_1 = \frac{\bar{z}_n^*}{(1 + \bar{z}_n^*)} < \frac{\bar{z}}{(1 + \bar{z})}.$$

Therefore, there is a cost level, c_3, $0 < c_3 < c_2$, such that the complete filter is better than no filter for $c < c_3$ and worse for $c_3 < c \leqq c_2$. A fortiori, the complete filter, though a competitive equilibrium, is not optimal for $c \geqq c_3$. Hence, if there is any range of costs for which the complete filter is optimal, the upper limit of that range, c_1, must be less than c_3.

Now consider equilibria which are not complete filters, those for which (10-30) holds. The argument here is simple: from (10-27) and the condition in (10-30) that $w_1 = w_2 \bar{z}_n$, it follows immediately that

$$(10\text{-}35) \qquad w_1 = \frac{\bar{z}_n}{(1 + \bar{z}_n)} < \frac{\bar{z}}{(1 + \bar{z})},$$

from (10-34), so that again the equilibrium filter is worse for everyone than the absence of college education.

One technical remark is needed here. If $c > c_2$, the only possible competitive equilibrium must satisfy (10-30). However, it is possible that for some values of $c \leqq c_2$ there may be more than one equilibrium; one will be the complete filter, but there are others which satisfy (10-30). Note that if we substitute (10-35) and the corresponding value of w_2, $1/(1 + \bar{z}_n)$, into (10-26), we have

$$c = \frac{\bar{y}_e(\bar{z}_g - \bar{z}_n)}{(1 + \bar{z}_n)} = A(y_0),$$

say, and therefore there is an equilibrium satisfying (10-30) for any c in the range of $A(y_0)$, with $y_0 \geqq y_0^*$. From (10-33), $A(y_0^*) = c_2$; hence, if $A(y_0)$ were an increasing function of y_0, there could not be any equilibria satisfying (10-30) for c-values for which the complete filter is also an equilibrium. (I have not studied whether this monotonicity condition is reasonable; if not, then it is possible that the minimum value of $A(y_0)$ for $y_0 \geqq y_0^*$, say $\bar{c}$, may be less than c_2. In that case, for any c, $\bar{c} < c < c_2$, the equation $A(y_0) = c$ may have one or more solutions, so that there will be several competitive equilibria, one a complete filter and the others not.)

Concluding Remarks

There are perhaps two final remarks that should be made, though I must be cursory in both. One is the comparison between this model and a human capital model. It has long been clear that measures of return to human capital may well be biased upward because ability differences are confounded with differences in the inputs of schooling. Attempts have been made to correct the measures of return to schooling (see, for example, Griliches and Mason, 1972; Hause, 1972) by introducing a variable designed to measure ability. But unfortunately these ability measures are wrong in principle. Typically, they are measures of intelligence; but "ability" in the relevant sense means the ability to produce goods, and there is simply no empirical reason to expect more than a mild correlation between productive ability and intelligence as measured on tests. Intelligence tests are designed to predict scholastic success, and this is a function they perform well. But there is considerable evidence in direct studies of productivity (for example, by the U.S. Navy) that ability to pass tests is weakly related to ability to perform specific productive tasks. It is only the latter ability that is relevant here.

Unfortunately, this argument raises another difficulty: the model of this chapter depends on an unmeasured and unmeasurable variable, "ability." There may be no way of ever achieving a direct measurement; after all, a premise of the model is that employers cannot measure ability directly, and there is no reason to suppose that the economist is going to do better. It remains to be seen if the theory can be made to yield interesting and testable implications in the absence of direct measurements of ability.

Indeed, if we revert to the one-factor model, the filter model has some implications for macroeconomic observations. It says that an increase in the resources devoted to college education will have no positive effect on output in the noneducational sector, if all other variables are controlled for. This is indeed a strong inference, but its usefulness in making intertemporal or international comparisons is limited by the need to hold the statistical distribution of ability constant. If "ability" is influenced by cultural factors, then it will certainly vary internationally and may also be thought to vary over time.

There is also one particularly needed elaboration of the model (which is not to say that it doesn't cry out for elaboration in many other directions). This is the relation between college filtering and on-the-job filtering. Once an employee has been hired, the employer can gradually draw on more directly obtained information to determine his productivity. However, this filtering may be costly. To the extent that the employer does filter and does so accurately, the value of the college filter is reduced. The employer pays the average product of a group with given educational achievement only during the period before his own filter has become effective. Conversely, however, an increase in the college population will mean (and has meant) a depreciation in the quality of noncollege students (this is *not* necessarily the same as a decrease in the quality of college students). It may be that, with the increased supply of college-filtered students and with a decrease in the quality of noncollege students, the alternative filters become less worthwhile and eventually cease to be profitable. This means that the improvement in the equality of income due to increased college education may therefore be offset by the decrease in alternative filters leading to qualification for type 2 jobs. In particular, it means that the criteria used to select for type 2 jobs become narrower in scope, and it can easily be true that both efficiency and equity suffer.

References

Arrow, Kenneth J., 1972a, Models of job discrimination, chap. 2 in A. H. Pascal (ed.), *Racial discrimination in economic life* (D.C. Heath, Lexington, Mass., Toronto and London).

Arrow, Kenneth J., 1972b, Some mathematical models of race in the labor market, chap. 6 in A. H. Pascal (ed.), *Racial discrimination in economic life* (D.C. Heath, Lexington, Mass., Toronto and London).

Berg, Ivar, 1970. *Education and jobs: the great training robbery* (Praeger, New York).

Griliches, Zvi, and William M. Mason, 1972, Education, income, and ability, *Journal of Political Economy,* 80, S74–S103.

Hause, John C., 1972, Earnings profile: ability and schooling, *Journal of Political Economy,* 80, S108–S138.

Hirshleifer, J., 1971, The private and social value of information and the reward to inventive activity, *American Economic Review,* 61, 561–574.

Spence, A. Michael, 1973, *Market signaling* (Harvard University Press, Cambridge, Mass.).

11   Information and Economic Behavior

The members of an economy — the firms, the consumers, the investors, and the government — make choices. To give a common name to them all, I will refer to them as agents, for indeed their most salient characteristic is that they act. That they make choices implies that they have alternatives, that what was chosen was not inevitable but was in fact only one in a range of opportunities. The opportunities available to a consumer are determined by the income he has and the prices he has to pay for commodities of different use-values. The opportunities available to a firm might be all the technologically feasible combinations of inputs and outputs, in the present and in the future; this description allows for time lags between input and output and for durable producers' goods whose product is realized over a period of time. The opportunities available to an investor are basically returns over the future from alternative present portfolios. If the investor plans to use his returns for consumption in the future, or, for that matter, for reinvestment, then the true meaning of his opportunities is understood only in terms of the consumer goods or investment opportunities that will be available in the future and the prices which they will command on the open market.

I have referred repeatedly to the future in the description of the opportunities open to individual economic agents. Certainly a most salient characteristic of the future is that we do not know it perfectly. Our forecasts, whether

Reprinted from "Information and Economic Behavior," lecture presented to the Federation of Swedish Industries, Stockholm, 1973.

of future prices, future sales, or even the qualities of goods that will be available to us for use in production or consumption, are surely not known with certainty, and they are known with diminishing confidence as the future extends. Hence, it is intrinsic in the decision-making process, whether in the economic world or in any other, that the opportunities available, the consequences of our decisions, are not completely known to us.

But it is important to note that uncertainty is a property of many decisions which do not extend into the future or at least only into the immediate future. For example, if I wish to purchase some good, especially one I have not bought recently, I may not know its price. Of course, I can ascertain it, but only by the expenditure of time and other scarce resources. I will in general end up making a purchase without the prices of all possible substitutes; it would be too costly to find them out.

Perhaps even more significant than uncertainty about prices is uncertainty about the nature of the goods being purchased, about their quality. This is most striking and obvious when it comes to the hiring of labor, at all levels up to and perhaps most especially including the highest executive and academic levels. Any university professor who has participated in making appointments knows how difficult it is to evaluate the research and teaching potential of junior faculty, and the same considerations hold for the hiring of most other forms of labor. Indeed, the same uncertainty occurs at every promotion opportunity, for previous experience is almost never a sure guide to future performance in new circumstances. Again, consider many complex durable goods, such as automobiles. A genuine evaluation by the buyer in individual cases can really only be made, if ever, after considerable experience. The performance of an automobile or producers' durable, its durability, its need for repairs, are surely uncertain. Because of random variation from item to item, even previous experience does not permit confident generalization to new cases, though it does reduce the degree of uncertainty. It is perhaps sufficient for me to mention the securities market to recognize an area in which considerations of uncertainty dominate.

One remark should, however, be made at this stage. In many cases of quality uncertainty, the economic effect is major only because of some degree of irreversibility or time lag. If the quality of a worker were displayed immediately upon being hired and could be recognized without undue cost and if the act of hiring were costless, the uncertainty about labor quality would have little economic significance; the worker could be fired if unsatisfactory, with little lost to the employer. Similarly, the purchase of a complex machine is risky because second-hand prices tend to be considerably lower than new prices, and therefore the machine can be resold only with loss if it proves unsatisfactory. I should make clear at this stage that in many cases, these irreversibilities are themselves the indirect result of the prevalence of uncertainty; but I must defer explanation of this remark for a bit.

The general effects of uncertainty on economic decision making have been the object of intensive research for some time; the risk aversion of the average economic agent and its implications for such matters as portfolio selection, choice among alternative kinds of producers' durable goods, the choice between saving and consumption, and the capital structure of firms have been analyzed theoretically at considerable length and some significant empirical applications made.

It is not the general theory of behavior under uncertainty that I wish to discuss here but a particular aspect which has only recently begun to receive analytic attention. When there is uncertainty, there is usually the possibility of reducing it by the acquisition of *information.* Indeed, information is merely the negative measure of uncertainty, so to speak. Let me say immediately that I am not going to propose a quantitative measure for information. In particular, the well-known Shannon measure which has been so useful in communications engineering is not in general appropriate for economic analysis because it gives no weight to the value of the information. If beforehand a large manufacturer regards it as equally likely whether the price of his product will go up or down, then learning which is true conveys no more information, in the Shannon sense, than observing the toss of a fair coin. The Shannon measure may, however, be a useful measure of the cost of acquiring information.

I will think rather of information as a general descriptive term for an economically interesting category of goods which has not hitherto been accorded much attention by economic theorists. One finds occasional discussions of the effects of changes in information, usually given some name like "expectation," in the old business-cycle literature, which seems to have been largely displaced by post-Keynesian developments; of course, practical economic forecasters have always realized the importance of expectational information and indeed place increasing reliance on it as the quality of those data has improved. Albert Hart's pioneering work (1942) on flexibility in the choice of capital goods and other aspects of capital structure was based on a recognition that the firm would acquire new information over time. Statistical theorists and communications engineers have gone the farthest in stressing the value of information. Statistics is, indeed, the science of extracting information from a body of data. More specifically, in the theory of design of experiments, R. A. Fisher, Jerzy Neyman, Abraham Wald, and a long line of successors have grappled with the problem of allocating scarce resources to maximize the information attained.

The statisticians' model of information seems appropriate for our purposes. The economic agent has at any moment a probability distribution over possible values of the variables interesting to him, such as present and future prices or qualities of goods. Call these his *economic variables.* He makes an observation on some other variable; call it a *signal.* The distribution of the economic variables given the signal is different from the unconditional distribution. The decisions made depend, of course, on the distribution of economic variables; but if this distribution is in turn modified by the signals received, then economic behavior depends not only on the variables we usually regard as relevant, primarily prices, but also on signals which may themselves have little economic significance but which help reduce the uncertainty in predicting other as yet unobserved variables.

Let me give some examples of signals for economic variables. In forming a probability distribution for future prices we may use as information not merely current prices but also past prices; there is information in the development of the prices over time. This particular argument is familiar and has long been used in justifying the role of distributed lags in prices in the explanation of supply or investment (for an excellent review, see Nerlove, 1972). Though a cardinal point in the teaching of economics is that "bygones are forever bygones" and past prices should have no effect on future actions, nevertheless it is clear that they may convey information about the future and therefore affect present actions.

But signals can be even less direct. In many circumstances, past quantity movements may be signals for the distribution of future prices. If sales of a commodity have been declining, this may easily be taken as an indicator that its price will not rise, or more precisely, that the probability of a rise is lower than it would have been if sales had been rising. An example, familiar to business analysts but a stranger to formal economic theory, is the signaling role of government economic policy. A tax cut in a recession may have an effect not merely directly in terms of released purchasing power, but as a signal which raises the probability distribution of sales and therefore increases the incentive to invest.

Thus, at a very minimum, recognition of the concept of information and its possible changes over time implies a considerable revision of the theory of general economic equilibrium in the form in which it has evolved over the last century and which has reached such a high level of power and depth at the hands of Hicks, Samuelson, Debreu, and others in the last several decades. In this theory the economic behavior of individuals is governed primarily by prices. From the viewpoint of the society as a whole, prices are signals by which information about scarcities is transmitted among the members of society. The informational role of prices in resource allocation has especially been stressed by writers on the theory of socialism, from Barone through Lange and Lerner; the most sophisticated and general statement is that of Hurwicz (1960). The existence of uncertainty need not, in and of itself, destroy the primary role of prices in resource allocation, if markets exist not only for goods but for insurance against alternative possible outcomes. The basic contract to which a price attaches becomes one for delivery of a good contingent on the occurrence of some state of affairs.[1] Some such markets do exist, as for insurance and, in a modified form, for equities. Part of the reason that more do not exist derives from the existence and distribution of economic information, as will be discussed subsequently.

But in any case the presence of information, the existence of signals and the expectation of future signals, implies that, as we have already seen, actual economic behavior is partly governed by nonprice variables. This proposition at least opens the door for explaining the importance of quantity variables in the Keynesian system.[2] It also agrees to some extent with Janos Kornai's critique (1971) of general equilibrium theory for exaggerating the role of prices as compared with quantities in determining the behavior of firms in any decentralized economy, whether socialist or capitalist. I should add that I am far from regarding the allocative functions of prices as negligible; the demonstrable power of investment credits, tariffs, and excise taxes to influence the flow of resources does not allow that inference.

I have so far brought out one implication of the presence of information which reduces uncertainty, the economic relevance of nonprice signals. But there are two more implications, which are, I think, of even more fundamental importance in a reorientation of economic theory: (1) that information or signals have economic value and therefore are worth acquiring and transmitting even at some cost; (2) that different individuals have different information. In the rest of this chapter I will argue that these two rather

---

1. For the theory of contingent markets, see Arrow (1971, chap. 4 [Chapter 3 in Volume 2 of these Collected Papers]); Debreu (1959, chap. 7).
2. See especially the interpretation of Leijonhufvud (1968).

simple observations taken together are potentially rich in implications for the working of an economic system.

I should stress the word "potentially." This is a report on a line of research, the bulk of which took place in the 1960s. Some theoretical results were obtained; very little empirical analysis was attempted. The initiators were Jacob Marschak (1959) and George Stigler (1961), with subsequent contributions by many writers but perhaps especially Armen Alchian (1969), Roy Radner (1961), Jack Hirshleifer (1971), Michael Rothschild (1973), and A. Michael Spence (1973), together with some contributions of mine (Arrow, 1971, chaps. 5–10, 12; 1973a; 1974). These works do not form a coherent stream; they start from different points of view, deal with different aspects, and use different terminologies. It is of some doctrinal interest to observe that they all come out of the much-criticized neoclassical tradition, though they certainly represent developments of it; that is, they start from some concept of individual advantage seeking in a world in which each agent has little market power, and they assume the equilibrium allocations which are arrived at are such that expectations are not falsified. A general definition of equilibrium in this context has been given by Hahn (1973, especially pp. 18–20). To be sure, the "expectations" are probability distributions rather than points, so that what is meant is that individual agents learn whatever it is that they could learn given their opportunities to observe.

The economic value of information offers no great mysteries in itself. It is easy to prove that one can always do better, whether as a producer or as a consumer, by basing decisions on a signal, provided the signal and the economic variables are not independently distributed. But this remark has an implication for economic decisions; the economic agent is willing to pay for information, for signals.

We must now recognize that the signals available to an economic agent are not given to him but can be added to. The space of possible decisions has been enlarged to include the acquisition of information in addition to production and consumption. The research engineer can be thought of as eliciting signals from nature, analogous to the miner who draws minerals from the earth; research is a form of production. Information about the behavior of other economic agents, especially customers or workers, or about future or even present prices or qualities of goods are more straightforward examples of information whose acquisition is both possible and desired.

Clearly, firms do engage in information gathering. They spend resources on engineering and market research. Moreover, there are large and significant exchanges of information through the market—newspapers, business advice, and, in a somewhat modified sense of market, all of education—in short, the whole realm of the production and distribution of knowledge, which Fritz Machlup (1962) has so carefully measured. Thus, information is not merely a good that is desired and acquired but is to some extent a commodity like others whose markets we study.

But even though information can be a commodity, it is one only to a limited extent. The presumption that free markets will lead to an efficient allocation of resources is not valid in this case. If nothing else, there are at least two salient characteristics of information which prevent it from being fully identified as one of the commodities represented in our abstract models of general equilibrium: (1) it is, by definition, indivisible in its use; and (2) it is very difficult to appropriate. With regard to the first point, information about a method of production, for example, is the same regardless of the scale of the output. Since the cost of information depends only on the item, not its use, it pays a large-scale producer to acquire better information than a small-scale producer. Thus, information creates economies of scale throughout the economy, and therefore, according to well-known principles, causes a departure from the competitive economy.

Information is inappropriable because an individual who has some can never lose it by transmitting it. It is frequently noted in connection with the economics of research and development that information acquired by research at great cost may be transmitted much more cheaply. If the information is, therefore, transmitted to one buyer, he can in turn sell it very cheaply, so that the market price is well below the cost of production. But if the transmission costs are high, then it is also true that there is inappropriability, since the seller cannot realize the social value of the information. Both cases occur in practice with different kinds of information.

But then, according to well-known principles of welfare economics, the inappropriability of a commodity means that its production will be far from optimal. It may be below optimal; it may also induce costly protective measures outside the usual property system.

Thus, it has been a classic position that a competitive world will underinvest in research and development, because the information acquired will become general knowledge and cannot be appropriated by the firm financing the research (see, for example, Nelson, 1959, and Arrow, 1971, chap. 6; for a somewhat critical view, see Demsetz, 1969). But Hirshleifer (1971) has pointed out that, if secrecy is possible, there may be overinvestment in information gathering; each firm may secretly get the same information, either on nature or on each other, although it would of course consume less of society's resources if they were collected once and disseminated to all.

To dramatize the issue, let me give an example where information is socially useless but privately valuable. Imagine an economy of gatherers of different kinds of food. Weather is uncertain, and some types of food are in relatively greater supply in some kinds of weather than in others. There is an opportunity for mutually advantageous insurance contracts. Those who are relatively better off in one situation can pay the others then, in return for commitments to compensate in those weather situations in which the first group is relatively worse off. But now suppose that an opportunity arises for the accurate prediction of weather, though at some cost. Given the insurance market, it clearly pays any individual to buy the information and keep it a secret. He can then make large gains by betting on the weather that will in fact take place. But under the assumptions made there is no social gain; what is produced will be produced in any case. If the receivers of the weather information are small on the scale of the market, then there will be neither social gain nor social loss on the risk-sharing contracts. But if enough individuals buy the information, the market for risk trading is destroyed, for competition will change the odds to those conditional on the information received, which, if accurate enough, will leave little opportunity for insurance against unfavorable risks. Hence, there is a double social loss — the resources used unnecessarily in acquiring information and the destruction of a market for risk sharing.

This example has been extreme, because it has, by assumption, excluded any possible gains in production. Ordinarily, we would assume that a knowledge of future weather would permit a reallocation of resources to activities which would be relatively more productive under the forecast weather. In that case, the signal has a positive effect on welfare. But this does not blunt the essential point, that there will very likely be an overinvestment in the acquisition of information whose private value is to gain at the expense of others. One would suppose that the securities markets and the extensive apparatus for private information gathering there would exemplify this point. Further, the very acquisition of this information is apt to make the securities market less valuable as a means of risk sharing.

When information is unequally distributed, there are incentives not only to acquisition of information but also to the emission of signals. If I know something about my product which will make it more attractive to others, or if my (low) price is not generally known, I will be willing to incur costs to transmit this information to the outside world. Advertising is an obvious example of the emission of signals, but not the only one. I want to abstract here from the emission of false signals, of deception, because in long-run statistical equilibrium the receivers of the signals will have had enough experience to know the statistical distribution of the economic variables (price or qualities) conditional on the signal. However, it is hard to define the process by which a signal gets to be recognized as such and how the receiver learns to discriminate among them. It would seem that in many cases, at least, collective action is needed to define signals. Suppose, for example, that one firm labeled different qualities of its product according to some scheme. This signal might have little effect in a market with many competitors, because the consumers would not find it worthwhile to expend the intellectual resources needed to learn the signaling scheme. However, a grade-labeling scheme adopted by collective agreement of the entire industry would be worth learning. It would become easier to observe the signals and correlate them with factual observations.

This argument was used by Kaysen (1949, pp. 294–295) to explain the then-current use of the basing-point system for pricing in steel and other industries. It is not easy to give a conventional economic explanation for this system, and even less for the agreement among steel producers that price differentials among different grades of steel be fixed. But if the steel industry is thought of as an oligopoly forbidden, however, from engaging in explicit collusion, it becomes very important for the attainment of a mutually satisfactory equilibrium that each firm may be able to observe the prices of other firms. If not, each firm will have the possibility of cutting prices without retaliation. If, in fact, the prices for every point of delivery and every grade are freely variable, then the capacity of the firms to observe each others' price behavior is very limited compared with their possible scope. But if relative prices of locations and qualities are fixed, then each firm's entire behavior is summarized in one number, and mutual observation becomes possible.

The educational system has become, partly inadvertently, an industry which sells signals for individuals to emit to the world. Its primary intended function is the acquisition of knowledge. But in the course of its own internal measuring of its success in this function, it automatically generates signals of ability in education. If it is in fact the case, or at least believed to be the case, that ability to produce is correlated with ability to absorb education, then the educational system does produce signals about productive ability. I have already argued that the observation of the productive quality of labor is costly to employers. Hence, it pays them to use signals emitted at no cost to them. In turn, however, this creates an incentive for the student to continue his education beyond that level which he would otherwise desire and beyond the level which is socially desirable.

The welfare analysis of the signaling function of education is similar to that of the private demand for weather information in the previous example. It may be, for example, that the educational system simply identifies individuals who are generally more able. They might be equally productive whether or not they are recognized. In that case, as in the simple case where weather information has no productive value, the screening would produce a redistribution of income among individuals but no increase in total product. The resources devoted to education beyond that desired as a consumption good would be simply wasted socially; further, if there is any aversion to risk about one's own abilities, the screening reduces welfare in the aggregate. If, however, individuals have differing advantages in different positions in the economy, then education may serve as a sorting process which will increase total product. This sorting process may, by the way, operate on both sides of the market; not only do employers know more about potential workers, but the latter may learn more about their own abilities. But note that the social productivity of screening has to do with identification of comparative, not absolute, advantages. Since educational attainment inevitably signals the latter as well as the former, there is almost bound to be a socially excessive demand for education if offered at cost with adequate credit facilities for the student investing in his future earnings.

We have now seen that the differentiation of information among individuals together with the existence of costs of acquiring information may lead to the emission of signals to others. But, as already suggested, the creation of new types of signals which can be understood and believed in is by no means a simple task. The education system yields ability signals as a by-product of its main activities; it was not developed for that purpose. Creating a credible screening device *de novo* will in general be more difficult.

Let me turn to two other kinds of responses to the differentiation and the costs of acquisition of information: (1) adaptations to improve efficiency of information processing may arise; (2) markets may fail to exist or else they may perform their functions in ways different from those usually assumed.

Let us take up the first point. How can a firm, for example, become more efficient in the acquisition of information? Now there are many elements in the cost of information acquisition, but surely the most fundamental is the limitation on the ability of any individual to process information. No matter how much the technology of information processing is improved, the ability of the human mind and senses to absorb signals will be a permanent limitation. Clearly, one strategy for increasing the input of information is to increase the number of individual receptors. One can have many individuals linked together in a firm or other organization, each making different observations on the world. (There is no value in having them observe the same signals, provided they are observed without error.) Indeed, the market system as a whole has frequently been considered as an organization for the allocation of resources; the typical argument for its superiority to authoritative central allocation has been the greater intake of information through having many participants.

But multiplicity of observers creates a new problem, that of coordination. The items of information are typically complementary in value and have to be pooled in some way for best use. There is a need for communication channels, and these are costly. Clearly, if every signal received by each observer had to be transmitted to another, the total amount of information handling would be greater than in the absence of organization. Economy arises only if the signals transmitted within the organization are summaries of the information received. The theory of sufficient statistics suggests one instance of economy; in certain contexts, all the information in a sample of many observations can be transmitted as two numbers, a statistic and an indicator of its reliability. Thus, the costs of transmission are much lower than those of acquisition, and it is possible that joining the observers into a single organization can represent a net economy. (See Radner, 1961, for some aspects of the design of information structures for organizations.)

However, the establishment of a system of many observers linked by communication channels has long-run dangers of petrifaction. A communication system has some cost of initial investment which is irreversible. In particular, a communication channel is used to greatest capacity when it has an optimal code for transmitting messages. This "code" need not be interpreted literally; the term refers to all patterns of communication and interaction within an organization, patterns which make use of conventional signals and forms which have to be learned. Once learned, however, it is cheaper to reuse the same system than to learn a new one; there is a payoff on the initial learning investment but no way of liquidating it by sale to others. If external conditions change, an originally optimal communication system may no longer be the one that would be chosen if the organization were to begin all over again. Eventually the communication system may be very inefficient at handling signals, and the firm may vanish or undergo a major reorganization.

To put it another way, the firm's organization is designed to meet a more or less wide variety of possible signals. The wider the range planned for, the greater is the flexibility of the firm in meeting the unforeseen (that is what flexibility means), but the less efficient it is in meeting a narrower range of possibilities, as Hart (1942) pointed out.

I see the communication-economical point of view as explanatory of the internal structure of firms and more generally of other economic organizations. The assumptions about the firm made in classical economic theory will have to be altered. It is assumed there to be a point; instead, it is an incompletely connected network of information flows. Thus, a change in the price of, say, a factor of production may be observed in some parts of the firm but not in the rest. The response will surely be different in general than if the firm reacted by altering its entire plan immediately.

Indeed, the whole idea of a firm with definite boundaries cannot be maintained intact. For example, the customers of a firm are, to some extent, part of it, as Chester Barnard (1938, p. 77) has maintained. There are direct information flows from customers in the form of complaints, requests for product alteration or special services, or threats to change to another firm, in addition to the anonymous alterations of demand at a given price which constitute the sole information link between a firm and its market in neoclassical theory. Some employees of a firm will have closer links to customers than to at least some of the other employees.

Finally, let me note that the fact of differential information as between contracting parties will prevent some efficient contracts from being made. The best examples are those in which uncertainty enters explicitly into the nature of the contract, various types of insurance being the most obvious instances. The most striking category of market failure due to differential information is that known in the insurance literature as *adverse selection.* Suppose a population at risk, for example, in life insurance, is divided into strata with differing probabilities of an untoward event. Suppose further that each individual desiring insurance knows which stratum he belongs to and hence the probability of risk for him, but the insurers cannot distinguish among the insured according to risk and therefore are constrained to make the same offer to all. At any given price for insurance the high-risk individuals will buy more, the low-risk individuals less, so that the actuarial expectations will become more adverse than they would be with equal participation by all or than they would be in an ideal allocation with different premiums to different strata. The resulting equilibrium allocation of risk bearing will be inefficient, at least relative to that which would be attainable if information on risks were equally available to both sides.

What is more, the patent fact of inefficiency under adverse selection may lead to altering the nature of the market transactions. The insurance company may find it profitable to engage in information-gathering activities to reduce the extent of adverse selection, for example, by medical examinations. Since there is a mutual gain to be made, such activities may become general even in a competitive market. But then the parties to a transaction have closer links than the simple impersonal exchange of money for services; the information must be gathered on identified individuals, not on anonymous customers.

Adverse selection in insurance is relatively transparent, but the same phenomenon is at work elsewhere in the economic system. George Akerlof (1970) has called our attention to this question with regard to the sale of used automobiles, where the seller will in general have more information about the properties of the object sold than the buyers; again, something like adverse selection can seriously impair the operations of the market.

I would mention the whole capital market as another and very important example. Virtually all extension of credit involves some risk of default. Hence, indebtedness can never be in the form of anonymous promises to pay interest and principal. The purchaser of credit instruments buys them from specific individuals who are responsible; and in general he gathers information about the potential debtors. A good part of the activity of a bank is precisely in performing these tasks.

Closely related to adverse selection is the occurrence of "moral hazard," that is, the difficulty of distinguishing between decisions and exogenous uncertainty. (The adjective "moral" is misleading in many contexts but is hallowed by long use.) An insurance policy, for example, may induce the insured to change his behavior, therewith the risks against which the insurance is written. Thus, insurance against fire will lead a rational individual to be less careful if care is at all costly. "Health insurance," more precisely insurance against medical costs, is a currently important illustration; the insurance, once taken out, is equivalent to a reduction of the price of medical care, and therefore the rational individual will increase his consumption, which increases the amount of medical insurance payments and ultimately causes an increase in the premiums. This is a social cost, since an increase in medical expenditures by any individual increases the premium for all, and thus the use of both the services of risk bearing and those of medical care is inefficient (see Pauly, 1968; Arrow, 1971, chaps. 5, 9).

Again, economic institutions may compensate by introducing nonmarket informational devices. In the case of fire insurance, a company may inspect the premises and demand that certain precautions be taken as a condition for the policy, or, at least, adjust the premium according to the observed safety standards. In the case of health insurance, it is theoretically possible to investigate medical treatments to see if they are really necessary, and there has indeed been a trend toward peer review, at least.

It is important to observe that the problem of "moral hazard" is one of differential information. Consider the case of fire insurance. For simplicity, suppose there are three possible conditions not under the control of the insured: fire regardless of the insured's precautions; a condition which could create fire if the insured were careless but not otherwise; or no fire in any case. If the insurance company could observe which of these states has occurred, it would be possible for it to insure separately against the first two cases. The rational buyer would purchase insurance against the first according to simple principles of risk aversion; with regard to the second, however, he would weigh the costs of insurance against those of the alternative of being more careful. Such an insurance market would lead to an efficient allocation. It is the cost of determining the occurrence of these states which leads the insurance company to write policies against fire as such, which is less efficient in terms of resource allocation but cheaper in terms of information. Similarly, an efficient health insurance system would be possible if the insurer could observe some measure of the severity of illness and simply pay a sum determined by that measure and independent of actual expenditures by the insured.

The general principle underlying these last few examples has been set forth by Radner (1968). An insurance contract (in the most general sense, including any situation in which the final payoffs to the participants have an uncertain component) can be made only if the conditions under which the contract is to be executed can be observed by both parties. If one will observe a condition but not the other, then the contract cannot hinge on that condition's being satisfied, even though it would be in the interests of both parties to make such a conditional contract if it could be credibly enforced. Whenever some markets are barred from existence, there is inefficiency, which is frequently reflected in strains on other markets.

It is important to note that if the informational inequality is regarded as an irremovable condition, there will in general be substitutes for competitive markets which will increase welfare, though not to the point achievable under full equality of information. One possibility is that of nonlinear price systems, where the premium paid for an insurance policy is not proportional to the amount of the policy. Roughly, the idea is that individuals who seek to buy more insurance are more apt to be high risks and hence should pay a higher marginal premium. The formal structure of these problems is analogous to that of imposing taxes on income as a substitute for the theoretically superior imposition of a tax on innate ability, the point being that income is partly a result of an individual's labor-leisure choice; see Mirrlees (1971, 1972).

One adaptation of the economic system to differential information is scarcely mentioned in our models; it is the development of ethical codes and the internalization of certain values (see Arrow, 1973b). Every profession, such as the medical, owes its economic function to the inequality of information between the professional and his client; what the latter is buying is most of all the superior knowledge of the former. But this is just the situation in which it is most difficult to expect a market to function, as just explained. The patient has little protection against the physician's recommendation of unnecessarily costly treatments. It is probably no coincidence that ethical constraints on economic behavior are so strongly developed in the professions; they serve as an alternative to equal information, the physician's ethical motivation for the client's welfare being relied on to replace contracts which the latter could not enforce due to lack of knowledge.

In fact, ethical elements enter in some measure into every contract; without them, no market could function. There is an element of trust in every transaction; typically, one object of value changes hands before the other one does, and there is confidence that the countervalue will in fact be given up. It is not adequate to argue that there are enforcement mechanisms, such as police and courts; these are themselves services bought and sold, and it has to be asked why they will in fact do what *they* have contracted to do. In any case, the cost of enforcement becomes bearable only if most transactions take place without attempts at fraud, force, or cheating. Further, in transactions of any complexity, it would be too costly to draw up contracts which would cover every contingency. Some aspects have to be left for interpretation when needed, and it is implicitly understood that it will be possible to agree on the meaning of the contract, even though one party loses.

I expect that ethical codes and informal nonprice organizations will continue to evolve where needed, for example in the control of product quality, to permit transactions which would be impossible because of differential information in markets where all individuals behaved in a purely selfish manner. The evolution of ethical codes is facilitated by the fact that productive units are organizations, not individuals, and individuals are mobile among these organizations. Hence, ethical codes held by individuals, perhaps derived as part of business education, may survive even though detrimental to the profits of the firms because the managerial element can accept a trade-off between profits, which only partly inure to it, and learned ethics, which have been found to facilitate business in general.

These remarks are merely preliminary to a genuine study of the development of ethical codes in the economic world. The basic question is how best to emit those signals which will lead to accepted and understood ethical and authority relations and the conditions for their stability. The latter depends on some combination of perceptions and of the reality of mutual self-interest.

References

Akerlof, G. 1970. The market for "lemons": Qualitative uncertainty and the market mechanism. *Quarterly Journal of Economics* 84:488–500.

Alchian, A. 1969. Information costs, pricing, and resource unemployment. *Western Economic Journal* 7:109–128.

Arrow, K. J. 1971. *Essays in the Theory of Risk-Bearing.* Chicago: Markham, and Amsterdam: North-Holland.

Arrow, K. J. 1973a. Higher education as a filter. *Journal of Public Economics* 2:193–216. [Chapter 10 of this volume.]

Arrow, K. J. 1973b. Social responsibility and economic efficiency. *Public Policy* 21:303–318. [To appear in a later volume of these Collected Papers.]

Arrow, K. J. 1973c. The agenda of organizations. In R. L. Marris and A. Wood (eds.), *The Corporate Economy: Growth Competition and Innovative Power.* London and Basingstoke: Macmillan. Chapter 7, pp. 214–234. [Chapter 13 of this volume.]

Arrow, K. J. 1974. *The Limits of Organization.* New York: Norton.

Barnard, C. 1938. *The Functions of the Executive.* Cambridge, Mass.: Harvard University Press.

Debreu, G. 1959. *Theory of Value.* New York: Wiley.

Demsetz, H. 1969. Information and efficiency: Another viewpoint. *Journal of Law and Economics* 12:1–22.

Hahn, F. 1973. *On the Notion of Equilibrium in Economics.* Cambridge: Cambridge University Press.

Hart, A. G. 1942. Risk, uncertainty and the unprofitability of compounding probabilities. In O. Lange, F. McIntyre, and T. O. Yntema (eds.), *Studies in Mathematical Economics and Econometrics.* Chicago: University of Chicago Press. Pp. 110–118.

Hirshleifer, J. 1971. The private and social value of information and the reward to inventive activity. *American Economic Review* 61:561–574.

Hurwicz, L. 1960. Optimality and informational efficiency in resource allocation processes. In K. J. Arrow, S. Karlin, and P. Suppes (eds.), *Mathematical Methods in the Social Sciences, 1959.* Stanford, Calif.: Stanford University Press. Pp. 27–46.

Kaysen, C. 1949. Basing point pricing and public policy. *Quarterly Journal of Economics* 63:289–314.

Kornai, J. 1971. *Anti-Equilibrium.* Amsterdam: North-Holland.

Leijonhufvud, A. 1968. *On Keynesian Economics and the Economics of Keynes.* New York: Oxford University Press.

Machlup, F. 1962. *The Production and Distribution of Knowledge in the United States.* Princeton, N.J.: Princeton University Press.

Marschak, J. 1959. Remarks on the economics of information. In *Contributions to Scientific Research in Management.* Los Angeles: Western Data Processing Center, University of California. Pp. 79–98.

Mirrlees, J. 1971. An exploration in the theory of optimum income taxation. *Review of Economic Studies* 38:175–208.

Mirrlees, J. 1972. Notes on welfare economics, information, and efficiency. Unpublished, Oxford University.

Nelson, R. R. 1959. The simple economics of basic scientific research. *Journal of Political Economy* 67:297–306.

Nerlove, M. 1972. Lags in economic behavior. *Econometrica* 40:221–252.

Pauly, M. 1968. The economics of moral hazard. *American Economic Review* 58:531–537.

Radner, R. 1961. The evaluation of information in organizations. In J. Neyman (ed.), *Proceedings of the Fourth Berkeley Symposium on Mathematical Statistics and Probability,* vol. 1. Berkeley and Los Angeles: University of California Press.

Radner, R. 1968. Competitive equilibrium under uncertainty. *Econometrica* 36:31–58.

Rothschild, M. 1973. Models of market organization with imperfect information: A survey. *Journal of Political Economy* 81:1283–1308.

Spence, A. M. 1973. *Market Signaling.* Cambridge, Mass.: Harvard University Press.

Stigler, G. J. 1961. The economics of information. *Journal of Political Economy* 69:213–225.

12 Limited Knowledge and Economic Analysis

The content of presidential addresses to the American Economic Association provides a fine example of a random variable with a high variance. It might even be a good subject for econometric analysis; the variation might be explained in terms of the economic conditions of the moment, previous intellectual investments, or even, for boldly interdisciplinary analysis, the psychological states or class origins of the speakers or the audience. But no doubt captious theorists like myself will object that the endogenous variable is not cardinally measurable and probably not even ordinally measurable; tougher-minded econometricians will worry about collinearity in the predetermined variables; and practical-minded policy analysts will see no discernible effect on the gross national product, the price level, or the balance of payments through effects on either fiscal policy or the stock of money. The last group, the policy-oriented, are perhaps the least accurate; at least according to Keynes, the effect of ideas on policy is

Reprinted from *American Economic Review*, 64 (1974):1–10. Presidential address delivered at the eighty-sixth meeting of the American Economic Association, New York, New York, December 29, 1973. The views expressed here are a personal synthesis of a widespread viewpoint which has appeared in many different contexts in the published work of and in some cases personal discussions with G. Akerlof, A. Alchian, G. Calabresi, R. H. Coase, H. Demsetz, P. A. Diamond, J. Green, F. H. Hahn, A. G. Hart, F. A. von Hayek, J. Hirshleifer, L. Hurwicz, C. Kaysen, F. H. Knight, A. Leijonhufvud, F. Machlup, J. Marschak, T. Marschak, J. Mirrlees, M. Nerlove, R. Radner, M. Rothschild, T. Schelling, H. A. Simon, A. M. Spence, and G. J. Stigler. For some additional aspects of the role of information problems in economics, see Chapter 11.

dominant, though the lag may be as variable as and a good deal longer than that of the stock of money on money gross national product.

It is now more fashionable than it used to be for statisticians to be told to take a good look at their data before fitting models. Taking presidential addresses as our data, we find most frequently a review of the speaker's main research concerns but also expressions of methodological or ethical concerns, historical surveys of varying degrees of erudition and humor, and, least frequently, new points of view on significant problems of economics.

I am taking a somewhat different tack here; this presentation will be an expression of discontents and expectations. As I shall try to argue, the uncertainties about economics are rooted in our need for a better understanding of the economics of uncertainty; our lack of economic knowledge is, in good part, our difficulty in modeling the ignorance of the economic agent.

Critical aspects of this need for reorientation of theory have been recognized by many scholars in the last quarter-century and particularly in the last decade [1974]. I view my remarks here as a summary and perspective on a widely shared development of thinking.

The starting point of discussion must still be the much-abused neoclassical theory. No really cohesive alternative which aspires to the same level of completeness exists. The neoclassical model is founded on two concepts, which are considerably different in nature. One is the notion of the individual economic agent, whose behavior is governed by a criterion of optimization under constraints which are partly peculiar to the agent, such as production functions, and partly terms of trade with the economic system as a whole. The other is the market; here, the aggregate of individual decisions is acknowledged, and the terms of trade adjusted until the decisions of the individuals are mutually consistent in the aggregate, that is, supply equals demand.

The neoclassical theory, especially in its competitive form, can be and has been given a rich formal development. Parenthetically, one cause for the persistence of neoclassical theory in the face of its long line of critics is precisely that for some reason of mathematical structure, the neoclassical theory is highly manipulable and flexible; when faced with a specific issue, it can yield meaningful implications relatively easily. Although I intend here to air complaints and desires for change, I must express my unabashed admiration for the accomplishments of the neoclassical viewpoint. In its most formal statement, we simply use for analysis the equilibrium conditions of the individual agent and of the market, without inquiry as to how they come to hold. Yet even these statements turn out to yield revealing insights into the workings of resource allocation. Why have medical costs risen so rapidly relative to other prices since 1967? The upward shift in demand due to Medicare and Medicaid with a price-inelastic supply of physicians and hospitals provides a simple, straightforward answer; I cannot really imagine how a Marxian or a neo-Ricardian would even approach the question, though I suppose they might dismiss it as unimportant. The explanation of environmental problems as due to the nonexistence of markets is similarly an insight of purely neoclassical origin. The now-demonstrated fact that flexible exchange rates are a feasible way of conducting international finance is a triumph of theoretical insights over practical men's convictions. More broadly, the shifts in long-run resource allocation as motivated by returns and, in particular, the absence of a secular trend in technological unemployment, to the perpetual surprise of the layman, fit in well with the neoclassical formulation but have no ready explanation in alternate models.

Of course, the implications of neoclassical theory have also been conspicuously falsified in important ways. Most notably, the recurrent periods of unemployment which have characterized the history of capitalism are scarcely compatible with a neoclassical model of market equilibrium. A post-Keynesian world in which unemployment is avoided or kept at tolerable levels by recurrent alterations in fiscal or monetary policy is no more explicable by neoclassical axioms, though the falsification is not as conspicuous.

Inequality in economic development among countries and among groups and regions within a country provides a second, somewhat complicated difficulty for neoclassical theory. A purely neoclassical answer would explain differences in per capita income by differences in physical and human assets per capita. This, of course, raises the further question of how this came to be, a question which would require a fully dynamic model to answer; but I think the more compelling problem is that the differences in income seem much too vast to be explained by factor differences. Indeed, in the presence of international trade and especially international capital movements, wage differences should be very strongly reduced compared with what would occur in autarchic states where domestic capital is the limiting factor. Hence, we come immediately to the explanation that there are differences in the production possibility sets of the different countries. This conclusion is a legitimate and important use of neoclassical analysis; but obviously it raises new questions, to which we will return.

I pass by the whole tangle of questions relating to the holding of money and the general level of prices. In its pure form, neoclassical theory is a theory of relative prices. Monetary theories vaguely related to it in spirit can be grafted onto it, but none have succeeded in achieving a genuine synthesis.

The two failures of the neoclassical explanatory mechanism reflect on its foundations in quite different ways. The existence of unemployment is clearly a direct contradiction to the notion of the smoothly clearing market. One must, of course, be aware that the official measure of unemployment is by no means a simple inequality between supply and demand; it aggregates a whole range of distinct markets, it does not separate out voluntary and involuntary unemployment according to the tests of economic theory, and it does not take account of unfilled jobs. I do not subscribe, I hasten to say, to the sometimes expressed view that all unemployment is essentially voluntary, an unwillingness to search or whatnot; indeed, the official measure may underestimate the degree of disequilibrium in the labor market, particularly with regard both to underutilization of advanced skills and discouraged job seekers. With all these qualifications, it is clear that statistical unemployment does correspond to a disequilibrium as that term is used in the basic neoclassical model; there are two individuals, identical in productive capacity and both willing to work at a given wage, but one is working at that wage and the other is not.

Differential levels of economic development, on the other hand, point to a difficulty with the other fundamental concept, the conditions of optimization. If countries differ in their production possibility sets, then firms occupying similar economic positions are facing different constraints on their optimization. This does not contradict the fundamental assumption of optimizing behavior, but it does raise severe questions about its interpretation. The simplest hypothesis is to take the technological conditions as data, possibly varying over time due to exogenous changes in scientific knowledge. But here we are asserting that two contemporaries have different access to productive knowledge. Clearly, we are saying something about the conditions of transmission of knowledge across national boundaries, and of course the same questions arise among firms or workers within a single economy. The constraints on the firm's optimization begin to seem more like variables to be explained than like constants exogenously given.

Let me look now at the two basic concepts from the inside, from the point of view of our direct perceptions which motivate the modeling. The two are far from parallel. The optimization by individual agents has a sense of concreteness about it, for all the sophisticated mathematical ability with which we theorists endow the agents. They behave in ways whose logic we understand. They seek to achieve goals which are reasonable to postulate, and we can specify constraints which clearly are real. It can be and has been correctly objected that our models are too simple; we ignore other arguments in the utility function—power, status, social approval, or whatever—that also motivate individuals, and we ignore some constraints, capacity for calculation and social controls. But the model is comprehensible, and the motives and constraints we deal with are real and important.

The market, on the other hand, is a much more ethereal construct. Who exactly is it that is achieving the balancing of supply and demand? Where in fact is the information on bids and offers needed for equilibration actually collected and stored? Right from the beginning of neoclassical theory, the difficulty of explaining markets in terms of individual self-seeking behavior was perceived. Parenthetically, this is one example of the superiority of neoclassical analysis to its predecessors, despite the current fashion for exalting Ricardo over his successors; Ricardo implicitly equated supply and demand on all his markets without ever realizing the problematic nature of this process. Jevons felt obliged to enunciate explicitly a Law of Indifference, enforced by arbitrage; but this does not really meet the problem when the market is out of equilibrium, for the arbitrage might well not be feasible. Menger, at least according to Hayek and Streissler, concentrated on individual trades and ignored the market completely. It was Walras' auctioneer which proved to have the most enduring effect on subsequent theoretical development, and the stability theory which flows from that concept is still the subject of vigorous theoretical development, though very little empirical application. What is envisioned is a feedback mechanism in which errors in the price are successively corrected by reference to the disequilibria they generate. This view specifies and makes feasible the operations of the market. But on one hand, the stability models are far from adequate representations even of the dynamics of the neoclassical models, and—what may be connected—the results are by no means necessarily favorable to the stability of the adjustment process; and on the other hand, the motivations for the feedback to operate are obscure.

Let me be clear on one methodological point. The fact that our intuitive understanding, our *verstehen* as the German social methodologists call it, of the market as an institution is not entirely satisfactory does not mean that we should not use the perfect market as a model, at least pending further development. Certainly, as Popper and Friedman hold, the acceptability of a theory is to be judged by its ability to predict and understand phenomena.

The theory of the perfect market is in an interesting way complementary to Keynesian theory. We have never been able to integrate Keynesian viewpoints into standard neoclassical theory, in terms of individual motivation, yet this theory, with its various modifications, has been a most serviceable tool of prediction and control. In fact, it is useful in domains where competitive theory fails and vice versa. Neither theory is good, however, at predicting dynamic processes, the short-run changes which are responses to disequilibria, and it is here that the pressure for a more satisfactory model arises.

Hold in abeyance for a moment our considerations about the market. Let us return to the optimization problem of the individual. One aspect on which we put a good deal of weight, particularly in our less formal discussions, is that a market system is informationally economical. That is, we tend to regard it as a virtue of the system that the individual agent need not know very much. Specifically, he is supposed to know the motivation and production conditions which define him, that is, his utility function and production possibility set, together with the prices of the commodities he buys and sells. The economic system, taken as a whole, has vastly more in it than any one individual knows; it contains the utility functions and production possibilities of all individual agents. Indeed, the apparent modesty of the information needed is one of the most appealing aspects of the neoclassical model, both in the descriptive sense that the individual's decision problems appear manageable for him and for the economist studying him, and in the normative sense that the system permits its members to spend their time and effort at producing goods rather than in unnecessary duplication of information.

But clearly this simplification of the individual's decision making is made possible only because the markets have supplied the information economized on, in the form of prices. In equilibrium, at least, the system as a whole gives the impression of great economy in the handling of information, presumably because transmission of prices is in some significant sense much cheaper than transmission of the whole set of production possibilities and utility functions. It is this point which emerged in the great debate over the feasibility of socialism begun by Ludwig von Mises' attack and usually thought of as concluding with the work of Oskar Lange and Abba Lerner in the 1930s; though it should be added that many of the essential points had already been made earlier by Vilfredo Pareto and Enrico Barone. What was argued, in effect, was that a socialist system could use the price system and therefore achieve whatever economies in information it does achieve; and if the equilibrium conditions are written out they do give the appearance of relative simplicity. But what was left obscure is a more definitive measure of information and its costs, in terms of which it would be possible to assert the superiority of the price system over a centralized alternative. Although I feel that current work has brought about a considerable clarification, we still have no definite measure. Indeed, in some respects, more recent developments have made the answers less clear. Several writers, in both Western and socialist countries, have noted that alternative decentralized schemes exist where quantity messages rather than price messages are transmitted in the successive stages of approximation and that such schemes also have efficient equilibrium points. Indeed, with the development of mathematical programming and high-speed computers, the centralized alternative no longer appears preposterous. After all, it would appear that one could mimic the workings of a decentralized system by an appropriately chosen centralized algorithm. Although there is more to the story than these few remarks, they do make the point that if we are going to take information economy seriously, we have to add to our usual economic calculations an appropriate measure of the costs of information gathering and transmission.

But actually the comparisons between socialist and capitalist resource allocation systems have tended to overlook some of the most obvious facts while examining fine points closely. As we all know, both production and consumption decisions are in fact made with reference to the future as well as to the present. A rational production plan includes, very importantly, decisions or at least plans about the future; and similarly with consumption plans. Investment and savings are not only integral parts of our current decisions but in the long run shape the possibilities for further development. As we know, the formal neoclassical model can be extended to decisions over time by dating commodities and regarding the same commodity at different dates as different commodities. All previous conclusions follow; allocative efficiency, for example, is achieved with the same appearance of informational efficiency.

But, of course, there is a slight problem with this reasoning. The information about future commodities needed includes their prices. These prices must be those found on a suitable market, one in which future supply and future demand are equated. Unfortunately, no such markets exist. Even the futures markets in certain commodities, limited in extent as they are, do not in fact lead to balancing *all* future decisions. Rather they balance present commitments to the future; but it is understood by all parties that when the future becomes the present, there will be a spot market on which the futures commitments may be undone; and indeed those making no futures commitments at all can enter and know now that they will be able to enter.

Even as a graduate student, I was somewhat surprised at the emphasis on static allocative efficiency by market socialists, when the nonexistence of markets for future goods under capitalism seemed to me a much more obvious target.

However that may be, the nonexistence of these markets must be faced. Now in general equilibrium, any part of the system affects every other part in at least two different ways. Thus, we may ask two questions about the nonexistence of futures goods markets; what its implications are for the rest of the system, and what the reasons are for its nonexistence.

The implication first of all is that the information needed by the optimizer is not provided by an existing market. It will be provided by a market which will exist in the future, but that is a bit too late to help in decisions made today. Hence, the optimizer must replace the market commitment to buy or sell at given terms by expectations: expectations of prices and expectations of quantities to be bought or sold. But he cannot know the future. Hence, unless he deludes himself, he must know that both sets of expectations may be wrong. In short, the absence of the market implies that the optimizer faces a world of uncertainty.

The exact modeling of behavior under uncertainty is probably not crucial to the subsequent discussion; let us use the conventional expected-utility hypothesis. When there is uncertainty, risk aversion implies that steps will be taken to reduce risks. This partly affects decisions within the firm, such as the holding of inventories and preference for flexible capital equipment, and partly leads to new markets which will shift risks to those most able and willing to bear them, particularly through the equity market. The rich development of inventory theory and portfolio theory in the last few decades reflects growing understanding of these matters.

But when we speak of expected utilities, we need to have some probabilities. Where do these come from? We may in the first instance regard them as subjective. But the economic agent observes his world and has the opportunity to learn from his experience, for there is a considerable degree of continuity. By Bayes's theorem or perhaps psychological learning theory, the probabilities, say of future prices, will gradually adjust so as to conform to the facts. If indeed the economic world exhibited the same structure in some sense from period to period, and if everybody observed everything relevant, then the probabilities ascribed by different individuals to the same events might be expected gradually to converge to the correct values and therefore be the same for all. In fact, of course, the basic economic facts are changing, partly endogenously because of capital accumulation in its most general sense, partly exogenously with predictable and unpredictable changes in technology and tastes; equally if not more important, though, is the fact that the dispersion of information which is so economical implies that different economic agents do not have access to the same observations. Hence, it is reasonable to infer that they will never come into agreement as to probabilities of future prices.

A further implication is that the past influences the future. Jevons' well-known slogan, "bygones are forever bygones," ceases to be fully accurate. The past is relevant because it contains information which changes the image of the future; the probabilities which govern future actions are modified by observations on the past. It follows that present decisions with implications for the future are functions of past values of variables as well as present values.

This point of view has been exploited in the econometric models which have used distributed lags in explaining investment decisions. What still needs to be exploited more, however, is that the inference to the future is necessarily uncertain, and the decisions made still exhibit risk aversion.

Expectations for the future are related to quantities as well as prices. The importance of quantity expectations has been stressed in macroeconomic models, even in such pre-Keynesian concepts as the acceleration principle, and most especially in relation to inventories. It sometimes is held that in a neoclassical world only prices matter; in the absence of prices, presumably they are replaced by price expectations. But this is not strictly true. Under constant returns, at least, quantity information for the individual firm is needed even when neoclassical assumptions are strictly fulfilled. Neoclassically founded investment theories usually predict capital-output ratios or capital-labor ratios; they still need output forecasts explicitly or implicitly. This gives considerable, perhaps major weight to past quantity information in predicting the future and therefore in guiding current investment decisions. It is perhaps along these lines that Keynesian theory, with its overwhelming emphasis on quantity changes as equilibrating variables, can be founded firmly on individual optimizing behavior.

I have referred to the fact that information is dispersed throughout the economy but have not suggested how. In the pure neoclassical model, each agent knows only his own production possibilities and his tastes, together with market information on the rest of the economy. In the world I have just sketched, however, any variables which improve his ability to predict the future have a very meaningful economic value to him. He will seek to acquire additional information. Such information is presumably costly; that is the basis for such great emphasis on the value of informational economy. But there is clearly a great incentive to acquire information of predictive value, and, as neoclassical theory would predict, there will be an incentive to produce such information. We have then an economic information industry: data assembly and analysis, business journalism, economic forecasting, with a longer-run perspective business education. Since information as a commodity does not satisfy all the neoclassical norms, it is not surprising that the government plays a large role in this process. Information-acquisition activities and information markets now appear on the economic landscape. Efficiency in the operation of firms ceases to be purely productive efficiency; it involves efficiency in prediction as well.

I would conjecture that the incomplete diffusion of information along the lines just sketched has a good deal to do with the operations of the securities markets and the decisions on corporate financing. The predominant role of internal financing and indeed the whole special importance of the managerial factor in corporate decision making are clearly connected with differential access to information about the firm.

I promised earlier to consider not only the implications of but also the causes for the absence of markets for future goods. One might wonder why one should explain the absence of a phenomenon. Sherlock Holmes once maintained to the dimwitted local police inspector so typical of English detective stories that the significant question in the case at hand was the dog's barking at night. "But," said the inspector, "the dog didn't bark." "That," said Holmes, "is what is significant." So too is the absence of these markets significant for a full neoclassical theory. A truncated theory of temporary equilibrium in which markets for future goods are replaced by some form of expectations, themselves functions of current prices and quantities, has indeed been developed, though its empirical content is necessarily meager if the formation of expectations is left unanalyzed. But the true neoclassical spirit is being denied in such a model. Although we are not usually explicit about it, we really postulate that when a market could be created, it will be. I sometimes think that welfare economics ought to be considered an empirical discipline. Implicitly, if an opportunity for a Pareto improvement exists, then there will be an effort to achieve it through some social device or another. In our theories and to a considerable extent in practice, the cheapest way in many cases is the creation of a market; and markets do emerge. If a market is impractical for one or another of the reasons we usually call "market failure," then very likely some other social device will at least be tried: government intervention, codes of professional ethics, or economic organizations with some power intermediate between the competitive firm and the government.

Thus, the failure of markets for future goods must be regarded as an analytic problem as well as a presupposition. It seems to me there are two basic causal factors. One is that contracts are not enforceable without cost, and forward contracts are more costly to enforce than contemporaneous contracts; the other is that because of the many uncertainties about the future, neither buyers nor sellers are willing to make commitments which completely define their future actions. Let me take up these two points in turn.

The ability to make enforceable contracts is a necessary but not sufficient condition for a market. However, there is no way to ensure complete enforceability. An individual may make a contract which he cannot in fact fulfill. Penalties may indeed be imposed on failure to live up to one's agreement, but they are not a substitute for compliance from the viewpoint of the other party, and there is always a degree of cost in enforcing the penalties. The laws of bankruptcy are a social recognition that complete enforceability is impossible, and that it is even socially desirable to set limits on the penalties for failure. However, when the exchange of values for values is simultaneous or nearly so, the contracts may almost be self-enforcing. If a good has been sold and not paid for, it can be recovered; if there is a continuing relation of buyer and seller, a failure to settle bills can be met by refusal to make further deliveries, in which case the loss is minimized. With contracts extending into the distant future, on the contrary, the possibility of failure to comply becomes greater, partly because the self-enforcement aspects become weaker, partly because unexpected changes may intervene to make even a sincerely intended compliance difficult or impossible.

The outstanding examples of forward contracts are credit instruments. The buyer, who is taking the risks of default, is motivated to protect himself by seeking more information about the seller. The lender wants to know the borrower's assets, the prospects for changes in them, possibly even what he is going to do with the money. This very individualized information-seeking relation is quite far from the arm's-length impersonal model of a market. The so-called capital markets are in many structural aspects very different from our model markets. It is, of course, an empirical question how far their behavior departs from the model. But the recurrent theme of credit ration-ing and availability doctrines, the essential imperfections of the credit market which underlie monetarist theories of cyclical fluctuations, suggest that the incomplete enforceability of credit contracts and the protective steps taken by lenders are significant factors in explaining the working of the market.

Although the enforceability question explains why those forward contracts that are made do not constitute a perfect market, we need more to understand why even these are so limited in their coverage of future goods transactions. There are forward contracts in money, some commodities, and real estate, but very little else. The explanation lies in uncertainties of both buyers and sellers about prices and quantities and about technology and tastes. Using uncertainties about prices and quantities as an explanation for market failure is a circular argument, though not necessarily a fallacy. That is, if all markets for future goods existed and cleared all transactions, then there would be no price-quantity uncertainties. But this much is true; if some markets for future goods do not exist, then the agents have uncertainties which are relevant to their behavior on markets for complementary or substitute goods. As Hicks showed a long time ago, complementarity and substitution can occur over time as well as simultaneously. If, as I will argue, uncertainty can tend to destroy markets, then we can conclude that the absence of some markets for future goods may cause others to fail.

To illustrate, the demand for capital goods at any point of time is dependent on the prices and sales of the product at future points of time. Therefore the demand for future capital goods will depend on expectations about the product at some still more removed time. If we assume only that we will not have markets for products at some distant point of time, then the resulting uncertainty will reflect itself in a failure of the market for capital goods in the nearer future, which will in turn create still further uncertainties.

Thus, if some markets for future goods are nonexistent, there will be uncertainties on the other markets; in addition, demand and supply conditions for the future are uncertain because of technological and taste shifts. Assume that both buyers and sellers are risk averters. Then, without going into details, it is reasonable to conclude that both demand and supply will have a downward bias as compared with the situation in which uncertainty is absent. A buyer will be unwilling to contract for purchase of a good if a superior or cheaper substitute may be available; and the seller will be unwilling to accept a price sufficiently low to be suitable to the buyer, particularly if he thereby foregoes a possible opportunity to shift his resources to other closely related goods. It would seem possible, at least, that there will be no price at which transactions in future goods will take place. From a theoretical viewpoint, one might say that the market is in a strange sort of equilibrium; there is some shadowy sort of price at which supply and demand are equated at zero. But this price is not performing much of a signaling function.

There is one ultraneoclassical approach to the market treatment of uncertainties, in which I take some pride. That is the notion of a contingent market. Instead of letting uncertainty ruin existing markets, we can take it explicitly into account by buying and selling commitments to be carried out only if some uncertain event occurs. We could in principle imagine agreements to transact which will hold if and only if a given conceivable technological innovation does not take place, with a second market for transactions valid if the innovation does take place. Then we can restore the possibility of markets.

Such contingent markets are not entirely unknown; insurance contracts are the purest example, and equity markets and cost-plus contracts provide more muddied illustrations. But they are relatively rare. Why this should be so follows again from the general problem of information costs and dispersal. If contracts are contingent on the occurrence of some event, then it must be verified whether or not the event occurred. But this is information, and as the example of a technological innovation suggests, it is information likely to be much more easily available to one party than to the other. Hence, the range of possible contingent contracts becomes limited to those for whom the events are easily verifiable for both parties. The implications of these limits are known in the insurance literature as adverse selection and moral hazard, and they are of immediate practical significance in such matters as health insurance. But more broadly, they so limit the scope of contingent markets in practice that, as argued before in connection with markets for future goods, they prevent the emergence of even technically possible markets because of the large unresolved uncertainties.

I hope enough has been said to indicate the widespread implications of costly, dispersed information for the process by which future-oriented economic decisions are made. Let me remark briefly that informational costs and values play a key role in modifying the structure even of contemporaneous transactions. The individual optimizing agent is supposed to know at least his technology or tastes and the prices he faces. I have already argued that there is a good deal of uncertainty with respect to the future economic implications of present economic choices. But in addition there is the possibility that technological information, which would be useful to the agent, exists somewhere in the world but outside his firm. There are grounds for engaging in the active pursuit of information. We begin to enter the realm of diffusion of innovations, to which some sociologists as well as economists have contributed. The interesting points here are the biases in the information channels, some of which, at least, can be explained in terms of differential costs of acquiring information. For example, the well-documented role of personal influence in accepting innovations can be interpreted as being due to a perceived high reliability of such information; in economic terms, this means more information per unit of expenditure of time or money.

The terms of trade with the outside world should not be regarded as freely given to the firm. In a world with a large number of commodities, even knowing the prices of relevant commodities involves the costly acquisition of certain kinds of information. This remark has given rise to a large literature on search in recent years. One implication which has been only slightly explored is that the concept of the market begins to weaken, and Jevons' Law of Indifference becomes more of an equilibrium condition than a statement valid about a market even in disequilibrium. At a moment of time, prices of what would usually be thought of as the same commodity bought or sold by different firms can differ because buyers or sellers may not, in their ignorance and in the presence of costs of search, find it worthwhile to shop further. Obviously, the important application of this principle may be to the labor market. There are clearly important informational differences between the employees currently working for a firm and potential substitutes elsewhere, although these are interchangeable in pure neoclassical theory. Indeed, there are differences both in the information the firm possesses about its employees as compared with alternatives and the information which employees have about the economic opportunities and the specific production conditions of the firm as compared with outsiders. It appears that considerations of this type must play some role in understanding the continued possibility of unemployment and particularly the sluggish response of wages to market disequilibria.

I am far from exhausting the implications of an information-economical viewpoint for the economic world. I look forward to exciting developments in the future.

13   On the Agenda of Organizations

In classical maximizing theory, it is implicit that the values of all relevant variables are at all moments under consideration. All variables are therefore *agenda* of the organization, that is, their values have always to be chosen. On the other hand, it is a commonplace of everyday observation and of studies of organization that the difficulty of arranging that a potential decision variable be recognized as such may be much greater than that of choosing a value for it. What the federal government regards as appropriate agenda has changed rapidly; nor can it be maintained that the new agenda necessarily correspond to changes in demand or supply, that is, the emergence of new problems in the world or of new techniques for their solution. Unemployment insurance is an old idea, and the need for it did not emerge only in the Great Depression; but it suddenly changed from a nonagendum to an agendum. (I shall occasionally make use of this singular form, though the dictionaries label it obsolete.) Similar examples can be cited for all sorts of organizations; innovation by firms is in many cases simply a question of putting an item on its agenda before other firms do. We can also see some items now in the process of becoming agenda. In the case of the federal government, the possibility of flexible exchange rates is at least on the horizon.

Reprinted from *The Corporate Society,* ed. R. Marris (New York: Wiley, 1974), pp. 214–234. This highly speculative essay is an amalgam of ideas that I learned from or read into the writings and personal conversations of many scholars, among whom I may mention especially Leonid Hurwicz, Carl Kaysen, Burton Klein, Janos Kornai, Jacob Marschak, Thomas Marschak, Roy Radner, Thomas Schelling, and Herbert Simon.

On the other hand, there is clearly a real value to putting an item on the agenda. The Employment Act of 1946 amounted to nothing more than a statement that full employment was at last a federal agendum, and many felt that this was a hollow victory indeed. But those who opposed it so violently were not deceived; in the long run, this recognition was decisive, though the process of implementing the responsibility was slow indeed. Once an item has arrived on the agenda, it is difficult not to treat it in a somewhat rational manner, if this is at all possible, and almost any considered solution may be better than neglect. I hasten to add that this generalization has its exceptions; there are problems for which there are no satisfactory solutions, but placing such an item on the agenda may create a demand for a solution, which will of necessity be unsatisfactory. Thus there is some justification for the principle of "salutory neglect," but on the whole this exception is not likely to be real. An unsatisfactory solution may be what is needed to provoke the needed information gathering to produce a better one, whereas neglect is never productive.

I want to sketch here some thoughts on the factors determining agenda. This problem already exists for the individual, and some time will first be devoted to him. But it will be suggested that the nature and purpose of organizations create additional implications for the determination of agenda and, in particular, for sluggishness in the introduction of new items.

What will be presented is not, strictly speaking, a theory or model but the kinds of considerations that will or should enter into the formulation of such a model. There does not seem to be great difficulty in formalizing the concepts to be presented, though handling them analytically to produce strong implications may be very difficult indeed. But at this stage it seemed more appropriate to raise these questions in a broad way, to avoid concentration on analytic problems. The point of view is that of an optimizing model but in a rich framework of uncertainty and information channels. Decisions, wherever taken, are a function of information received; then when information remains unchanged, no decision is made, or, to put the matter in a slightly more precise way, the implicit decision is made not to change the values of certain variables. In turn, the acquisition of information must be analyzed, since it is itself the result of decisions to collect information.

Of course, it is essential to this argument that information is scarce or costly; it can be assumed that any free information is acquired. As will be argued, the fact that for any given individual or organization different sorts of information have different costs has many implications for organizational behavior.

The theme to be presented is that the combination of uncertainty, indivisibility, and capital intensity associated with information channels and their use implies (1) that the actual structure and behavior of an organization may depend heavily on random events, in other words on history, and (2) that the very pursuit of efficiency may lead to rigidity and unresponsiveness to further change.

The Economics of Information

Each individual is assumed to start with the ability to receive some signals from the (natural and social) environment. This capacity is not, however, unlimited, and the scarcity of information is an essential feature for the understanding of organizational and individual behavior. The individual also starts off with a prior probability distribution over the space of all possible signals that he or anyone else might conceivably receive now and in the future. These signals are to be interpreted broadly; some might inform the individual of the outcome of his decisions, some might be used as the basis of decisions, if only of implicit decisions not to act. A signal is then any event capable of altering the individual's probability distribution; in more technical language, the posterior distribution of signals conditional on the observation of one may, in general, differ from the prior. This transformation of probabilities is precisely what constitutes the acquisition of information.[1]

This definition of information is qualitative, and so it will remain for the purposes of this chapter. The quantitative definition which appears in information theory is probably of only limited value for economic analysis, for reasons pointed out by Marschak; different bits of information, equal from the viewpoint of information theory, will usually have very different benefits or costs. Thus, let A and B be any two statements about the world, for neither of which its truth or falsity is known a priori. Then a signal that A is true conveys exactly as much information, in the sense of Shannon, as a statement that B is true. But the value of knowing whether or not A is true may be vastly greater than the value of knowing B's truth-value; or it may be that the resources needed to ascertain the truth-value of A are much greater than those for B. In either case, the information-theoretic equivalence of the two possible signals conceals their vast economic difference.

Some economic characteristics of information will be important for the present analysis. First and most important, the individual himself is an

---

1. See Marschak (1959); Radner (1968).

input, indeed the chief input if quantification is at all meaningful here, into any of his information channels. Immediately or ultimately, the information must enter his brain through his sensory organs, both of which are limited in capacity. Information may be accumulated in files, but it must be retrieved to be of use in his decision making. The psychological literature has many studies of the limits on the sensory perception abilities of human beings and some (for example, Miller, 1956) on their limits as information processors. I do not want to argue for fixed coefficients in information handling any more than in more conventional production activities; substitution of other factors, especially computers, for the individual's mind is possible. But the individual's very limited capacity for acquiring and using information is a fixed factor in information processing, and one may expect a sort of diminishing returns to increases in other information resources. Organization theorists have long recognized limits of this kind under the heading of "span of control."

A second key characteristic of information costs is that they are in part capital costs; more specifically, they typically represent an irreversible investment. I am not placing much weight on the physical aspects of communication, telephone lines and the like, though they are in fact a nonnegligible cost and they do provide a concrete, understandable paradigm. Rather I am thinking of the need for having made an adequate investment of time and effort to be able to distinguish one signal from another. Learning a foreign language is an obvious example of what I have in mind. The subsequent ability to receive signals in French requires this initial investment. There are in practice many other examples of codes that have to be learned in order to receive messages; the technical vocabulary of any science is a case in point. The issue here is that others have found it economical to use a large number of possible coding methods, and for any individual it is necessary to make an initial investment to acquire it.

However, even when the codes are not deliberately contrived, there is a need for an initial attempt at understanding. The empirical scientist in any area has to make preliminary observations (or learn them from others, which also involves an investment) in order to read nature's signals. Similarly, as E. H. Gombrich has emphasized, our understanding of a particular school of art, and indeed the understanding by artists themselves, depends on a degree of familiarity with it. Thus, there tends to be a cycle in which an innovation in artistic vision is first diffused; then, as it becomes more familiar, the value of repetition of similar signals decreases, and the ability to understand new signals, that is, departures from the new tradition, increases.

One might attempt to formalize the capital aspect of information in this way. A signal hitherto unheard is useless by itself; it does not modify any probability distribution. However, a preliminary sampling experiment in which the relation between the new signal and more familiar ones can be determined or at least estimated will serve to make valuable further signals of the new type. This experiment, which may be vicarious (education, scientific literature) is an act of investment.

Such investment, being locked up in an individual's mind, is necessarily irreversible. It can of course be transmitted to others, but it remains in the possession of the individual and cannot be alienated by him, although, like most irreversible investments, it is subject to depreciation.

In the last few decades, there has developed some literature on irreversible investment. Obviously irreversibility is of no consequence when the future is one of steadily growing demand for the capital good; but it becomes of importance when there are fluctuations, particularly stochastic fluctuations. Now by its very nature the value of an information channel is uncertain, and therefore we have an economic problem which resembles the demand for inventories under conditions of uncertainty. We may venture on some possible generalizations. One is that the demand for investment in information is less than it would be if the value of the information were more certain. The second, more important I would guess, is that the random accidents of history will play a bigger role in the final equilibrium. Once the investment has been made and an information channel acquired, it will be cheaper to keep on using it than to invest in new channels, especially since the scarcity of the individual as an input, already alluded to, implies that the use of new channels will diminish the product of old ones. Thus, it will be difficult to reverse an initial commitment in the direction in which information is gathered. Even if the expected value of the difference between two possible channels were relatively small, and even if subsequent information suggested that the initial choice was wrong, it would not pay to reverse the decision later on.

A third basic characteristic of information costs is that they are by no means uniform in different directions. At any given moment, an individual is a bundle of abilities and accumulated information. He may easily find it cheaper to open certain information channels rather than others in ways connected with these abilities and this knowledge. Thus, an explorer in hitherto unknown territory will find it easier to explore new areas near to those he has already covered. Geographic propinquity is but a special case. It is cheaper to proceed to the chemical analysis of compounds similar to those already studied. Learning generalizes naturally and cheaply in some directions, but with much greater difficulty in others. A rat shocked at one point will generalize by staying some distance away; the avoidance effect falls off with distance.

It is also easier to communicate with other individuals with whom one has a common approach or a common language, literally or metaphorically. The capital accumulation of learning, a code referred to earlier, may have to be engaged in at both ends of the channel. In the usual economic analysis, collusive agreements in an industry are not stable because there always exist alternative allocative deals involving some producers and some consumers which are preferable from the viewpoint of the participants. But if, as Adam Smith once suggested, members of the same trade find it easy to communicate with each other, presumably because of their common experiences, it may well be that the exchange of information leading to a collusive agreement among producers of one commodity is much cheaper than that needed to achieve a blocking coalition. Hence, the collusive agreement may in fact be stable. (The concept of class interest and identification may be related to ease of communication among individuals with similar life experiences.)

The relative costs of communication channels may also be influenced by activities of the individual other than the collection of information. There is a complementarity between a productive activity and some kinds of information. An individual cannot help making observations while working at some task. These observations are signals which in some circumstances change his knowledge about this productive activity, so-called learning by doing. In other circumstances, they may yield information relevant in other, seemingly remote, areas of decision making, a phenomenon known as serendipity. We are all familiar with the accomplishments of explorers who were seeking the Northwest Passage.

To sum up, the costs of information, in the general sense of utilization of scarce resources, (1) are in some sense increasing for the individual because he is himself a scarce input, (2) involve a large irreversible capital element, and (3) vary in different directions.

There is little systematic to say about the benefits from information. The main remark that can be made now is the familiar one that there are increasing returns in the *uses* of information. The same body of technological information, for example, can be used in production on any scale. This fact serves as an incentive toward increases in scale and therefore toward productive enterprises with some degree of monopoly power, in accordance with familiar principles.

The Agenda of Individuals

Decisions are necessarily a function of information. Hence, if it is decided to collect no information relevant to a certain class of decisions, those decisions are nonagenda.

The last sentence, by its uses of the words "decided" and "decision," highlights the need for a distinction between two kinds of decisions, decisions to act in some concrete sense and decisions to collect information. This distinction is very familiar in statistical decision theory; these two types are referred to as "terminal acts" and "experiments," respectively, by Raiffa and Schlaifer (1961). The distinction cannot be made with absolute clarity in general. Both are relevant to resource utilization, since experiments are here deemed costly. If we suppose a model in which utilities are expressible as the sum of two functions, one of which depends on the terminal act and the state of the world and the other of which depends on the experiment and the state of the world, and if only the signals derived from the latter experiment modify the probability distribution while only the terminal act can yield positive benefits (the experiment can lead directly only to costs even though indirectly it will be beneficial), then a clear distinction can indeed be made. In view of the emphasis in the last section on the interrelations between costs of acquiring information and other productive activities, I would not myself want to insist on this model. But it is suggestive.

Imagine in addition that the space of possible terminal acts can be factored into several subspaces, that the space of possible experiments can be factored in some parallel way, and that there is some sense, which I shall not formalize here, in which the valuation of terminal acts in any given subspace is influenced primarily by the outcome of experiments in the corresponding subspace. Then one can imagine conceptually a trichotomy of these decision areas (a decision area being one subspace of the space of terminal acts with the corresponding subspace of the space of experiments). A decision area may be *active, monitored,* or *passive.* An active area is one in which experiments are performed, signals received from them, and terminal acts chosen as a function of the signals. A monitored area is one in which some experiments are being performed; the signals received convey too little information to take terminal acts, but if appropriate signals are received, it is optimal to make further experiments, which in turn yield enough information to bring the terminal acts onto the agenda. Finally, a passive area is one in which no experiments are being conducted, and therefore neither experiments nor terminal acts are on the agenda.

The partition of decision areas among these types will depend of course on the relative benefits and costs. As noted, there is little that can be said about anticipated benefits, but the classification of costs in the previous section may have some explanatory power. As an illustration, consider an individual investor choosing a portfolio of securities. There will be one class of securities in which the individual is actively investing; he has positive investments in them or else they are being watched closely, with the decision to invest or not to invest being thought about steadily. The investor will be watching the market prices, receiving reports on the activities of the firms, and so forth. There will be a second class of securities which he is watching, so to speak, out of the corner of his eye. He occasionally checks prices and looks at relatively cursory information. If interesting movements or other information appear, he may increase the intensity of his surveillance and move the security into the active group. Finally, he will pay no attention whatever to the largest number of securities.

The previous analysis suggests some systematic reasons for classifying securities into one group or another. Familiarity with a particular firm or industry, because of previous experiences or current productive relations, will mean that information about some securities will be cheaper than about others; the investor has a background which enables him to understand the signals better. The fact that information has a strong capital component means that once an investor has chosen a selected list of securities, he will stay within the group, because additional information about the same securities is cheaper than acquiring the initial information about other securities needed to begin meaningful analysis.

The investor is likely to monitor securities for which some information is cheap because its acquisition is complementary to other activities. Thus, as a background for analysis of the securities he is primarily interested in, he may pick up some information about others from the point of view of the latter group; this process amounts to inexpensive monitoring. Professional information services, brokers and the like, may supply him with broadly spread, if shallow, information; at the same time they supply detailed information. General news sources about business conditions may be read simply because of their intrinsic interest and hence at virtually no cost; but these may constitute a certain amount of monitoring. Finally, social associations with business connections may constitute a source of information, perhaps a stronger one because much evidence shows that personal influences are regarded as more reliable, which means there will be more information, subjectively measured, at a given cost.

How, then, do we expect the agenda of an individual to change — that is, how do decision areas get changed from one class to another? The monitoring process is a built-in explanation of part of the process. There are a lot of potential decision areas which are in fact being looked at a little bit. A classic illustration of monitoring is the process of quality control in industry. The quality of the product is tested on a sampling basis. As long as the results are satisfactory, nothing is done; but when deterioration occurs, there is a more thorough investigation of its causes, with the possible eventuality that a machine is repaired or replaced. But clearly there is more to the matter than agenda changes as the result of foreseen possibilities. One possibility is a sharp change in payoffs to terminal acts. In particular, this is most likely to be a change in the opportunity benefit, that is, a decrease in the return to the present, unexamined, action. In plain language, we have a "crisis." In William James's term, a "coercive fact" may be more persuasive than any speculation about potential benefits from change. The sinking of the *Titanic* led to iceberg patrols.

No doubt the changes in payoffs may be changes in perceptions rather than in actuality. The current ecological concerns have grown much more rapidly than the actual problems (which is not to say that they are not important; they are). What sometimes happens is that the cost of signals goes down, for one of many reasons. There may simply be a threshold effect; beyond a certain point, the effects of, say, pollution or the low performance of your portfolio become obvious with virtually no investment in observation or experiment. In some cases it may be that some other individuals, for their own reasons, are supplying signals cheaply. These are the reformers and agitators of all sorts; no doubt their work only flourishes when the value and cost structures are appropriate, but the torch, though ready, still has to be lit by someone.

Another cause of agenda changes is that information channels do not, despite the model that has been tentatively used, stand in a simple relation to the different subspaces into which the space of terminal acts has been factored. Signals with quite different policy implications may be closely interrelated in origin and be received over the same channel; or it may be that an experiment conceived for one purpose can yield additional information relevant to very different terminal acts with only slightly additional cost. An interesting paradigm is that of opportunistic replacement (see Jorgenson, McCall, and Radner, 1967); when a complex mechanism, such as a missile, is being examined to check for possible malfunctioning of one subunit, it becomes much cheaper to examine or replace others.

The Agenda of Organizations

I am not going to attempt a formal definition of organization, which would probably be impossible. Rather, the concept is really a primitive term in a system, its significance being revealed by assumptions and their consequences. However, the term should be understood quite broadly. Formal organizations — firms, labor unions, universities, governments — are not the only kind. The market system is to be interpreted as an organization with indeed elaborate methods for communication and joint decision making. As this example makes clear, the participants in organizations may be organizations themselves as well as individuals. Further, it is important to note that individuals typically belong to many organizations.

The purpose of organizations is to exploit the fact that many (virtually all) decisions require the participation of many individuals for their effectiveness. In the discussion of the internal economics of the firm, this point is of course customary with regard to what has been called here terminal acts. But it is equally and even more valid with regard to experiments, that is, information channels.

An organization can acquire more information than any one individual, for it can have each member performing different experiments. Thus, the limitations on an individual's capacity are overcome. But as always, there is a price to be paid. In fact, the relevant considerations have been adduced in some of the old discussions of the U-shaped cost curve. The information has to be coordinated if it is to be of any use to the organization. More formally stated, communication channels have to be created within the organization.

Now if all information received by any member of the organization were transmitted to all others or even to one headquarters, there would be no gain in information-processing costs. Indeed, there would be a loss, since there are additional information channels within the firm. The economies of information in the organization occur because in fact much information received is irrelevant. The terminal acts within the competence of the organization do not require for assessment the entire probability distribution of states of the world but only some marginal distributions derived from it. Hence, in general, the information received by a member of the organization can be transformed into a much smaller volume for retransmission without losing value for choice of terminal acts. The theory of sufficient statistics is an example of this reduction of information without loss of value. In this case, the reason is that the value of any terminal act depends only on the parameters of the underlying distribution and not on the values observed in the sample; hence it suffices to transmit the values of a function of the sample which exhausts its information about the parameters.

It is this reduction in retransmission which explains the utility of an organization for information handling. Since information is costly, it is clearly optimal, in general, to reduce the internal transmission still further. That is, it pays to have some loss in value for the choice of terminal act in order to economize on internal communication channels. The optimal choice of internal communication structures is a vastly difficult question. It underlies, not always explicitly, the great controversies on the economies of socialism and has received deep exploration in certain directions in the Marschak-Radner theory of teams.

Since it is, in general, optimal not to transmit all the relevant information, an individual member will have accumulated information which is not under present circumstances judged worthwhile to transmit. It is possible that at a later time this information will turn out to be of value, due to receipt of some other signal which is complementary to it. Whether this information will then be used depends on a number of factors; among them are the cheapness of transmission over time, by means of memory or files and subsequent retrieval. This creates the possibility that different members of the organization, who have had different experiences which have not been transmitted, will interpret new signals in different ways. There seem to be interesting implications for a reduction of informational efficiency in organizations whose external environment has changed considerably.

Since internal communication channels can be designed, their structure can be chosen with a view to cost minimization. In particular, the efficiency of a channel can be increased by suitable choice of a code. This term is used both literally and metaphorically; it refers to all the known ways, whether or not inscribed in formal rules, for conveying information. As is well known from information theory, the optimal code will depend on the a priori distribution of possible signals, as well as on the costs of communicating differently coded signals.

The role of coding has two economic implications: (1) it weakens but does not eliminate the tendency to increasing costs with scale of operations; (2) it creates an intrinsic irreversible capital commitment of the organization. With regard to the first point, we have seen that the organization's gains from increasing scale are derived by having its members make different experiments, that is, by specialization. As we have seen in discussing the economics of information for the individual, this means that the members will be accumulating differing types of skills in information processing, learning (acquiring capital) in the areas in which they are specializing and unlearning elsewhere. As a result, communication among them becomes more difficult (as academic specialists are learning), and the codes used in their intercommunications have to become more complex. Hence, although coding permits a greater number of individual information sources to be pooled usefully, there are still increasing costs eventually as the scale of operations grows.

With regard to the second point, I have already argued that the learning of a code by an individual is an act of irreversible investment for him. It is therefore also an irreversible capital accumulation for the organization. It follows that organizations, once created, have distinct identities, because the costs of changing the code are those of unanticipated obsolescence.

Becker and others have stressed that a significant part of the accumulation of human capital consists of training specific to the needs of a firm, an input of information to the worker which increases his value to the firm but not to other firms. If the function of labor is to cooperate in production with capital goods which are held widely by different firms, it would appear that virtually all training is general. But learning the information channels within a firm and the codes for transmitting information through them is indeed a skill of value only internally.

One might ask, as one does frequently in the theory of the firm, why all firms do not have the same codes, so that training in the code is transferable? In the first place, in this combinatorial situation, there may easily be many optimal codes, all equally good, but to be useful in a firm it is important to know the right code. The situation here is very much that of the games of coordination which have been stressed so much by Schelling (1960). If it is valuable for two people to meet without being able to communicate with each other during their trips, the meeting-place must be agreed on beforehand. It may not matter much where the meeting is to be. But a person who learned one meeting-place is not much use to an organization which has selected another.

In the second place, history matters. The code is determined in accordance with the best expectations at the time of the firm's creation. Since the code is part of the firm's capital, or more generally the organization's capital, as already argued, the code of a given organization will be modified only slowly over time. Hence, the codes of organizations starting at different times will in general be different even if they are competitive firms. Indeed, individuals starting with firms at the same time may well have different a priori distributions and therefore different codes.

The need for codes that are mutually understandable within the organization imposes a uniformity requirement on the behavior of the participants. They are specialized in the information capable of being transmitted by the codes, so that, in a process already described, they learn more in the direction of their activity and become less efficient in acquiring and transmitting information not easily fitted into the code. Hence, the organization itself serves to mold the behavior of its members.

This process may well have interesting implications for the behavior of the organization. The code of the organization may be supposed to be governed most strongly by its primary functions. But an organization has in general many functions, auxiliary indeed to its primary ones but important to its welfare. Alternatively, it may be thought desirable to add some secondary functions to the organization because their accomplishment appears to be complementary to the primary ones. But if the code appropriate to the primary functions is inappropriate to the auxiliary or secondary functions, the organization may function badly. Burton Klein has provided one illustration: the primary function of the military is the coordination of large masses of men and material in circumstances where coordination is according to a previously planned timetable. Research and development on military weapons is, in the present era, an important auxiliary service. But, Klein has argued, it tends to be run by men who think in military terms and therefore expect coordination of achievements at predictable time points in the future. In fact, of course, research and development are prime examples of information gathering with a considerable degree of uncertainty, and achievements are certainly not predictable. As a result, the precisely laid out timetables and cost forecasts are dramatically unfulfilled, as Summers (1967) has shown. The costs in the end are much higher than they would have been if the uncertainty had been taken into account initially. His recommended solution, indeed, is to remove military research and development from military control and put it in the hands of a separate civilian agency.

An example of the difficulty of additional functions in an existing organization is provided by the tendency to add management control function to existing accounting and budgetary departments. Since the quantitative basis of scientific decision making overlaps so heavily with classical accounts, it is appealing to economize by joining the two functions. But in fact the purposes differ considerably, and therefore the code, the way of looking at the world, differs also. The accountant, whose aim is in part to insure against dishonesty, is interested in a degree of precision in certain data that is unnecessary for management science but is not interested in other and rougher kinds of data. Budgetary control is also different in many ways from scientific management, and some students of public administration are highly critical of the addition of management control to the functions of the former Bureau of the Budget.

Because of these difficulties of communication, there has been a tendency in both the public and private sectors to hive off incompatible functions into new organizations. Stigler (1951) has pointed suggestively to the steady vertical disintegration which has accompanied the growth of large firms; the forces of the market make it profitable for the specialization in auxiliary services. Similarly, in the federal government, Franklin D. Roosevelt seems to have been the innovator who first saw the need of assigning new tasks to new bureaus, even though according to some logic a new task belonged in the sphere of an existing department.

Let us return to the original purpose of this chapter, the determination of the agenda of organizations. Basically, the possible causes of changes in the agenda of organizations are the same as those of individuals: a signal may be received in a monitored area on the basis of which it is judged worthwhile to make the area active; the payoffs to terminal acts may change or may be perceived to change abruptly; or an information channel used primarily for one purpose may turn up a signal with implications for taking action in a hitherto passive area. The discussion just concluded has been directed toward developing the cost factors specific to organizations which influence agenda changes in these organizations. In many ways, indeed, the cost of change may be greater for an organization. More precisely, it has a greater ability to monitor but a lesser ability to change from a passive attitude to a monitoring or active role.

There is one effect on organizations which has no parallel in individuals. An organization is typically composed of changing individuals. Now any individual generally has access to many communication channels, of which this particular organization is only one. In particular, education is such a channel. Thus, the organization is getting the benefit of a considerable amount of information which is free to it. Even though the code of the organization may make the internal transmission of such information costly, if there is enough of it, the behavior of the organization will change. In particular, new items will appear on the organization's agenda. If we think of education as the primary source of new information, then it is introduced into an organization by its youngest and newest members. Thus we have the possibility of changes in organizational agenda induced by generational changes.

Possible Implications for Policy toward Externalities

Consideration of the communication and structural problem in productive organizations may suggest some modification of the economists' usual recipes for improving resource allocation in the presence of externalities. Indeed, the difficulties of changing agenda may explain why proposals which seem like the veriest common sense to the economist are incomprehensible to the citizen and the affected industrial interests. The strategy of the welfare economist is to charge or reward the firm for its externalities, its now unpriced effects on others. But taken literally, such a policy may impose an undue informational and organizational burden on the firm.

The firm has been organized to specialize in the production of some particular set of commodities, for example, automobiles. By the processes already described, its internal channels, its knowledge, its effective agenda are all specialized to this and associated ends (such as marketing and finance). The effects of the automobile on the quality of air, for example, or even on urban congestion belong to very different realms of intellectual discourse. Further, these are realms not parallel in structure to the production and sale of definite material objects with measurable performance properties and well-defined property rights.

Suppose a public policy is established that the costs of congestion and pollution are to be charged to the motorist. His ability to estimate these effects of his actions is, of course, likely to be very low. The manufacturers may try to step into the breach. They may offer alternative automobiles which are smaller or in other ways reduce congestion or which offer or claim to offer reduced emission of pollutants. But in fact their ability to know the consequences of their production decisions is not so high either. Their well-developed internal channels of communication are specialized in very different directions, and the costs of adapting to new requirements are high. These costs are real, and if incurred, will under competitive conditions be shifted to the buyers. More likely, the firms will adapt by moving along the least steep cost gradient, given their previous structure and their primary aims. The activity they currently engage in which is closest to meeting the problems of externalities is their advertising; they are most likely to regard the problems of minimizing pollution and congestion as problems in public relations. If information about the relationship between the nature of the product and the occurrences of negative externalities is sufficiently limited to both the manufacturers and the buyers of automobiles, then the solution of providing pseudo-information may be the cheapest—cheaper than the acquisition of new information.

Thus the simple welfare economics solution of directly taxing the unpriced consequences may have limited effectiveness; the usual analysis ignores the costs of change created by new informational needs. To some extent, the argument just given is more valid for the short run than for the long. Over time, new communication channels will be created anyway, and the cost of acquiring new information about externalities will be lower if more time is allowed to pass. But the difficulties of operating an organization concerned both with manufacture and with tenuous and complex external effects may not disappear even in the long run.

In fact, and perhaps because of considerations such as these, the control of externalities has not so far relied on the pricing of external effects directly. Instead, it has taken the form of direct regulations and standards. Emission standards are set; physicians and lawyers are licensed. From the viewpoint of the firm being regulated, the relevant information is reduced to a much more manageable form. It becomes just a question of adding a new dimension to the physical characteristics of the commodity. Quantitatively, the additional information needed by the firm has become very limited; qualitatively, the information and communication needs parallel those in which the organization is efficient.

Of course, there is a loss as well as a gain in specific standards: the flexibility of response theoretically inherent in the price system is sacrificed. There might be very different and better ways of balancing the external costs against the conventional ones, but these reactions are now barred. Certainly, the rigidity of control through building codes is not an encouraging precedent in other directions. No simple rules for choosing between the pricing of consequences and more specific forms of regulation and licensing are now available.

So far we have discussed the adequacy of signals to the producer of externalities. But this is only one part of the problem of policy toward externalities. For some organization, which we usually refer to as the "government," has to take the basic decision to tax or price or regulate, as the case may be. In the usual welfare-economics treatments both the benevolence and the competence of this government authority are taken for granted, a point of view which has been criticized by such defenders of laissez-faire as Demsetz (1969) and McKean and Minasian (1966). But the government or any government-like authority is also an organization with limited capacities for information acquisition and utilization. The difficulty of making a possible externality an agendum of the government is a matter of common observation. Even when the principle is established, the mechanism for new decision making under changing information or changing circumstances may be limited in its capability. The history of regulatory agencies has not, on the whole, been encouraging.

The problem is the design of public organizations to mimic the ideal of the market system. The forces of demand are separated from those of supply, and with very good reason, for they represent very different informational structures. In our general-equilibrium models, these forces have to be ultimately reconciled; at this stage of our analysis, we resort to uncomfortable metaphors of auctioneers adjusting prices to achieve an equality of supply and demand. A parallel pattern is to be found in the judicial system. Plaintiff and defendant have different interests and different information channels. The usual theory of the adversary system is that each party will be best motivated and able to present not a complete picture, but the information most helpful from its point of view. The judiciary then uses only the information made available to it by the parties to arrive at a verdict. Thus decisions are the resultant of three organizations, each informationally specialized.

I suggest that an analogue is appropriate for the handling of externalities. Once an externality is recognized, there is a need for two public organizations, as distinct from each other as a prosecuting attorney and a court. One is charged with an adversary role—to establish the social costs of the externality and suggest remedies, whether of the tax-price variety or regulation. Having a well-defined goal, it should be possible for this organization to structure its informational channels appropriately. There is no reason to give such an agency a monopoly in its role of expressing the cost side of the externality pseudo-market. Citizens' groups, private foundations, other government agencies, and the like should all be highly eligible to enter briefs for the existence, costs, and mode of regulation of an externality.

The final decisions will be made by a quasi-judicial agency. It will receive the cases as presented by the complainants, whether the officially designated agency or a volunteer organization, and by the firms affected by the order. Over a period of time, rules should emerge for the form in which evidence is accepted, in part a codification of present practices in benefit-cost analysis. Like the ideal market or the judiciary, there will be an appropriate specialization of informational function.

To be absolutely clear, I am *not* assenting to a common view, that externalities can be handled through the usual processes of the civil law. In such a procedure, each individual example of an externality is the object of a separate action. A procedure like this seems extremely uneconomic from the viewpoint of information. Essentially the same arguments have to be used again and again; either there is vast repetition, or instead it will not pay to collect the costly information for any one use, so in fact the cases will be incorrectly decided. Instead, I suggest that the judicial method be used for the establishment of rules to handle many individual cases, for example, to set a tax rate. The provision, of course, has to be made for periodic revaluations as circumstances change, just as prices change over time. But what is sought here is a recognition of the need for informational economy in the establishment of procedures for the assessment of external costs.

References

H. Demsetz, Information and efficiency: Another viewpoint, *Journal of Law and Economics,* 12 (1969) 1–22.

D. W. Jorgenson, J. J. McCall, and R. Radner, *Optional Replacement Policy* (Chicago: Rand-McNally, 1967).

J. Marschak, Remarks on the economics of information, in *Contributions to Scientific Research in Management* (Los Angeles: Western Data Processing Centre, University of California, 1959) pp. 79–98.

R. McKean and J. R. Minasian, On achieving Pareto optimality regardless of cost, *Western Economic Journal,* 51 (1966) 14–23.

G. A. Miller, The magical number seven, plus or minus two: Some limits on our capacity for processing information, *Psychological Review,* 63 (1956) 81–97.

R. Radner, Competitive equilibrium under uncertainty, *Econometrica,* 36 (1968) 31–58.

H. Raiffa and R. Schlaifer, *Applied Statistical Decision Theory* (Boston: Graduate School of Business Administration, Harvard University, 1961).

T. C. Schelling, *The Strategy of Conflict* (Cambridge, Mass.: Harvard University Press, 1960).

G. J. Stigler, The division of labour is limited by the extent of the market, *Journal of Political Economy,* 59 (1951) 185–193.

R. Summers, Cost estimates as predictors of actual costs: A statistical study of military development, chap. 4 in T. Marschak, T. K. Glennan, Jr., and R. Summers, *Strategy for R&D Studies in the Microeconomics of Development* (New York: Springer, 1967) pp. 140–189.

14 Vertical Integration and Communication

The possible motives for vertical integration are many.[1] In this chapter I want to emphasize the role of uncertainty in the supply of the upstream good and the need for information by the downstream firms. Though in fact it will be shown that imperfect competition is a necessary outcome, the initial conditions will be of the sort that we usually associate with perfect competition.

In the model there are two kinds of firms. The upstream firms have a product, to be referred to as "raw materials." The production conditions are marked by uncertainty; to make the point more dramatic, I shall assume that the output of each upstream firm is a random variable, unaffected by any possible decision on its part. It will be clear that generalization to make the output of an upstream firm a random function of inputs will not make much difference—indeed, no difference at all if the inputs have to be chosen before the random factors are known to the firm. The outputs of different upstream firms may be and in general will be correlated with each other.

Each downstream firm has a production function for its output, called the "final product," as a function of two inputs, raw materials and "capital." The latter is purchased on a competitive market whose price is a known

Reprinted from the *Bell Journal of Economics*, 6 (1975):173–183.

1. See, for example, O. E. Williamson, "The Vertical Integration of Production: Market Failure Considerations," *American Economic Review*, 61 (May 1971):112–123.

constant. There is no uncertainty in the production function for the final product. The production function has constant returns to scale, so that essentially there is free entry and therewith the basic prerequisites for competition.

Finally, we assume that raw materials are traded on a market which clears in each time period. Hence, the downstream firms have no uncertainty about raw material supply per se, but only about its price.

The competitive equilibrium for this system of markets in the absence of vertical integration is easily understood and will be developed in the next section. The question that has to be asked is the following: Is there any incentive for vertical integration which will upset that equilibrium? It is fairly obvious that in the absence of production lags, there would be no incentive. We therefore assume that capital has to be purchased one time unit before the acquisition of raw materials in the downstream production process. Even so, as will be seen, there is no incentive to vertical integration unless there is also an information lead; in the simplest case, the upstream producer knows his output one time unit before it appears on the market. Then indeed there is an incentive to integrate; but the incentive is *not* to insure in advance a quantity of raw materials, but rather to acquire information relevant to its market price.

In the second section the model and the competitive equilibrium conditions in the absence of vertical integration are set forth in detail. In the third section it is shown that there is an incentive for any one downstream firm to acquire one or more upstream firms. In the following section it is argued that a competitive equilibrium with vertical integration in which no firm has a large fraction of the raw material production is also impossible; given any such conceivable equilibrium, it will always pay one of the integrated firms to buy more upstream firms. In the fifth section it is argued that, in the absence of monopoly power to a fully integrated industry (that is, given a highly elastic demand for the final product), there will be an equilibrium which is, in a sense, competitive but in which there exists only one firm owning the entire upstream production and producing all the final product. Finally, in the last section some possible extensions of the model are discussed briefly: some inconclusive comments on the possibility of imperfectly competitive equilibria, an exploration of the possible substitution of a futures market for vertical integration, the possible inefficiency of vertical integration in the marketing of intermediate products, and the role of risk aversion.

Competitive Equilibrium without Vertical Integration

I will now give an explicit formulation of the model and discuss its equilibrium when both vertical and horizontal integration are forbidden. There are n upstream firms referred to, for convenience, as u-firms. The number n is finite but sufficiently large that each u-firm regards itself as engaged in perfect competition. The output of the ith u-firm is x_i, taken to be a random variable with a distribution known to all participants on the market. The variables $x_1, \ldots, x_n$ have a joint distribution and, in general, will not be independent; hence, any one u-firm has, by observing its output, some information on the outputs of other firms. We do assume that the successive drawings of the random vector of x_i's are independent over time. Finally, we assume that the value of x_i is known to the ith firm one time unit before it is ready for sale. The significance of this predictive ability will be seen later.

With regard to the downstream firms, referred to as d-firms, it is assumed that there are an indefinite number, a continuum if you will, each producing the final product under conditions of constant returns. Each firm has the same production function $F(x,y)$, concave and homogeneous of degree one, expressing output as a function of the use of the raw material, x, and of another input, y, which has been called "capital." It will be assumed that the capital input has to be chosen one time period before the raw material. Any lag of output behind the acquisition of raw material will have no significance to our problem, so we shall assume without loss of generality that there is no such lag.

We assume risk neutrality on the part of all firms; I wish to avoid the analysis of vertical integration as a portfolio problem. Capital is available to our industry in perfectly elastic supply; its price is constant over time, and we shall take it to be 1.

There are two markets endogenous to the model, those for raw materials and for the final product. They are cleared simultaneously, since there is no lag between raw material acquisition and final production in the downstream industry. The amount of raw material on the market is a random variable,

$$(14\text{-}1) \qquad x = \sum_{i=1}^{n} x_i.$$

Let p and q be the prices of the final product and raw material, respectively. At the time the markets open, the capital must have already been purchased.

Hence, y is given to these markets and is independent of the realized value of x. The demand for raw material is then governed by the marginal productivity relation,

(14-2) $pF_x(x,y) = q$.

The output of the final product is $F(x,y)$, and the demand function for the final product then determines p as a function of x, for given y. If, as we shall sometimes assume, the demand for the final product is perfectly elastic, p will be a constant. Given p, constant or a function of x for given y, we find q as a function of x, again for given y.

The capital is determined so as to maximize *expected* profits; the d-firm in a competitive market takes the functions $p(x)$ and $q(x)$ as given and is unaware of the influence of y on them. Remember that, because of the lag structure of production in the d-firms, y must be chosen before the prices of the raw material and of the final product are known. The d-firms are assumed to be aware of the dependence of p and q on the random total output of raw material:

(14-3) $E[p(x)F_y(x,y)] = 1$.

The equilibrium is defined by (14-2), (14-3), and the demand function for the final product; specifically, these relations determine the functions $p(x)$ and $q(x)$ and the value y. If, in particular, the demand for the final product is perfectly elastic, then p does not depend on x, y can be solved for from (14-3), and $q(x)$ immediately determined from (14-2).

The Incentive for Incipient Vertical Integration

Now assume that vertical but not horizontal integration is permitted. This amounts to opening a new market, that for u-firms. The previous equilibrium remains an equilibrium if, at the market price for u-firms, there is no demand by d-firms. Under risk neutrality, the market price for a u-firm would be simply the expected value of its profits, the price being reckoned on a flow or equivalent income basis rather than as a capital value. Let P_i be the price of the ith u-firm:

(14-4) $P_i = E[q(x)x_i]$.

At these prices and at the random prices $p(x)$ and $q(x)$, would it pay for a d-firm to purchase one or more u-firms? Suppose it did. What would its optimal policy and payoff be? Let y' be its purchase of capital and x' its use of the raw material. Once the market for raw materials is opened, the integrated firm could just as well sell all of the raw material output from its u-department and buy what it needs and wants for use in its d-department. The two activities are thus completely separable. From the viewpoint of any decision making in the d-department, the price of the raw material is effectively the market price, $q(x)$; the fact that the firm owns some of the raw material is irrelevant at that stage, since it can sell it in the market. Thus, in a sense, owning a u-firm is no protection against scarcity as reflected in high prices; the shadow cost to the integrated firm of the raw material is not affected by owning any. There might conceivably be a portfolio diversification benefit, but I am ruling that out by my assumption of risk neutrality.

Since P_i is the expected value of the raw material output of u-firm i, the expected value of the u-department is zero, and by the assumptions it is not affected by any decision. Let us then concentrate on the decision making in the d-department. This is significantly affected by the vertical integration in terms of information. The integrated firm knows the value of x_i; and by assumption it knows this value early enough to make use of it in deciding on the level of capital used. Thus vertical integration in this model is essentially a way of acquiring predictive information.

Let x' and y' then be the amounts of raw material and capital, respectively, used by our integrating firm in the production of the final product. Let x and y be the total amounts used in the industry; x is a random variable, given to all participants, and in seeking a competitive equilibrium we can regard y as given parametrically to all and in particular to our integrating firm. Once investments have been made, then, since we are testing whether the equilibrium without vertical integration remains an equilibrium, the raw material market clears in such a way that the ratios of the two inputs are the same throughout the industry:

(14-5) $$\frac{x'}{y'} = \frac{x}{y}.$$

The profits from the d-department are

(14-6) $$p(x)F(x',y') - q(x)x' - y' = y'G\left(\frac{x'}{y'}\right),$$

since F is homogeneous of degree one. From (14-5),

(14-7) $$G\left(\frac{x'}{y'}\right) = G\left(\frac{x}{y}\right).$$

Since the integrated firm knows x_i at the time y' is determined, its aim is to maximize the conditional expected profit given x_i,

$$(14\text{-}8) \qquad E_x\left[y'G\left(\frac{x'}{y'}\right)\Big|x_i\right] = y'E_x\left[G\left(\frac{x}{y}\right)\Big|x_i\right],$$

where the subscript x reminds one of the variable with respect to which the expectation is taken. Since y is taken as parametric by the integrated firm, the expression in (14-8) is simply proportional to y'; hence optimization requires a positive, indeed an indefinitely large, value of y' for those values of x_i for which

$$(14\text{-}9) \qquad H(x_i) = E_x\left[G\left(\frac{x}{y}\right)\Big|x_i\right] > 0,$$

and $y' = 0$ whenever the contrary holds. In the long run, the profits of the firm are given by the unconditional expectation of $y'G(x'|y')$, where y' is taken to be a function of x_i. Thus, in particular, let $y_0 > 0$ be some fixed value of y', and let $y' = y_0$ whenever (14-9) holds, and $= 0$ otherwise. By a well-known principle of probability theory, the unconditional expectation is the expected value of the conditional expectation. That is, if U and V are any two random variables, the conditional expectation $E_U(U|V)$ is a function of the random variable V and therefore a random variable itself; then its expectation is the unconditional expectation of U,

$$E_V[E_U(U|V)] = E(U).$$

Then

$$(14\text{-}10) \qquad E_x\left[y'G\left(\frac{x'}{y'}\right)\right] = E_{x_i}\left\{E_x\left[y'G\left(\frac{x'}{y'}\right)\Big|x_i\right]\right\}$$

$$= E_{x_i}\left\{y'E_x\left[G\left(\frac{x}{y}\right)\Big|x_i\right]\right\}$$

$$= y_0 E_{x_i}[H^+(x_i)],$$

where

$$H^+(x_i) = H(x_i)$$

when it is positive and $= 0$ otherwise.

Since $H^+(x_i) \geqq 0$ always, the expectation in (14-10) is nonnegative and is positive if and only if (14-9) holds with positive probability. But from constant returns and risk neutrality, we must have in equilibrium

$$(14\text{-}11) \quad 0 = E_x\left[yG\left(\frac{x}{y}\right)\right] = E_{x_i}\left\{E_x y\left[G\left(\frac{x}{y}\right)\Big|x_i\right]\right\} = yE_{x_i}[H(x_i)],$$

so that $H(x_i)$ is a random variable with mean 0. Clearly, under any reasonable set of assumptions, $G(x|y)$ will be correlated with the output of any one firm, and $H(x_i)$ will not be a degenerate random variable. Hence, it must be positive with some positive probability. But then we have shown that the integrating firm can make a positive profit, indeed an indefinitely large one. Positive profits are, however, incompatible with equilibrium, since they would be destroyed by entry of d-firms.

The information about total profits conveyed by knowing the output of one u-firm arises from an improved ability to predict total raw material output. This can arise in two ways: (1) the obvious one, that total output is the sum of the outputs of the individual u-firms, and therefore knowing the output of one firm conveys information about the total in the absence of negative correlations; (2) in general, we may suppose that there is a positive correlation among the raw material outputs of the different firms, arising perhaps from a common factor (for example, weather) which affects them all.

It follows that the competitive equilibrium in the absence of vertical integration can no longer continue to be an equilibrium in its presence. If vertical integration is permitted, then any equilibrium must in fact contain some. But it must be emphasized that the value of vertical integration is the information acquired about total raw material in production.

Competitive Equilibrium with Many Firms and Vertical Integration

Can there then be a competitive equilibrium in which in fact there are one or more integrated firms? Suppose there were. The first point is that, because of free entry of d-firms and a competitive market for u-firms, the expected profits of any integrated firm must be zero. Let the firm own a set, A, of u-firms. Then it chooses its capital, y', as a function of $x_i (i \in A)$, and its raw material input x' on the market for raw materials. In general, each firm has chosen its capital as a function of some set of x_i's, so that the aggregate amount of capital, y, is a function of $x_1, \ldots, x_n$. Given y, the demand for the raw material is its marginal productivity, while the supply is, as before, simply the random total. Thus, p and q are related,

$$pF_x(x,y) = q,$$

as in (14-2) above, and p and q are determined jointly by this equation and the demand for the final product. But since y is now a function of the x_i's, q will be a function $q(x_1, \ldots, x_n)$, not in general determined merely by the total x. As before Eq. (14-5) holds. The following modification of (14-6) holds for the profits of the d-department:

$$(14\text{-}12) \quad p(x_1, \ldots, x_n)F(x',y') - q(x_1, \ldots, x_n)x' - y' = y'G\left(\frac{x'}{y'}\right);$$

and from (14-5),

$$y'G\left(\frac{x'}{y'}\right) = y'G\left(\frac{x}{y}\right).$$

For simplicity of notation, let X_A be the vector $x_i (i \in A)$, and let X be the vector of all x_i's. The integrated firm wishes to maximize

$$(14\text{-}13) \quad y'E_X\left[G\left(\frac{x}{y}\right)\middle|X_A\right]$$

for given X_A. Clearly, then, equilibrium requires that

$$(14\text{-}14) \quad E_X\left[G\left(\frac{x}{y}\right)\middle|X_A\right] \leq 0 \quad \text{with probability 1.}$$

On the other hand, if the strict inequality held with probability 1, the integrated firm would not in fact be in business, which is hardly a relevant case:

$$(14\text{-}15) \quad E_X\left[G\left(\frac{x}{y}\right)\middle|X_A\right] = 0 \quad \text{on a set of positive probability.}$$

The market price of the ith u-firm must be at least expected sales, otherwise the owner of the firm would not sell:

$$(14\text{-}16) \quad P_i \geq E[q(x_1, \ldots, x_n)|x_i].$$

On the other hand, any owner of a u-firm would certainly sell at a price above the right-hand side. Hence, if any u-firm is not sold, the equality must hold in (14-16). Consider now a u-firm which has been sold to an integrated firm. The expected profits of that firm are zero. The expected profits of its

d-department must be zero by (14-14). Hence, the expected profits of its u-department must be zero, and that means that the price paid for the u-firms it owns must equal their expected sales:

$$\sum_{i \in A} P_i = E\left[q(x_1, \ldots ,x_n) \sum_{i \in A} x_i \right],$$

and, in view of (14-16), this can hold only if equality holds in (14-16) for each i:

(14-17) $P_i = E[q(x_1, \ldots ,x_n)x_i].$

Some aspects of the competitive equilibrium with some vertical integration have been described on the hypothesis that it exists. It will exist if and only if there is no incentive for any firm to acquire an additional u-firm. As before, the incentive, if any, must be solely in the improvement in the d-department. If the firm acquires another u-firm, i, not in A, the change is that it can choose y' as a function of both X_A and x_i. This will be profitable only if

(14-18) $E_X\left[G\left(\dfrac{x}{y}\right)\Big| X_A, x_i \right] > 0$ with positive probability.

Take any X_A for which (14-15) holds. Then

$$0 = E_X\left[G\left(\frac{x}{y}\right)\Big| X_A \right] = E_{x_i}\left\{ E_X\left[G\left(\frac{x}{y}\right)\Big| X_A, x_i \right] \right\}.$$

Under almost all reasonable conditions, x_i gives information additional to X_A concerning the value of $G(x|y)$. (Remember that, under competitive assumptions, the potential integrator assumes that the functions $p(x_1, \ldots ,x_n)$ and $q(x_1, \ldots ,x_n)$ do not change with his planned acquisition of firm i.) Then

$$E_X[G(x,y)|X_A, x_i],$$

as a function of x_i for fixed X_A, is a random variable with a nondegenerate conditional distribution; since its mean is zero, it is positive with positive conditional probability for each X_A for which (14-15) holds; but since (14-15) holds on a set of positive probability, (14-18) is verified.

Just as in the previous section, we can conclude that no competitive equilibrium is possible where there is vertical integration but no firm owns all the u-firms.

A Monopoly Equilibrium with No Monopoly Power

The argument in the preceding section showed that if a competitive equilibrium formed with a given pattern of vertical integration, it would be upset because any firm would always have an incentive to acquire one more u-firm. This suggests that there will be a tendency to increase consolidation of u-firms into integrated firms to the point where the competitive nature of the markets is destroyed.

Of course, there is in any case an impulse to merge to achieve market power, and I want to avoid confusing the incentive of monopolization with that of minimizing the inefficiency due to uncertainty, the point I am trying to stress here. The model has prohibited horizontal mergers at either level; but vertical integration, if pursued sufficiently, will include a horizontal integration upstream. To purge the model of monopolizing incentives, let me assume that *the demand for the final product is perfectly elastic.* We might think of the upstream and downstream industries as belonging to a small country whose final products are sold on world markets in competition with other companies.

Under these conditions there can be a "competitive" equilibrium in which there is but one active firm, one which has bought up the entire u-industry. Capital decisions are now made with no uncertainty. The total supply, x, is known to the firm at the time of choosing capital, so that

$$(14\text{-}19) \quad F_y(x,y) = 1,$$

yielding y as a function of x. The price of the raw material is again determined by (14-2):

$$pF_x(x,y) = q(x),$$

where p is now assumed to be a constant. Because of competition and free entry in the d-sector, the original owners of the u-firms reap the full benefit of the rationalization of industry, in the form of the prices paid for the firms:

$$P_i = E[q(x)x_i],$$

in form the same as before, but the value of $q(x)$ will in general be higher.

The only way this equilibrium could be upset is if an outsider were to enter and possibly buy one or more of the u-firms (or even try to operate a d-firm with no u-department). Clearly, however, any such firm will have less information than the "monopolist." Hence, his expected profits in the d-department will have to be less, because his adaptation of capital to the supply of raw material is less good. Since the "monopolist," however, is making zero profits in the d-department, the potential entrant will be making negative profits there. Under competition and risk neutrality, he can have zero expected profits in the u-department. Therefore the potential entrant will find it unprofitable unless, indeed, he buys out all the u-firms. But then that is simply a change of monopolists and no true change in the equilibrium configuration.

The outcome is socially optimal, since all the available information is used perfectly. Of course, it must be repeated, this beneficent result of the invisible hand occurs only when there is no monopoly power in the system as a whole. Otherwise, we do have a situation in which the advantages of merger to improve information are accompanied by an opportunity to exercise monopoly power.

Concluding Comments

It is conceivable that there are imperfectly competitive equilibria. That is, one can imagine the possibility that there are a few large vertically integrated firms, each aware of its effect on the market and on the others; they play some sort of noncooperative game. Even in the absence of monopoly power in the industry as a whole, each firm could have an influence over the raw materials market. Any one firm might be restrained from expanding by consideration of its increasing portion of the raw materials market.

It is difficult to construct a believable model of this possibility and, therefore, to see whether this imagined world is consistent. The trouble is that there will necessarily be few individuals on either side of the raw materials market in that case, and so the rules of the game are hard to define. I would conjecture that these imperfectly competitive worlds cannot in fact exist — that is, no matter how they are defined, it would always pay an integrated firm to acquire the additional information contained in additional u-firms.

I have not considered various auxiliary markets which might convey the information without integration. I assume first of all that the information about upstream production cannot itself be sold; the argument for that is fairly familiar. Second, I assume the absence of suitable contingent markets. Since they do not in fact exist, there are presumably good reasons in terms of cost factors, such as the specification and verification of the possible outcomes.

In this model, a third possibility cannot be so easily ruled out — that of futures markets. Since the sellers of raw materials do know their future product, they could offer valid contracts one period in advance. If the market works smoothly enough so that it does not create an additional delay in diffusing the needed information, the d-firms could make the correct investment decisions on the basis of the futures price.

However, a small modification of the model would deprive the futures market of much of its usefulness. Suppose what each u-firm knows one period in advance is not its actual output but an indication of it, that is, a signal correlated with its output (and/or with total output) but not perfectly. Assume further that a futures contract must in fact always be honored, or else that there is a severe penalty for failure to deliver. Then the individual u-firm can make futures contracts only up to the minimum output which is absolutely assured, given the signal. Thus there will remain an active spot market whose price will not be known in advance with certainty. The futures price will be socially useful primarily as a signal, but it will not convey the same information as acquiring all the u-firms. On the other hand, the arguments presented earlier concerning vertical integration remain valid without change; it was not necessary that the "monopolist" have perfect information, only that the acquisition of successively more u-firms represent an increase in information.[2]

Another possible modification is that the vertically integrated firm might be less efficient than the sum of the firms. (Jerry Green has used this assumption in a different approach to vertical integration.)[3] A particular form of this, which has some realism, is that a vertically integrated firm will not sell the raw material, though it may buy additional amounts on the open market. This condition will certainly operate to restrict the incentive for vertical integration. Preliminary analysis suggests that this restriction will lead to extremes; either there will be no vertical integration at all, or, as in this chapter, it will proceed to the limit.

Finally, the hypothesis of risk neutrality might be relaxed. However, it is not clear that risk aversion provides much of an incentive to vertical integration. If demand for the final product is highly elastic, then it is easy to show that upstream sales and downstream profits are positively correlated. Hence, acquiring a u-firm does not seem to be the best possible portfolio diversification.

---

2. I am indebted to the members of the Interdisciplinary Colloquium on Mathematics in the Behavioral Sciences, University of California at Los Angeles, for raising the question of the futures market as an alternative to vertical integration.

3. In J. Green, "Vertical Integration and Assurance of Markets," Harvard Institute of Economic Research, Discussion Paper no. 383, 1974.

15 Risk Allocation and Information: Some Recent Theoretical Developments

I propose to set forth here some new developments in the theory of risk allocation in a market economy. In contrast to earlier work, these revolve about the effects of information on the viability and efficiency of risk-bearing markets. Specific questions raised are the allocative effects of additional publicly available information and of possibly differing private information.

Markets are means for the mutually beneficial exchange of goods and for inducing the transformation of goods from one form to another. We will take it as axiomatic that individuals are risk-averse, so that the bearing of risks is a cost and the shifting of risks to others a good. The existence of insurance, common stocks, and many other devices testifies to the validity of the assumption of risk aversion, though it must be admitted that gambling and perhaps some speculative activity might be regarded as evidence for risk preference in some contexts.

As part, then, of the general use of the market for exchanging goods, we expect to find markets in which risks are traded. The risks are shifted to those more able to bear them until at the margin the cost to the risk bearer is equal to the benefit to the risk shifter. More specifically, there are, in addition to the usual commodities, a set of *contingent commodities;* a unit contingent commodity is an agreement to deliver one unit of a specific good

Reprinted from *The Geneva Papers on Risk and Insurance,* no. 8 (1978). Originally presented as the First Annual Lecture of the Geneva Association, November 1977.

or (more generally in practice) to pay one unit of money if and only if a specified event has occurred. An insurance policy is a good example.

If an event is certain to occur, then a commodity contract contingent on its occurrence is identical with the corresponding unconditional contract, and creation of the contingent commodity market has no economic significance. If an event is certain not to occur, then a commodity contingent on that event must have price zero, and again existence of the contingent market has no economic significance. However, if there is uncertainty about the event, then in general a market for contracts contingent upon that event will be viable; there will be a price at which supply and demand will balance with some buyers and some sellers.

In fact, if markets are created for every commodity for every contingency, then the general competitive equilibrium leads to an efficient allocation of risk bearing (Arrow, 1953; Debreu, 1953; 1959, chap. 7).

The existence of competitive equilibrium with universal contingent contracts follows by suitable reinterpretation of the usual existence results. Even if the markets only exist for some contingencies, existence of equilibrium can still be demonstrated (Radner, 1968). However, as is usual when markets are absent, the market allocation of risk bearing is no longer efficient; there exist conceivable reallocations which would make everyone better off.

It is a matter of some controversy how to represent the concept of uncertainty. The most usual doctrine represents uncertainty by probabilities, and I shall follow that convention here. It certainly is the only theory that has shown itself to be useful in deriving any results. Within this framework, however, is a point which has created controversy for generations: is probability objective or subjective? That is, given an event, is there one probability to which all reasonable people must subscribe, or can individuals differ? The currently most accepted doctrine is the subjective probability theory; probabilities express individual beliefs just as utilities express individual tastes. Individual behavior is determined by maximizing expected utility, where the expectation is computed according to the individual's own probabilities.

Under the subjective probability theory, there are two motives for trading in contingent commodities. One is the desire to avoid risks fundamental to insurance; this depends on the existence of uncertainty and would hold even if everyone agreed on the probabilities. The other motive derives from differences of opinion; if I judge an event more probable than you do, then, other things being equal, there will be a price at which I am willing to sell a contract contingent on that event and you are willing to buy it. Betting on horse races is a pure example. For a more serious example, it is clear that many of the participants on the commodity futures or stock markets are basing their actions on anticipations of the future; since some sell and some buy, these anticipations must differ. From this viewpoint, the efficiency of the competitive market in contingent claims remains valid, in the sense that there is no alternative feasible allocation which will yield every individual a higher expected utility based on his or her own probabilities.

Both the subjective and the objective probability theories, however, recognize that there may be differences of opinion based on different observations. As part of the complete structure of probability beliefs about the world, every individual has conditional probabilities. The probability that an event A occurs will in general be changed by the knowledge that another event B has occurred. Thus, the probability that it will snow on 1 January 1990 in Cambridge, Massachusetts, will be some number which will be approximately the proportion of the times it has snowed on 1 January over the years for which observations have been made. But on 31 December 1989, a more relevant probability will be that given by the weather map on that date — roughly, the proportion of times that a similar weather map has been followed by snow the next day.

Therefore, two individuals with the same probability beliefs may nevertheless have different probabilities for the same event when entering the market, because they have observed different other events. The existence of information derived from observations can have profound effects on the working of the risk-sharing markets. Indeed, the problem of differential information has long been known in the insurance literature under such headings as "moral hazard" and "adverse selection."

In this chapter I want to survey some aspects of the effects of information on the markets for contingent goods, by means of a toy example studied under different informational assumptions. The theory is still under development and was influenced by many scholars; I give specific references in appropriate places.

First, some definitions. By "information," I mean any observation which effectively changes probabilities according to the principles of conditional probability. The prior probabilities are defined for all events, an event being described by statements about both the variables that are relevant to individual welfare and those that define the range of possible observations. Given an observation, there is a conditional or posterior distribution of possible values of the welfare-relevant variables.

Consider first the case of a single individual. Suppose information is offered to him or her at no cost. Should the individual accept it? Clearly, the answer is yes. He or she cannot be worse off because the information can always be disregarded. In more technical language, the individual, in the absence of information, will have to make a decision. That is, he or she will have to choose among a set of alternative actions. Since the consequences of each action are uncertain, the choice will be made so as to maximize expected utility. Now suppose the individual is told that information will be made available; that is, an observation which specifies which of a number of possible alternative events occurred will be made and transmitted to him. The decision can be made after the observation has been received and therefore maximizes expected utility computed according to the probabilities conditional on the observation. The decision made will now depend on the actual event observed. To put it slightly differently, the individual can, before receiving the information, choose a *decision function,* which specifies the decision made for each possible observation. The decision made in the absence of information is a special kind of decision function, one which specifies the same decision for any possible observation. Therefore, the optimal decision function must be at least as good, in the expected-utility sense, as a constant decision, simply from the definition of the word "optimal." In general, the best decision function will be better, in the expected-utility sense, than the best decision which disregards the observation.

This analysis neglects the cost of acquiring and using the information. The most important and most stubborn of these costs are the limits on individual information-processing capacity. These costs are extremely important in actual economic life, but I wish to neglect them for the present discussion. The point to be stressed here is rather the difference between the individual and the social values of information, even apart from costs. As will be seen, when risks are allocated by the market, information may be harmful rather than beneficial.

Let us review briefly the theory of allocation under contingent contracts by means of the simplest possible example. Suppose the world can be in only two possible states, although it is not known to any party which is the truth. Further, suppose there are only two individuals. More precisely, to preserve the competitive flavor, we should assume two types of individuals, with indefinitely many in each type and with identity of tastes and endowments among all individuals within a type. The effect is the same as if there were two individuals, each of whom, however, behaved like a perfect competitor in taking prices as parameters. Call the members of our tiny economy Walras and Böhm-Bawerk. Suppose further that their subjective probabilities for the two events are the same. (I shall maintain throughout the hypothesis that the subjective probabilities of the events held *prior* to any observations are the same to all individuals. Any difference in probability judgments when entering a market are attributed to different observations.) In fact, to make the examples even simpler, it will be assumed that the probability of each event is 1/2 for each individual. Suppose that, of the two states, state 1 is relatively more favorable to Walras than to Böhm-Bawerk. Then Walras sells contracts payable if state 1 occurs and buys contracts payable if state 2 occurs.

Let me state a whimsical, more specific example which will be used throughout the chapter as a theme for variations. Suppose there are two commodities, "wheat" and "barley," which are perfect substitutes in consumption but produced under different conditions. If v is the total amount of wheat and barley consumed by an individual, then the individual's von Neumann–Morgenstern utility is assumed to be log v. Walras has initially a stock of 1 unit of wheat, Böhm-Bawerk a stock of 1 unit of barley; there is no production. There are two weather states, with probability 1/2 each: in state W, all the barley is destroyed and none of the wheat; in B, all the wheat is destroyed and none of the barley. The effective initial holdings of the consumers' good, "wheat plus barley," are given in Table 15.1.

There are two contracts on the market; delivery of the consumers' good if W and delivery of the good if B. Because of the total symmetry of the assumptions, the two contracts have equal unit prices. In equilibrium, Walras sells 1/2 unit of wheat if W and buys 1/2 unit of barley if B. Böhm-Bawerk does the opposite. The expected utilities of Walras and Böhm-Bawerk are the same, both being (1/2) log (1/2) + (1/2) log (1/2) = log (1/2). For ease of understanding, it is preferable to state the *certainty-equivalent income* instead of expected utility, that is, that income

Table 15.1 Output as a function of state of the world

Individual	State of the world	
	W	B
Walras	1	0
Böhm-Bawerk	0	1

which, if obtained with certainty, would have a utility equal to the given expected utility. If y^* is the certainty-equivalent income, then

$$\log y^* = E (\log y),$$

or

$$y^* = \text{antilog } E (\log y),$$

where y is the variable consumption.

To cover the general case, let p_W and $p_B = 1 - p_W$ be the probabilities of states W and B, respectively, from the viewpoint of any particular individual. Let y_W and y_B be the individual's consumption under the respective states. Then, his or her certainty-equivalent income is

$$y^* = y_W^{p_W} y_B^{p_B}.$$

In the present case, $p_W = p_B = 1/2$, so that

(15-1) $y^* = (y_W y_B)^{1/2}.$

It is seen that with perfect contingent markets but no information,

(15-2) $y_W^* = y_B^* = 1/2.$

A major theme of this chapter is the surprising fact that an increase in information may *lower* the efficiency of the market, as first noted by Hirshleifer (1971). The simplest illustration already occurs if information is introduced into the above example. Suppose the information is *public,* by which is meant that both parties know it. Because there are only two possible states of the world, information consists of knowing which state will prevail. Clearly, if W is known, Böhm-Bawerk will have no purchasing power; therefore no transactions will take place (this is in fact the competitive equilibrium allocation, with all prices for the contingent commodities as possible equilibria). Then Walras will consume 1 unit, for utility 0, Böhm-Bawerk 0 units, for utility $-\infty$, if W occurs. If B occurs, the allocation is reversed. Ex ante, states W and B occur with probability 1/2 each; hence, for each individual the expected utility is $-\infty$, and therefore,

(15-3) $y_W^* = y_B^* = 0.$

Thus, the existence of public information effectively prevents the sharing of risk bearing and destroys the corresponding utility gain.

In the preceding example, public information effectively reduced the market to autarchy. The information eliminated the possibility of trading risks without doing any offsetting good. The reason for this is that the information has no social use in a pure exchange economy. If production is introduced, however, it is reasonable to suppose that information enhances productive capability. If inputs are made before outputs, then, under uncertainty, outputs are a random function of inputs. Information reduces the uncertainty of output for any given input, and therefore should improve the allocation of resources for production.

Let me now introduce a simple example, which generalizes the previous one and at the same time demonstrates the possibility that information increases productivity. Instead of being endowed with wheat or barley, let each member of the market be endowed with land which can be sown to either wheat or barley according to the decision of the owner. We retain the assumption about the unknown state of the world; in W weather, only wheat grows, in B weather, only barley. Walras is better off than Böhm-Bawerk in W weather in the sense that if they both plant their entire land (one unit for each) in wheat, then Walras' output is greater than Böhm-Bawerk's; the opposite holds in B weather. The production hypothesis is summarized in Table 15.2. The parameter a satisfies the condition, $0 \leqq a < 1$. The utility functions and prior probabilities of the two states are as before. If $a = 0$, this production model is equivalent to the pure exchange model; Walras' land can only be used for wheat, so that his output is the same as his endowment in the pure exchange model for each state, and the same is true of Böhm-Bawerk.

Each individual can sow part of his land to wheat and part to barley; the amounts produced under each state are proportional to the amounts sown. Thus, if Walras plants 2/3 of his land in wheat and 1/3 in barley, his output is 2/3 if W, $a/3$ if B.

If $a = 1$, then Walras and Böhm-Bawerk have identical production possibilities. No trade will occur in either the presence or the absence of informa-

Table 15.2   Output as a function of production decision and state of the world

	State of the world	
Individual	W	B
Walras	1 if sown to wheat	a if sown to barley
	0 if sown to barley	0 if sown to wheat
Böhm-Bawerk	a if sown to wheat	1 if sown to barley
	0 if sown to barley	0 if sown to wheat

tion. But public information is certainly productive; if it is known that state W obtains, both will plant to wheat, if B both to barley. Retain the assumption that information is public. We can compare attained welfare levels with or without information and with or without the existence of contingent markets. There are four possible cases.

Case 1: No Information, No Contingent Markets. Since each has to be autarchic, each plants so as to maximize the expected utility of consumption. Let Walras, for example, plant w in wheat and $b = 1 - w$ in barley. His output is w if W, ab if B. His expected utility is $(1/2) \log w + (1/2) \log (ab)$ $= (1/2) \log w + (1/2) \log b + (1/2) \log a$. The optimal policy is clearly independent of a; it is $w = b = 1/2$. The situation for Böhm-Bawerk is symmetric. Straightforward calculation shows that

$$y_W^* = y_B^* = a^{1/2}/2.$$

Case 2: Contingent Markets without Information. There are now markets for wheat-claims conditional on W and for barley-claims contingent on B. Because of the symmetry of the assumptions, it is obvious that the prices of the two kinds of claims are the same.

Each individual can be thought of as made up of a firm and a consumer. The consumer's income is the profit of the firm. The firm can be thought of as supplying two joint products, wheat-claims if W and barley-claims if B. As in the usual theory of firms and households under certainty, the firm should maximize its profits independently of the tastes of the owning household. In this case, profits equal the total value of contingent claims sold. We assume honesty in sale, in that the number of claims sold for a given state does not exceed the amount the firm could supply in that state.

Since the prices of the two kinds of claims are equal, it is clear that Walras should sow his entire land to wheat and sell 1 unit of wheat claims; any land transferred to barley would yield a lesser value sold in the ratio $a:1$. Similarly, Böhm-Bawerk sows his land to barley and sells one unit of barley claims. Under expected-utility maximization, each individual will spend half his income on claims of each kind; hence, each will receive $1/2$ unit of wheat if W and $1/2$ unit of barley if B, so that his income is $1/2$ with certainty.

Since $a < 1$, $1/2 > a^{1/2}/2$; hence, introducing contingent markets without information increases the welfare of both.

Case 3: Information without Contingent Markets. In the absence of contingent markets, there is no trade either before or after realization of the state of the weather. Clearly, both individuals plant wheat if W and barley if B. Walras realizes and consumes 1 if W and a if B, while Böhm-Bawerk has the same up to a permutation of the states. Therefore, each has a certainty-equivalent income of $(1 \cdot a)^{1/2}$. Each is obviously better off than in case 1. Introduction of public information increases welfare if there are no contingent markets, because it permits adaptation of production.

Is the outcome of case 3 better than that of case 2? Is it better to introduce public information or contingent markets, if only one is possible? Comparison of the certainty-equivalent incomes shows that case 3 yields better outcomes if and only if $a^{1/2} > 1/2$, or $a > 1/4$. The coefficient a measures what may be termed the *flexibility* of the economy, its ability to increase production in response to information.

Public information is better than the introduction of contingent markets if the economy is sufficiently flexible and not otherwise.

Case 4: Information and Contingent Markets. It has already been pointed out that public information prevents the execution of mutually advantageous contingent contracts. But it should be noted that, technically speaking, the contingent markets are not "destroyed." Rather, the prices are such that each individual finds it most advantageous neither to buy nor to sell. Specifically, if state W obtains, barley claims have zero price. Then both individuals plant only wheat. Neither can plan to buy wheat claims, since they cannot sell barley claims. On the other hand, since both know that W obtains, neither will want to sell wheat claims, since all they could do with the proceeds would be to buy barley claims, which have no use. Hence supply and demand balance on both markets. However, from the welfare point of view, the situation is identical with that of public information and no markets.

The results of this section are set forth in Table 15.3. Certainty-equivalent

Table 15.3 Certainty-equivalent incomes for different combinations of public information and contingent markets

Public information	Contingent markets	Certainty-equivalent income
No	No	$a^{1/2}/2$
No	Yes	$1/2$
Yes	No	$a^{1/2}$
Yes	Yes	$a^{1/2}$

income for (No, No) is less than any of the other three. Certainty-equivalent income for (Yes, No) is greater than that for (No, Yes) if and only if $a > 1/4$.

Now suppose that information is not public; specifically, assume that one member of our toy economy has information that the other does not have. For definiteness, we suppose that Walras knows the state of the weather while Böhm-Bawerk does not. Call this the hypothesis of *differential* information.

The concept of differential information is becoming increasingly recognized as central to many features of economic organization. The problems of adverse selection and moral hazard in insurance are special cases, as will be discussed subsequently; their implications for the general theory of risk bearing were suggested in Arrow (1965, lecture 3) and have been greatly developed in recent years. Akerlof (1970) showed how markets might disappear altogether when the parties have different information and know it.

When there is differential information, the prices obtaining on markets may be a means of transmitting information. The existence and efficiency properties of equilibria under these circumstances have been studied by Green (1973), Kihlstrom and Mirman (1975), Grossman (1976), Grossman and Stiglitz (1976), and Shubik (1977), among many others. These concepts will be illustrated in our very simple model.

Case 5: Differential Information without Contingent Markets. Walras plants entirely to wheat if W, to barley if B. His output is 1 if W, a if B; hence, his certainty-equivalent income is $a^{1/2}$, just as in the case of public information and no contingent markets. Böhm-Bawerk is in the same situation as if there were no public information and no contingent markets; hence, his certainty-equivalent income is $a^{1/2}/2$.

If there are contingent markets, then all depends on what Böhm-Bawerk can infer about what Walras knows. First, we must note that in any case, the equilibrium on the contingent markets cannot be the same as if there were no information. In the last case, prices for the two kinds of contingent contracts (wheat if W, barley if B) must be equal. But suppose the state is in fact W; Walras will buy no barley claims and will therefore sell no wheat claims. At the original prices, Böhm-Bawerk's demands and supplies are unchanged. Hence, there is now excess supply of barley claims and excess demand for wheat claims, so the original prices can no longer be in equilibrium.

How does Böhm-Bawerk respond to the discovery that the previous equilibrium no longer holds? There are (at least) two possibilities. One is in the spirit of competitive theory — he simply takes market prices as parameters and responds to them by profit-maximization and utility-maximization. We may call this the *parametric price* assumption. Alternatively, he may be aware that Walras knows the true state; since the market prices reflect Walras' behavior, Böhm-Bawerk can infer the true state and act accordingly. The equilibrium price for each state must be such that if it is read as a signal for the truth of that state, the resulting behavior will sustain it as an equilibrium. This is the assumption of *rational expectations.*

Before taking up the two cases, some terminology and general remarks are in order. In either case, there will be in general a different set of prices if W occurs than if B occurs; this was also true in the (trivial) case of public information and contingent markets (case 4). Take barley-claims to be numéraire in each state of nature. Then the price system in each state reduces to the price of wheat-claims in terms of barley-claims (possibly infinite if barley-claims are free goods). Let p^W and p^B be the prices of wheat-claims in terms of barley-claims in the states W and B, respectively; the pair (p^W, p^B) will be referred to as the *equilibrium price system.*

It is important to note that the supply conditions are independent of information once the prices are given; this is a fundamental property of contingent markets. Each of our agents can be thought of as combining a firm and a consumer. The firm sells claims contingent on the state of the weather. Its aim is to maximize its profits in the transactions; given the contingent prices, it cannot do better by using information. To validate any planned sales of contingent claims, the firms must actually plant the corresponding amounts. Note that demands indeed respond to information; hence, the system as a whole is influenced by information, and supplies may indeed respond to information, but only through the prices of the contingent contracts.

In our simple linear technologies, there will be for each firm one wheat-claim price, p, at which it is indifferent between producing barley and wheat (and therefore between selling barley-claims and wheat-claims). For all smaller wheat-claim prices it produces only barley, for all larger ones only wheat. Walras would realize p if he produced only wheat, a if he produced only barley. Therefore, he produces barley if $p < a$, wheat if $p > a$, and is indifferent between them when $p = a$. In the last case, he is also indifferent among all alternatives which allocate a fraction r of his land to wheat and

$1 - r$ to barley and therefore produces r of wheat and $a(1 - r)$ of barley for any r, $0 \leq r \leq 1$. It also follows that Walras' income as a function of the wheat-claim price is

(15-4) $Y_W(p) = \max (p,a)$.

Similarly, Böhm-Bawerk produces only barley if $p < a^{-1}$, only wheat if $p > a^{-1}$. If $p = a^{-1}$, he is equally willing to produce ar of wheat and $1 - r$ of barley for any r, $0 \leq r \leq 1$. His income is

(15-5) $Y_B(p) = \max (ap,1)$.

With these remarks, we can study the equilibrium price systems and associated quantity allocations under the alternative assumptions of parametric prices and rational expectations.

Case 6: Differential Information with Contingent Markets and Parametric Prices. The determination of the equilibrium price system is elementary but slightly tedious; it will be found in the appendix at the end of the chapter. The results are

(15-6) $p^W = a^{-1}$, $p^B = a$ if $a \geq 1/2$,
                          $= 1/2$ if $a < 1/2$.

The production and consumption allocations are interesting. Since $p^W = a^{-1} > a$, Walras will produce only wheat-claims if W prevails. His supply will be 1. Also, from (15-4), his income is p^W; since he only buys wheat-claims (knowing that W prevails), he buys 1 unit of wheat-claims, and therefore exactly consumes his own supply. Böhm-Bawerk, not knowing which state prevails, buys both kinds of claims. To meet his demand for wheat-claims, he must therefore produce some of his own, as well as some barley-claims. At $p^W = a^{-1}$, he will in fact be willing to produce both. Precisely, he plants one-half his land in wheat, one-half in barley, and therefore consumes $a/2$ if W prevails.

Suppose B is true, so that the price is p^B. The case $a < 1/2$, where the technology is relatively inflexible, is most interesting. Since $p^B = 1/2 > a$, Walras will find it profitable to plant only wheat and therefore sell only wheat-claims, even though he knows that B is true! Since $p^B = 1/2 < a^{-1}$, Böhm-Bawerk plants only barley and sells barley-claims. Therefore, one unit of barley is produced if B holds. However, Walras' income is $1/2$, which he spends entirely on barley-claims. Walras and Böhm-Bawerk therefore consume 1/2 each. The production, though not the consumption, reflects a striking misallocation.

If $a \geq 1/2$, then still $p^B < a^{-1}$, so that Böhm-Bawerk plants only barley. However, Walras will plant some of his land in each, $(2a)^{-1}$ in wheat and $1 - (2a)^{-1}$ in barley. His product, if B prevails, is $a - (1/2)$ of barley, while Böhm-Bawerk's output of barley is 1, for a total output of $a + (1/2)$. Walras' income is a, spent entirely on barley-claims, so that he receives a units of barley, while Böhm-Bawerk's consumption is the remainder, 1/2.

If we work through the certainty-equivalent incomes, we find

$$(15\text{-}7) \quad \begin{aligned} y_W^* &= 2^{-1/2} \quad \text{if } a < 1/2, \\ &= a^{1/2} \quad \text{if } a \geq 1/2; \end{aligned}$$
$$y_B^* = a^{1/2}/2 \; [a^{1/2}/2] \quad \text{in any case.}$$

Comparison with the results in Table 15.3 shows that Walras is at least as well off under differential information as in any previous case. Böhm-Bawerk, on the other hand, has the same welfare level as in the absence of both contingent markets and information and is worse off than in the presence of either.

Case 7: Differential Information with Contingent Market and Rational Expectations. It is obvious that if both wind up knowing the true state, the situation is the same as with public information and contingent markets (case 4). Barley-claims are free goods in state W, wheat-claims in state B; the contingent markets are ineffective, and the real outcome is the same as with public information and no markets (case 3).

It may be a useful exercise to restate this conclusion more formally. It is asserted that the equilibrium price system is $p^W = \infty$, $p^B = 0$. Clearly, with these prices, both individuals plant only wheat if W, only barley if B. Further, if W holds, both know it, Walras by assumption and Böhm-Bawerk by inference from observing p^W, and therefore both demand only wheat-claims; the same holds, *mutatis mutandis,* if state B holds.

In the spirit of general equilibrium theory, one may ask if the equilibrium price system is unique. In this case, it is not, and the formal argument is instructive. Suppose there is another equilibrium price system, p^W, p^B. First suppose that $p^W \neq p^B$. Then Böhm-Bawerk can infer from the market price which state holds. If W is true, both demand only wheat-claims. Hence, both must supply only wheat-claims. But this policy will be profit-maximizing for both whenever $p^W \geq a^{-1}$. Similarly, equilibrium will hold if B is true whenever $p^B \leqq a$. Hence, any pair satisfying these conditions is an equilibrium price system.

Is it possible that $p^W = p^B$ in some equilibrium price system? If it did, then Böhm-Bawerk would *not* be able to infer which state prevailed. His demands for the two kinds of claims would therefore be the same as if he took prices parametrically. Since the rational expectations and parametric price models differ only with respect to Böhm-Bawerk's demand, it follows that, if $p^W = p^B$, the pair of prices would be a rational expectations price equilibrium system if and only if it is a parametric price equilibrium system. But, from (15-6), there is not in this example any parametric price equilibrium system with $p^W = p^B$.

In this example, there is no rational expectations equilibrium with $p^W = p^B$. But it is certainly possible to have such equilibria in other contexts. Therefore, rational expectations equilibria do not necessarily convey information held by one individual to the uninformed. As Table 15.4 shows, the informed party, Walras, is as well off with differential information as with public information and better off if the uninformed party takes prices parametrically and if the technology is not very flexible. The uninformed party, on the contrary, is as badly off as if there were neither information nor contingent markets unless he uses the observed prices to form rational expectations; in that case, the situation is essentially the same as with public information.

These examples all show compromise between spreading the risk bearing and efficiency of production. Can both kinds of efficiency be achieved?

First, what is the optimal allocation in an ideal system? Clearly, if W obtains, both parties should plant to wheat; the total production would be $1 + a$. Similarly, if B obtains, a total output of $1 + a$ is also obtainable. If, in

Table 15.4 Payoffs under alternative assumptions

Assumption on markets	Productivity parameter (a)	Individual	
		Walras	Böhm-Bawerk
None	$0 \leqq a < 1$	$a^{1/2}$	$a^{1/2}/2$
Parametric prices	$1/2 \leqq a < 1$	$a^{1/2}$	$a^{1/2}/2$
Parametric prices	$0 \leqq a < 1/2$	$2^{-1/2}$	$a^{1/2}/2$
Rational expectations	$0 \leqq a < 1$	$a^{1/2}$	$a^{1/2}$

Note: Walras knows the state of the world, Böhm-Bawerk does not.

each state, the total output is divided equally between the two, then each consumes $(1 + a)/2$ with certainty. Since $(1 + a)/2 > a^{1/2}$ and also $(1 + a)/2 > 1/2$ whenever $0 < a < 1$, this is better than any allocation achieved through the market structures analyzed so far. The allocation is Pareto-optimal; it is the only one which is also symmetric between the participants.

Could this allocation be achieved through a market mechanism? It can, if the contingent markets operate *before* information is available while production takes place after. In this case, Walras knows that he could produce 1 unit if W, a units if B, and will sell claims accordingly. The market prices for the two kinds of claims are equal, say to 1. Then Walras' and Böhm-Bawerk's incomes are each $1 + a$; they each purchase $(1 + a)/2$ of each kind of claim, thereby realizing the optimal allocation.

Whether this principle has significant application can only be determined in individual cases. It depends on the possibility of ensuring that contingent markets are in existence before information can be known.

To conclude, I give some real-world cases in which problems of market organization are illustrated by the new theoretical developments. Examples of differential information abound. In the field of insurance, both adverse selection and moral hazard arise from differential information. In the case of adverse selection, the insured has a greater knowledge of the risks than the insurer. His or her demand behavior will change accordingly. In equilibrium, the insurer is correct on the average but cannot distinguish among insured with varying risks. Those with higher risks find their insurance underpriced relative to the true risks and will thus buy more insurance than is efficient. Therefore, the average risk per dollar of insurance is higher; the premium must rise and might conceivably rise to the point of eliminating low-risk individuals from the market. If the insurance company can observe the total amount of insurance purchased by an individual, it might infer his risk status and use that information in setting rates. The differential information is that which enables the individual insured to know his or her particular risks.

In the case of moral hazard, the individual can make decisions which cannot be monitored successfully by the insurance company. Thus, in the case of health insurance, the ill person demands medical services based on his perception of his illness. But if the cost of medical services is partly or wholly covered by the insurance, he or she will demand more than if the full cost were not covered. The insurer is not, however, able to distinguish among medical needs.

It is for reasons such as these that other kinds of cost controls are widely proposed and beginning to be enforced, at least in the United States. The market is no longer regarded as thoroughly efficient, and nonmarket controls are invoked.

Differential information is manifested in another form in connection with quality of product. The quality of medical services is a particularly acute form of this problem. Here, the seller in general knows much more than the buyer; the latter is not in a strong position to insist on quality standards. It is unlikely that a market mechanism of any kind will be very useful. Society has been adapting to this example of market by regulation and by ethical codes, such as those governing the practices of medicine and law.

For a final example among a vast number of possibilities, I mention the allocation of resources to the production of information itself. The main form is research and development of new products. There are conflicting tendencies to overinvestment and underinvestment. In the case where public information renders contingent markets useless, there can be overinvestment by social standards. Since differential information is advantageous (at least in the parametric price case), each individual may be willing to expend resources to find the information; but if both succeed, they may have made both worse off. On the other hand, information is hard to make into a private good; if discovered, it is likely to leak in some form, and therefore the investor will not get the full reward.

My main stress in this chapter is not on the particular applications, most of which remain to be worked out, but to exemplify as simply as possible some new tendencies in economic thinking about risk bearing.

Appendix

As promised earlier, I work out here in detail the equilibrium price system and quantity allocations for case 6, where there are contingent markets, differential information, and parametric prices.

First, note that Böhm-Bawerk, who receives no information directly and makes no inferences from observed prices, is uncertain about the state of the weather. He therefore demands some claims of each kind. Hence, in equilibrium, there must be a willingness to supply claims of both kinds. From the discussion of supply in the text, we see that at any equilibrium, we must have

(A-1) $a \leqq p \leqq a^{-1}.$

With this range of prices, the incomes of the two individuals are

(A-2) $Y_W(p) = p,$ $Y_B(p) = 1.$

Let d stand for demand for wheat-claims, with subscripts representing the agents. Böhm-Bawerk's demand is independent of state. For any market price, p, his demands come from maximizing

$$(1/2) \log w + (1/2) \log b$$

subject to $pw + b = 1$, where w and b are the demands for wheat-claims and barley-claims respectively. Then,

(A-3) $d_B(p) = w = (2p)^{-1}.$

Walras' demand for wheat-claims depends on the state, to be indicated by a superscript. If W holds, Walras spends his entire income on wheat-claims; if B holds, he spends none of his income on wheat-claims:

(A-4) $d_W^W(p) = 1,$ $d_W^B(p) = 0.$

If d^W and d^B represent total demands in states W and B, respectively,

(A-5) $d^W(p) = 1 + (2p)^{-1},$ $d^B(p) = (2p)^{-1}.$

Walras will supply 1 unit of wheat-claims if $p > a$; he will supply any amount from 0 to 1 indifferently if $p = a$. Similarly, Böhm-Bawerk will supply no wheat-claims if $p < a^{-1}$ and will be indifferent at any amount from 0 to a if $p = a^{-1}$. Hence, total supply is indifferent over the interval $\langle 0,1 \rangle$ if $p = a$, equals 1 if $a < p < a^{-1}$, and is indifferently anything in the interval $\langle 1,1 + a \rangle$ if $p = a^{-1}$.

If $d(p)$ is the demand function, then p is an equilibrium in any of the three following circumstances: (1) $p = a,\ 0 \leq d(a) \leq 1$; (2) $a < p < a^{-1},\ d(p) = 1$; (3) $p = a^{-1},\ 1 \leq d(a^{-1}) \leq 1 + a$. (Note that clearing the wheat-claims market automatically clears the barley-claims market.)

Suppose state W holds. Since $d^W(p) > 1$, the only possible equilibrium is at $p = a^{-1}$. Since $1 < d^W(a^{-1}) = 1 + (a/2) < 1 + a$, it is in fact true that $p^W = a^{-1}$. Total output is $1 + (a/2)$, of which 1 is supplied by Walras. From (A-4), Walras' demand for wheat-claims is also 1, which is realized.

In state W, then, Böhm-Bawerk commits himself to producing $a/2$ of wheat if W; this can be done by sowing one-half his land in wheat and half in barley. He buys $a/2$ wheat-claims and $1/2$ barley-claims; the former is realized.

In state B, matters are a little more complex. Is it possible that $p^B = a$?

From (A-5) and the equilibrium conditions, $p^B = a$ if and only if $(2a)^{-1} \leq 1$, or $a \geq 1/2$. In that case, Böhm-Bawerk produces only barley. However, he demands $(2a)^{-1}$ of wheat-claims, which is supplied by Walras. This means that Walras must plant $(2a)^{-1}$ of his land in wheat, even though he knows that no wheat will grow; he plants the remainder in barley, with a realized output of $a[1 - (2a)^{-1}] = a - (1/2)$. Walras' demand for barley-claims, which is realized, is a (his total income). Böhm-Bawerk's demand for barley-claims is $1/2$.

It is impossible that $p^B = a^{-1}$; for $d^B(a^{-1}) = a/2$, from (A-5), and $a/2 < 1$. However, it is possible that $a < p < a^{-1}$; this occurs only when $d^B(p) = 1$, that is, $p = 1/2$, and it is an equilibrium when $a < 1/2 < a^{-1}$. Since the second inequality must hold, we have that

$$p^B = 1/2 \quad \text{when} \quad a < 1/2.$$

Here, Walras has an income $1/2$ and a demand $1/2$ for barley-claims. Because $p^B > a$, he plants only wheat, although he knows that no wheat will grow, a remarkable inefficiency. Böhm-Bawerk grows only barley; since Walras receives $1/2$, Böhm-Bawerk will also receive $1/2$.

References

Akerlof, G. A. (1970). "The market for 'lemons'; quality uncertainty and the market mechanism." *Quarterly Journal of Economics* 84:488–500.

Arrow, K. J. (1953). "Le rôle des valeurs boursières pour la répartition la meilleure des risques." *Econométrie,* Colloques Internationaux du Centre National de la Recherche Scientifique, vol. 11, Paris, 41–47. English translation, 1963–64.

Arrow, K. J. (1963–64). "The role of securities in the optimal allocation of risk-bearing." *Review of Economic Studies* 31:91–96. English translation of Arrow (1953); appears as Chapter 3, Volume 2 of these Collected Papers.

Arrow, K. J. (1965). *Aspects of the Theory of Risk-Bearing.* Helsinki: Yrjö Jahns-sonin säätio. Lecture 3, reprinted in Arrow (1970, chap. 5); appears as Chapter 6 in this volume.

Arrow, K. J. (1970). *Essays in the Theory of Risk-Bearing.* Amsterdam: North-Holland.

Debreu, G. (1953). "Une économie de l'incertain." Paris: Electricité de France, mimeographed.

Debreu, G. (1959). *Theory of Value.* New York: Wiley; New Haven: Yale University Press.

Green, J. (1973). "Information, efficiency, and equilibrium." Harvard Institute of Economic Research, Discussion Paper no. 284.

Grossman, S. (1976). "On the efficiency of competitive stock markets where traders have diverse information." *Journal of Finance* 31:573–585.

Grossman, S., and Stiglitz, J. (1976). "Information and competitive price systems." *American Economic Review* 66:246–252.

Hirshleifer, J. (1971). "The private and social value of information and the reward to inventive activity." *American Economic Review* 61:561–574.

Kihlstrom, R. E., and Mirman, L. J. (1975). "Information and market equilibrium." *Bell Journal of Economics and Management Science* 6:357–376.

Radner, R. (1968). "Competitive equilibrium under uncertainty." *Econometrica* 36:31–58.

Shubik, M. (1977). "Competitive equilibrium, contingent commodities, and information." *Journal of Finance* 32:189–193.

16   The Property Rights Doctrine and Demand Revelation under Incomplete Information

The conditions under which the price system might not achieve optimal resource allocation have gradually been refined since they were first given reasonably accurate expression by Young (1913) in a review of Pigou's *Wealth and Welfare* (the first edition of what became *The Economics of Welfare*). Landmarks on the way to better understanding were the work of Knight (1924) and that of Scitovsky (1954).

The basic thesis is that the optimal resource allocation will not be achieved by a competitive market system if there are technological externalities. These are goods (or bads) for which no market can be formed. The usual reason given is that the good is not property in law or in practice, the latter covering the cases in which the act of enforcing property rights is itself costly and may therefore not be worthwhile. An excellent survey of market failure and its implications is to be found in Bator (1958).

A conclusion which is usually drawn from the presence of externalities not mediated through competitive markets is that the state has to intervene in some form to improve resource allocation, whether in the form of taxes and subsidies or other regulatory forms. Such were the recommendations of Pigou (1952) after he had absorbed Young's critique; an enthusiastic formulation is that of Baumol (1952).

A recent counterattack has been that of the so-called property rights school, starting with the well-known and important paper of Coase (1960)

Reprinted from *Economics and Human Welfare,* ed. M. Boskin (New York: Academic Press, 1979), pp. 23–39.

and including the work of Buchanan, McKean, and others, as surveyed by Furubotn and Pejovich (1972). They start with the position, common to all, that market failures are associated with lack of definition of property rights. However, they then argue that in principle clear definition of property rights is sufficient to ensure efficiency. This position goes well beyond the standard neoclassical position that competitive markets suffice for efficiency. As is well known, defined property rights are only one of the necessary conditions for competitive markets; large numbers (actual or potential) of buyers and sellers, concavity of the production possibility sets, and informed buyers are others. Scitovsky (1951, chaps. 15 and 16) has given the classic characterization of competitive markets as means of achieving efficiency.

The property rights theorists do not usually set out their underlying assumptions with the utmost clarity; but it appears that the basic postulate is the same one that underlies the theory of cooperative games, in the original formulation of von Neumann and Morgenstern (1947, chaps. 5, 6, and 10) and virtually all later developments (see, for example, Luce and Raiffa, 1957, chaps. 6, 8, and 9). That is, whatever else may be true about the outcome of the bargaining process, it will certainly be Pareto-optimal. The argument is obvious. Suppose A and B are both possible outcomes of the game, achievable by suitable choices of strategies by the players. Suppose the players can bargain about the choices of strategies, including possible side payments, and suppose that every player prefers A to B. Then clearly they will not stop at B, since, if nothing else is achievable, they can all improve by going to A.

What is not always recognized is that this argument depends crucially on the unstated assumption that every player knows every other player's payoff (utility, profit, whatever) as a function of the strategies played. In the case of bargaining over externalities, the strategies might be offers and counteroffer strategies, that is, plans beforehand to make a counteroffer as a function of the initial offer. If player I misperceives the payoff function of player II, then he or she may make an offer judged to be Pareto-superior to the initial position but not in fact superior in player II's payoff function. Thus, getting stuck at a Pareto-dominated point is no longer impossible.

In the traditional smoke case, suppose the landowners in the neighborhood of a factory own the property rights to clean air. (The opposite assignment of property rights leads to a similar analysis, and discussion is omitted.) The factory owner must buy out the rights from all landowners before he can emit smoke. Each landowner has a reservation price for permitting smoke. Efficiency implies that the smoke be emitted if and only if the pure profits of the factory owner exceed the sum of the reservation prices of the landowners. It would appear that a mutually advantageous bargain will achieve the efficient allocation.

But the factory owner does not know the reservation prices of the landowners. If the land is used for residential purposes, then the reservation price is determined by the indifference surfaces of the residents, clearly private information. If the land is used for production, then the reservation price depends on the effect of smoke on productivity, and it is an essential virtue of decentralized private enterprise that businesses do not know in detail each others' production functions. By the same token, the landowners do not know the value of smoke emission to the factory owner; and, what is at least as important, no landowner knows the reservation prices of the other landowners. (A landowner might infer the reservation price of another landowner who was visibly identical to him in circumstances, by assuming it was the same as his own; but to the extent that landowners vary in land use and location relative to the factory, their mutual knowledge of reservation prices becomes correspondingly hazy.)

Consider, then, how bargaining might proceed. The factory owner might make an offer to each landowner. Since he does not know the reservation prices of the landowners, the offer might well be rejected by some as below the reservation price. This, by itself, is only a difficulty in the adjustment process, for the factory owner has now acquired information about the reservation prices. But a more serious problem is that a landowner might reject the offer even if it is above his reservation price, to convey the idea that it is still higher, for he knows that the factory owner cannot be sure of the deception. In turn, knowing this possibility means that the factory owner cannot draw any inference from a refusal.

Suppose instead that the landowners initiate the offers. Independently of the others, each landowner states a price at which he is willing to yield his rights to clean air. Even if, and perhaps especially if, each landowner has a fairly good idea of the factory owner's profits and of the reservation prices of others, he will be tempted to set a price much higher than his true reservation price. Each one will attempt to garner for himself the entire surplus in the economy, the excess of the producer's profits over the sum of the reservation prices (assuming it is positive and large relative to any one landowner's reservation price). Indeed, precisely this situation actually occurs in land assembly, where a large plot of contiguous land is needed, and the odd shapes of some department stores and office buildings testify mutely to failures to achieve efficient resource allocation.

The second case brings out more fully the essential identity between the achievement of efficiency through bargaining and the well-known "free-rider" problem in efficient allocation of resources to public goods. In the second case, each landowner may be tempted to ask for much more than his reservation price, relying on the others not to ask too much; similarly, in the public goods case, each may be tempted to understate his benefits if his taxes are related to his statement.

This connection reminds us of the recent literature which suggests the possibility of overcoming the free-rider problem by appropriate incentives (Clarke, 1971; Groves and Loeb, 1975; Green and Laffont, 1977a,b). These incentives have been referred to as achieving "demand revelation" (the term is due to Tideman and Tullock, 1976, who give a most spirited interpretation and an argument for practical implementation).

The dominant theme in this work has been the search for strategy-proof incentive structures. The agents are supposed to send messages which reflect or purport to reflect their valuations. In addition to the initial resource allocation problem, a system of rewards and penalties as functions of the messages is created; the resulting game is supposed to be such that the message sent by an agent reflects only his valuations and is independent of his guesses as to the evaluations of others. If the preference orderings of the agents over the possible outcomes are unrestricted a priori, then indeed there is no possible mechanism which will guarantee strategy-proof behavior, as brilliantly shown by Gibbard (1973) and, independently, by Satterthwaite (1975). However, strategy-proof procedures may be possible if the orderings are restricted, for example, by the assumption that there are no income effects, so that any rewards or penalties are additive to the results of the bargaining procedure. This assumption is in fact the basis of most of the demand-revelation literature and will be made here.

(There is a close relation between the existence of strategy-proof procedures and the existence of social welfare functions. In fact, as shown by Maskin, 1976, chap. 3, the two problems are essentially equivalent, in that an a priori restriction on the agents' preferences which permits one problem to be solved also permits the other to be solved.)

The demand-revelation procedures do indeed yield efficient decisions, with, however, a curious qualification. The decision made is indeed efficient, but the rewards and penalties do not in general add up to zero; to ensure against infeasibility, it is in general necessary to permit resources to go to waste, in the sense that the sum of the penalties exceeds the sum of the rewards. Green and Laffont (1977a) have shown that this lack of balance is necessary.

I wish to suggest a different approach to demand revelation, which achieves efficiency and avoids the waste of resources in the incentive payments. As might be expected, it makes stronger assumptions, in this case assumptions about the expectations that each agent has about the others' valuations.

In the next section I will exhibit one possible formalization of the bargaining process which would lead to efficient allocation when the agents know each others' utility functions. The third section illustrates how efficiency fails to be achieved when this knowledge is absent. In the fourth section the general approach to demand revelation under incomplete information will be discussed. In the fifth section I show how this approach can be used to develop a demand-revealing game for which truthful revelation is a local equilibrium point (in the sense of Nash) and for which all the side-payments balance. The final section is supplementary; it shows that the utilitarian criterion ensures that the collective decision rule has a responsiveness property assumed in the fifth section.

A Formalization of Bargaining

We are accustomed to proofs of the optimality of allocation resulting from the market under a competitive price regime. The rules of the system in equilibrium are well defined, and the propositions clearly stated. What is meant by an assertion, whether by Coase or by von Neumann and Morgenstern, that unrestricted bargaining with well-defined property rights will lead to efficient allocation? What are the rules of the game and how do we determine its outcome?

We have to describe bargaining as a series of permitted moves and then an equilibrium concept which determines when no agent will wish to change his or her strategy. This turns out to be a difficult task, and most proposed solutions have some unsatisfactory qualities.

In game-theoretic language, the problem is to devise a noncooperative game whose equilibrium point (in the sense of Nash) is an efficient allocation of resources. Thus, each agent will have the right to change unilaterally, but the game is so devised that at some efficient allocation no agent will in fact find it preferable to change.

I confine discussion to the case of two agents, Estragon (E) and Vladimir (V). To simplify further, assume that there is only one private good and one public good (or externality-producing activity). Suppose first that the public good is resource-using. Let x_E be the amount of the private good going to Estragon, x_V the amount of the private good going to Vladimir, and y the amount of the public good. Total initial resources are w, and there is no production. An allocation, then, is feasible if and only if

(16-1) $x_E + x_V + y = w$.

Assume that the two individuals can have any feasible allocation they agree to. If they do not agree, suppose that there is no public good ($y = 0$) and that each keeps his initial stock of the resource for private use, $x_E = w_E$ and $x_V = w_V$, where w_i is the initial resource holding of agent i ($i = E, V$). We shall refer to the allocation ($w_E, w_V, 0$) as the disagreement payoff and denote it by A^d.

Let $U^i(x_i, y)$ be the utility of agent i if he receives x_i of the private good and the amount of the public good is y. An efficient resource allocation then satisfies the well-known Samuelson condition that the sum of the marginal rates of substitution of the public good for the private for the two individuals equals 1:

(16-2) $$\frac{\partial U^E}{\partial x_E} \bigg/ \frac{\partial U^E}{\partial y} + \frac{\partial U^V}{\partial x_V} \bigg/ \frac{\partial U^V}{\partial y} = 1.$$

Equations (16-1) and (16-2) constitute two equations in the three unknowns, x_E, x_V, y, and define the Pareto frontier. However, because of initial holdings, the contract curve is restricted in addition to the allocations which satisfy the conditions of *individual rationality*,

(16-3) $U^i(x_i, y) \geq U^i(w_i, 0)$,   ($i = E, V$);

that is, no agreement will make any individual worse off than he could be without agreement. Note that the disagreement payoff A^d satisfies these conditions by definition.

Consider now the following simple procedure. Estragon proposes an allocation, that is, x_E, x_V, and y, satisfying the feasibility condition (16-1). Vladimir can accept or reject it. Suppose that Estragon knows Vladimir's utility function. Vladimir will accept if and only if the proposed allocation is individually rational from his point of view. Then clearly Estragon's optimal strategy will be to choose that allocation which maximizes his utility subject to the constraints

(16-4) $x_E + x_V + y = w$, $U^V(x_V, y) \geq U^V(w_V, 0)$.

In general, the optimal allocation to Estragon subject to (16-4) will be better for him than the disagreement point ($w_E, 0$), and therefore he will not choose an allocation which will be rejected by Vladimir, while among those which

Vladimir will accept, Estragon will, of course, choose the best from his viewpoint.[1]

The outcome of this procedure is clearly Pareto-efficient by definition, since it maximizes the utility of one agent for a given level of utility for the other. Hence, there is a game whose equilibrium is Pareto-efficient. The outcome, it must be noted, is not the competitive equilibrium.

The Failure of Bargaining under Privacy

One of the virtues of decentralization is the respect for privacy. The utility functions of different individuals cannot easily be known to each other. Indeed, since they have meaning only in terms of observable behavior, there may be no way of transmitting utility functions from one agent to another. There is in general no way of forcing an individual to reveal his utility function; if he knows that this knowledge will be used in some allocation process, what he will transmit will or at least can be designed to affect that allocation favorably to him.

Let us analyze the outcome of the procedure of the last section with one additional complication: Estragon does not know for sure what Vladimir's utility function is. More specifically, suppose that it could be one of two utility functions, $U_a^V(x_V,y)$ or $U_b^V(x_V,y)$, and Estragon does not know which.

---

1. Wilson (1978) has given a procedure for any number of economic agents which will achieve efficient allocation by means of a noncooperative game; the procedure above is the special case of Wilson's when there are but two agents.

The procedure given in the text is not quite standard in game theory. The game has been described in so-called extensive form. It is usual to reduce games to normal form, in which each agent describes his potential behavior at any point for every possible history of the game up to that point. These descriptions or *strategies* are thought of as chosen simultaneously at the beginning of the game. Then the equilibrium point is a choice of strategy by each agent such that neither could gain by changing if the other player does not change. In the game described above, Vladimir's strategy, in this sense, would be a statement describing which allocations he would accept if offered by Estragon. But then if he should choose a strategy of accepting only one allocation, Estragon's optimal strategy in reply would be to make that offer if it is at least as good for him as the disagreement allocation; and given that offer, Vladimir should announce that he would accept it if it is at least as good for *him* as the disagreement allocation. Hence, any individually rational allocation could be achieved as an equilibrium in this sense.

In the text, and in the work of Wilson (1978), the last player is not allowed to formulate a strategy in advance but rather is required to accept or reject previous offers on the basis of a comparison with the disagreement allocation. This concept of equilibrium, in which the second player is optimizing given all previous history, has been termed a *perfect* equilibrium by Selten (1975); it is the game-theoretic counterpart of the principle of optimality in dynamic programming.

Let us go further, and represent his uncertainty by an assignment of probabilities; Vladimir's utility function is U_a^V with probability p_a, U_b^V with probability p_b, $p_a + p_b = 1$. These probabilities may be regarded as objective facts or as subjective probabilities of Estragon's.

Now consider Estragon's choice problem. If he chooses a feasible allocation (x_E, x_V, y) which Vladimir would accept for either utility function, then the probability of acceptance would be one. Clearly, among such allocations, Estragon would choose the best from his point of view. Hence, one possible candidate for his choice would be

$$(16\text{-}5) \qquad A^* = (x_E^*, x_V^*, y^*) \quad \text{maximizes} \quad U^E(x_E, y)$$
$$\text{subject to} \quad x_E + x_V + y = w,$$
$$U_a^V(x_V, y) \geq U_a^V(w_V, 0),$$
$$U_b^V(x_V, y) \geq U_b^V(w_V, 0).$$

Another possibility would be to consider a broader class of feasible allocations, those which Vladimir would choose if his utility function were U_a^V. Again, among these, Vladimir would choose that one which maximizes his utility. This allocation might happen to satisfy also the condition that $U_b^V(x_V, y) \geq U_b^V(w_V, 0)$, in which case it would be the allocation A^*. If we disregard this possibility, we have another candidate for Estragon's choice,

$$(16\text{-}6) \qquad A^a = (x_E^a, x_V^a, y^a) \quad \text{maximizes} \quad U^E(x_E, y)$$
$$\text{subject to} \quad x_E + x_V + y = w,$$
$$U_a^V(x_V, y) \geq U_a^V(w_V, 0).$$

Note that Estragon will prefer this policy to any other which is rational for Vladimir under U_a^V because, if rejected, the payoff to Estragon is independent of the offer. Since the probability of acceptance is p_a, the expected utility of Estragon is

$$(16\text{-}7) \qquad p_a U^E(x_E^a, y^a) + p_b U^E(w_E, 0).$$

Symmetrically, of course, Estragon can choose an allocation which would be acceptable to Vladimir if his utility function were U_b^V. He would choose the best:

$$(16\text{-}8) \qquad A^b = (x_E^b, x_V^b, y^b) \quad \text{maximizes} \quad U^E(x_E, y)$$
$$\text{subject to} \quad x_E + x_V + y = w,$$
$$U_b^V(x_V, y) \geq U_b^V(w_V, 0),$$

and the expected return to him would be

$$(16\text{-}9) \qquad p_a U^E(w_E, 0) + p_b U^E(x_E^b, y^b).$$

Finally, Estragon could, if it were desirable, choose an allocation which Vladimir would reject whether his utility function were U_a^V or U_b^V. But Estragon would know that the disagreement allocation would result, an allocation he could also obtain by offering it, since it would satisfy all the individual rationality conditions for Vladimir. In that case, he would do at least as well by choosing A^*, so that we can assume that Estragon will always choose an allocation which satisfies Vladimir's individual rationality condition for at least one possible utility function.

Estragon then chooses that one of the three allocations A^*, A^a, A^b which makes his expected utility as large as possible; the expected utility of A^* to him is $U^E(x_E^*,y^*)$, since there is no uncertainty in that case, while the expected utilities of A^a and A^b are given by (16-7) and (16-9), respectively. Given all values of the utilities, the choice depends on p_a, being A^a if p_a is sufficiently large, A^b if it is sufficiently small; there may also be an intermediate range in which A^* is chosen.[2]

If A^a is offered and in fact Vladimir's utility function is U_a^V, the allocation will be Pareto-efficient. But there is a probability p_b that the disagreement allocation will be the equilibrium. Hence the system cannot guarantee efficiency; indeed, p_b might easily be nontrivial and the inefficiency of the disagreement point very considerable. Similarly, if A^b is offered, there is a probability p_a of winding up at the disagreement allocation. Finally, A^* is inefficient whichever utility function Vladimir has; hence, if it is offered, there will be inefficiency with probability 1.

Thus, it can be seen that a procedure which would achieve a Pareto-efficient allocation if each agent knew the other's utility function will have a positive probability of falling short of efficiency if this knowledge is absent.

Bargaining as a Game of Incomplete Information

The game analyzed in the last section is one of incomplete information in the sense introduced in an important series of papers by Harsanyi (1967–68). It can be reduced to a game in standard form by introducing, for each

---

2. For those interested in the detailed results, it will be easy to verify the following statements. Define $V^a = U^E(x_E^a,y^a) - U^E(w_E,0)$, $V^b = U^E(x_E^b,y^b) - U^E(w_E,0)$, $V^* = U^E(w_E^*,y^*) - U^E(w_E,0)$. Let $\bar{V}$ be half the harmonic mean of V^a and V^b. Then there are two cases: (1) if $V^* > \bar{V}$, then Estragon chooses allocation A^a if $p_a > V^*/V^a$, A^b if $p_a < 1 - (V^*/V^b)$, and A^* in the intermediate range; (2) if $V^* < \bar{V}$, then A^* is not chosen for any value of p_a, while A^a is chosen if $p_a > V^a/(V^a + V^b)$, and A^b otherwise.

agent, a chance move which determines his utility function, the outcome of the move being revealed to him but not to other agents. (In the particular game just discussed, uncertainty about Estragon's utility function is irrelevant, since Vladimir has to respond passively to Estragon's proposal; but in general, allocation games will be more symmetric.) The probabilities of different utility functions are part of the rules of the game and are known to both (or, more generally, all) agents. It might be asked why Vladimir, who comes to know his own utility function, has to know the ex ante probabilities; in the particular game in fact he does not have to know, but more generally, he should know what probabilities about his utility functions are in Estragon's mind.

The question to be posed is the following: Can we find a set of rules, a game, in which each agent is to announce his or her utility function, the allocation of resources is a function of the announcements, and the rewards are such as to induce each to announce truly? The answer to be demonstrated here is that such a game can be devised if (1) income effects are neglected, and (2) the probabilities of different possible utility functions for the agents are known and are independent of each other.[3]

It should be remarked that there has been a shift from revelation of indifference maps to revelation of utility functions. The reason is that once probabilities are introduced, the aim of each agent in the bargaining game is to maximize *expected* utility according to the conventional Bernoulli– Ramsey–von Neumann-Morgenstern hypothesis. The results will not be invariant under monotone transformations of the utility functions, since such transformations alter attitudes toward risk bearing.

The absence of income effects means that the utility function is linear in income (and therefore, in particular, implies risk neutrality toward income). This is a serious limitation, though one that is common to the entire demand-revelation literature.

More specifically, we model the making of a public decision, a variable x in some domain. (The decision might include the allocation of private goods, but it is the choice of public goods and externalities that is most in mind here.) Agent i has a utility function for the decision; the form of this

---

3. After working out the ideas to be presented, I found that the representation of incentives for satisfactory bargaining as a game of incomplete information had already been used by d'Aspremont and Gerard-Varet (1975). The ideas are essentially the same; their utility functions, arising out of a pollution problem, are more specialized, and this fact permits some simplification.

function is known to all up to some parameters which are private. Let p_i be the parameters of the ith agent; his utility function then is $U^i(x,p_i)$. Individual i has a net increment of income t_i (which may be negative); then his utility is $U^i(x,p_i) + t_i$. Since there could be infinitely many parameters, the restriction of the utility functions U^i to a class of known form in unknown parameters is no real restriction.

Each individual makes an announcement of his parameter values, which may or may not be true. For example, in a pollution problem, the manufacturer may announce the unit cost of antipollution measures to him while the neighbor announces the damage due to unit pollution. If the issue is whether or not to build a bridge, each agent may be asked to announce the value to him of the bridge. Let r_i be the announcement by agent i.

There is specified a rule for making the decision as a function of the announcements, $x(r_1, \ldots ,r_n)$, where n is the number of agents. At the moment we leave the rule unspecified; it might be derived on the hypothesis of maximizing the sum of the agents' utilities on the assumption that their announcements are true, a case that will be considered in the last section.

Each agent i has a probability distribution over the true parameter values of other agents. Let p^i be the parameters of all individuals other than individual i: $p^i = (p_1, \ldots ,p_{i-1},p_{i+1}, \ldots ,p_n)$. Suppose the ith agent assumes that everyone else will tell the truth (he does not, of course, know what those parameters are but knows their distribution). If he announces r_i, then the social decision is $x(r_i,p^i)$. In the absence of any money transfers, his utility will be $U^i(x(r_i,p^i),p_i)$; but, since he does not know p^i, he would be induced to maximize

(16-10) $E_{p^i}[U^i(x(r_i,p^i),p_i)]$,

where, as the notation indicates, the expectation is taken over p^i. One would like to see that $r_i = p_i$ for all p_i; that is, we would like to have individual i be induced to reveal his private parameters truthfully if everyone else did so. If this held for all i, truth telling would be an equilibrium point of the game.

There is no reason so far for truth telling, as we well know from the literature on the free-rider problem in the theory of public goods. The demand-revelation literature suggests that we modify the payoff to individual i by assessing a change in income as a function of his announcement. Specifically, we will prescribe a function $T_i(r_i)$ for each individual, which is the amount he pays if he makes the announcement r_i. This income has to go somewhere; it would be inefficient to throw it out if positive, and there is no source to supply it if negative. Hence, we add a specification that the income dispensed by one agent is paid out to all other agents. That is, we specify functions, $T_{ij}(r_j)$, the amount paid by individual j to individual i if j's announcement is r_j. These functions are defined only if $i \neq j$, of course. By definition,

(16-11) $\quad \sum_{i \neq j} T_{ij}(r_j) = T_j(r_j).$

From the viewpoint of individual i, then, his utility is decreased by his payments, $T_i(r_i)$, and increased by the payments made to him by others, $\Sigma_{j \neq i} T_{ij}(r_j)$. Therefore, once the functions T_i, T_{ij} satisfying (16-11) are selected, and each agent chooses his announcement r_i, the net payoff to individual i is

(16-12) $\quad U^i(x(r),\rho_i) - T_i(r_i) + \sum_{j \neq i} T_{ij}(r_j),$

where $r = (r_1, \ldots, r_n)$. Each agent must choose an announcement r_i for each possible value of the parameters ρ_i; that is, a *strategy* for i is a function $r_i(\rho_i)$. Once the strategies are selected by the agents, the expected utility to agent i is the expected value of (16-12) over the parameters of other agents, ρ^i. Let r^i be the announcements of agents other than i, and $r^i(\rho^i)$ the strategies of agents other than i. Then agent i's expected utility is

(16-13) $\quad E_{\rho^i}\{U^i[x(r_i(\rho_i),r^i(\rho^i),\rho_i]\} - T_i(r_i(\rho_i)) + E_{\rho^i}\left[\sum_{j \neq i} T_{ij}(r_j(\rho_j))\right].$

An equilibrium point is a specification of a strategy $r_i(\rho_i)$ for each agent, such that if every agent $i \neq j$ chooses $r_j(\rho_j)$, then (16-13) is maximized for agent i by the choice of the strategy $r_i(\rho_i)$. This is the same as saying that, for each particular value of ρ_i, the corresponding value of the strategy $r_i(\rho_i)$ maximizes (16-13).

The Demand-Revelation Game

A truth-telling strategy is given by $r_i(\rho_i) \equiv \rho_i$ (that is, identically in ρ_i). A truth-telling equilibrium is one in which each agent is playing a truth-telling strategy. Our problem is to find functions T_i, T_{ij} so that truth telling is an equilibrium.

Define $F^i(r_i,\rho_i)$ to be the expected payoff to agent i, when all other agents are telling the truth. This is defined by setting $r_j(\rho_j) \equiv \rho_j$ in (16-13); for a given ρ_i, we also replace $r_i(\rho_i)$ by r_i:

(16-14) $\quad F^i(r_i,\rho_i) = E_{\rho^i}[U^i(x(r_i,\rho^i),\rho_i)] - T_i(r_i) + E_{\rho^i}\left[\sum_{j \neq i} T_{ij}(\rho_j)\right].$

At an equilibrium, agent i chooses r_i to maximize $F^i(r_i, p_i)$. Assume now differentiability of all relevant functions, and also assume that the optimum choice is not a boundary. Also, for simplicity, assume that p_i, and therefore r_i, are one-dimensional variables; this restriction is solely expository and can be removed with only notational changes. Then r_i satisfies the condition $\partial F^i / \partial r_i = 0$. This condition in fact defines r_i for each value of p_i and therefore defines the strategy $r_i(p_i)$. Since the last term in (16-14) is independent of r_i, optimal behavior for agent i is defined by

(16-15) $E_{p^i}[U_x^i(x(r_i, p^i), p_i) x_{r_i}(r_i, p^i)] - T_i'(r_i) = 0.$

To have a truth-telling equilibrium, the solution of (16-15) in r_i should be p_i for all p_i. That is, (16-15) should hold with r_i replaced by p_i for all p_i:

$$T_i'(p_i) = E_{p^i}[U_x^i(x(p_i, p^i), p_i) x_{r_i}(p_i, p^i)]$$

for all p_i, or, if we replace the variable p_i by the variable r_i,

(16-16) $T_i'(r_i) = E_{p^i}[U_x^i(x(r_i, p^i), r_i) x_{r_i}(r_i, p^i)]$

for all r_i.

Equation (16-16) supplies a complete solution of the problem, if one exists. It defines the function $T_i(r_i)$, up to an irrelevant constant of integration. The right-hand side is well defined by the conditions of the problem. The transfer function T_{ij} does not affect the behavior of any individual and therefore can be chosen arbitrarily, subject to the condition that the transfer to all other individuals equals the payment required; see (16-11).

The right-hand side has a simple interpretation. If the true value of the parameter p_i is in fact equal to the announcement, then a perturbation dr_i in the announcement will change the social decision by $x_{r_i} dr_i$ and will therefore change the individual's utility by $U_x^i x_{r_i} dr_i$. This product depends, however, on the true values of other individuals' parameters p^i; hence, from agent i's point of view, he must consider the expected marginal utility. The payment function T_i has to be fixed to just offset any resulting incentive to change from r_i to $r_i + dr_i$.

Thus, each agent will find that truth telling satisfies the first-order conditions for a maximum. We must, however, check to see that the second-order conditions are also satisfied.

The derivative $\partial F^i / \partial r_i = F_{r_i}^i(r_i, p_i)$ is given by the left-hand side of (16-15). By our construction of T_i, we know that $F_{r_i}^i(r_i, p_i) = 0$ when $r_i = p_i$, that is,

$$F_{r_i}^i(r_i, r_i) \equiv 0$$

identically in r_i. Total differentiation with respect to r_i yields

(16-17) $\quad F^i_{r_i r_i}(r_i, r_i) + F^i_{r_i \rho_i}(r_i, r_i) \equiv 0.$

In order that truth telling be optimum for individual i, given that all others are telling the truth, it is necessary that the first- and second-order conditions for a maximum in r_i be satisfied at $r_i = \rho_i$, that is, that $F^i_{r_i}(\rho_i, \rho_i) = 0$, which is guaranteed by construction, and that $F^i_{r_i r_i}(\rho_i, \rho_i) < 0$. Since these conditions must hold for all ρ_i, we can replace ρ_i by r_i and require that they hold for all r_i. From (16-17), then, we require that $F^i_{r_i \rho_i}(r_i, r_i) > 0$ for all r_i.

In (16-14), note that the second and third terms are independent of ρ_i. If we differentiate (16-14) with respect to ρ_i and that derivative with respect to r_i and set $\rho_i = r_i$, we find that the second-order condition for individual i to have a truth-telling optimum is

$$E_{\rho i}[U^i_{x\rho_i}(x(r_i, \rho^i), r_i) x_{r_i}(r_i, \rho^i)] > 0.$$

This means that, on the average, for any given values of the utility function parameters of the others, if an individual is telling the truth, a shift in his parameter changes the amount of the public good, through the collective decision rule, and the marginal utility of the public good to him in the same direction. This is a minimum condition for the collective decision rule to represent positively the desires of the economic agents.

We can restate our results formally.

DEFINITION 1. *A collective decision rule is a function which determines the amount of the public good for any specification of the utility function parameters of the economic agents.*

DEFINITION 2. *A collective decision rule is said to be responsive if, for any given individual, a shift in his parameter changes on the average his marginal utility for the public good and the amount of the public good in the same direction. More precisely, the expected value of the product of these changes, averaged over the utility function parameters of others, is positive.*

THEOREM 1. *Suppose*

(a) *there are no income effects so that agent i has a utility function in the public good and other income of the form $U^i(x, \rho_i) +$ (other income);*

(b) *the form of the utility function is known to all, but the value of ρ_i is known only to the agent i;*

(c) *each agent has a probability distribution over the utility function parameters of others which is independent of his own parameter value;*

(d) *the collective decision rule is responsive.*

Consider the following social decision procedure. Each individual chooses a strategy which associates to each possible value of his parameter an announced value of the parameter. The public good quantity is determined by the collective decision rule as a function of the announced values of the parameters. Finally, there are specified functions $T_{ij}(r_j)$ ($i \neq j$) which specify amount of income paid by agent j to agent i as a function of j's announcement r_j of his utility parameter. These functions satisfy the condition

(16-18) $$\sum_{i \neq j} T_{ij}(r_j) = \int E_{\rho^j}[U_x^j(x(r_j,\rho^j),r_j)x_{r_j}(r_j,\rho^j)]dr_j.$$

Then the truth-telling strategies, $r_i(\rho_i) \equiv \rho_i$, form a local equilibrium point of the social decision procedure.

Remark 1. By a local equilibrium point is meant that, given that others tell the truth, agent i will find that for each value of ρ_i, the action $r_i = \rho_i$ is a local maximum. Examination of the second-order conditions cannot by itself show that the action is globally optimal for the agent.

Remark 2. Condition (16-18) is simply a restatement of (16-16), with i replaced by j and condition (16-11) substituted in. The constant of integration in (16-18) can be chosen arbitrarily.

The Utilitarian Decision Rule

I have so far only required that the collective decision rule be responsive. A natural condition is that the collective decision rule be defined by the condition that the amount of the public good be such as to maximize the sum of individuals' utilities. This rule is especially plausible if we maintain the assumption that utility is linear in money, for then the sum of utilities is the money value of net benefits. This rule will in fact imply that the collective decision rule is responsive if the utility functions are concave in the public good.

We are requiring that $x(r_1, \ldots, r_n)$ be defined as the value of x which maximizes the sum of utilities on the assumption that announcements are true:

(16-19) $x(r)$ maximizes $\sum_{i=1}^{n} U^i(x,r_i),$

where $r = (r_1, \ldots, r_n)$. Then $x(r)$ satisfies the identity in r,

$$\sum_{i=1}^{n} U_x^i(x(r),r_i) \equiv 0.$$

Partial differentiation with respect to r_i yields

$$\left[\sum_{i=1}^{n} U^i_{xx}(x(r),r_i)\right] x_{r_i}(r) + U^i_{xr_i}(x(r),r_i) \equiv 0.$$

Multiply through by $x_{r_i}(r)$:

$$\left[\sum_{i=1}^{n} U^i_{xx}(x(r),r_i)\right][(x_{r_i}(r)]^2 + U^i_{xr_i}(x(r),x_{r_i}(r) \equiv 0.$$

But, because U^i is assumed concave in x for each i, the first term is in general negative, so that the second term must be positive. But this certainly implies that x is a responsive collective choice rule.[4]

THEOREM 2. *If the collective choice rule x(r) is defined so as to maximize the sum of the agents' utilities, then it is responsive.*

References

Arrow, K. J., and Scitovsky, T., eds. (1969). *Readings in Welfare Economics.* Homewood, Ill.: Richard D. Irwin.

Bator, F. (1958). The Anatomy of Market Failure, *Quarterly Journal of Economics* 72, 351–379.

Baumol, W. J. (1952). *Welfare Economics and the Theory of the State.* Cambridge, Mass.: Harvard University Press.

Clarke, E. (1971). Multipart Pricing of Public Goods, *Public Choice* 11, 17–33.

Coase, R. H. (1960). The Problem of Social Cost, *Journal of Law and Economics,* 3, 1–44.

d'Aspremont, C., and Gerard-Varet, L. (1975). Incentives and Incomplete Information. CORE discussion paper (unpublished).

Furubotn, E., and Pejovich, S. (1972). Property Rights and Economic Theory: A Survey of Recent Literature, *Journal of Economic Literature* 10, 1137–1162.

Gibbard, A. (1973). Manipulation of Voting Schemes: A General Result, *Econometrica* 41, 587–602.

Green, J., and Laffont, J. (1977a). Characterization of Satisfactory Mechanisms for the Revelation of Preferences for Public Goods, *Econometrica* 45, 427–438.

Green, J., and Laffont, J. (1977b). Révélation des préférences pour les biens publics, *Cahiers du Séminaire d'Econometrie* 19, 83–103.

Groves, T., and Loeb, M. (1975). Incentives and Public Outputs, *Journal of Public Finance* 4, 211–226.

---

4. Laffont and Maskin (1978), in some unpublished work, have shown that the utilitarian rule actually implies that truth telling is a global equilibrium point in this game; that is, if everyone else is telling the truth, then truth telling is a global maximum strategy. They have also shown the close connections between the revelation mechanism developed here and the Groves mechanism and its generalization.

Harsanyi, J. (1967–68). Games with Incomplete Information Played by "Bayesian" Players, I–III, *Management Science* 14, 159–182, 320–334, 486–502.

Knight, F. H. (1924). Some Fallacies in the Interpretation of Social Cost, *Quarterly Journal of Economics* 38, 582–606. (Reprinted in Arrow and Scitovsky, 1969, pp. 213–227.)

Laffont, J., and Maskin, E. (1978). A Differential Approach to Expected Utility Maximizing Mechanisms, Notes, Groupe de Travail, Economie de l'Information, Ecole Polytechnique, Paris (unpublished).

Luce, R. D., and Raiffa, H. (1957). *Games and Decisions.* New York: Wiley.

Maskin, E. (1976). Social Choice on Restricted Domains, Ph.D. dissertation in Applied Mathematics, Harvard University.

Pigou, A. C. (1952). *The Economics of Welfare,* 4th ed. London: Macmillan.

Satterthwaite, M. A. (1975). Strategy-Proofness and Arrow's Conditions: Existence and Correspondence Theorems for Voting Procedures and Social Welfare Functions, *Journal of Economic Theory* 10, 187–217.

Scitovsky, T. (1951). *Welfare and Competition.* Chicago, Ill.: Richard D. Irwin.

Scitovsky, T. (1954). Two Concepts of External Economies, *Journal of Political Economy* 62, 143–151. (Reprinted in Arrow and Scitovsky, 1969, pp. 242–252.)

Selten, R. (1975). Reexamination of the Perfectness Concept for Equilibrium Points in Extensive Games, *International Journal of Game Theory* 4, 25–55.

Tideman, N., and Tullock, G. (1976). A New and Superior Process for Making Social Choices, *Journal of Political Economy* 84, 1145–1160.

von Neumann, J., and Morgenstern, O. (1947). *Theory of Games and Economic Behavior,* 2nd ed. Princeton, N.J.: Princeton University Press.

Wilson, R. (1978). A Competitive Model of Exchange, *Econometrica* 46, 577–585.

Young, A. (1913). Pigou's *Wealth and Welfare, Quarterly Journal of Economics* 27, 672–686.

17 Allocation of Resources in Large Teams

For a number of years I have given a course on the economics of information and organization, both at Harvard and at Stanford. One year I examined in detail the work of Roy Radner on teams with quadratic payoffs and normal disturbances, under alternative assumptions about the conditions of communication. I realized that his results had strong implications for the value of communication, for his work showed that the differences between two communication systems, one clearly stronger than the other, vanished if the number of units became large. There were some other implications that were unacceptable. I developed in class a new model that avoided some of the difficulties in Radner's. At this point Radner came to visit for a year at Harvard, and we jointly developed the chapter that follows.

One of the oldest themes in economics is the use of the market in the coordination of widespread and diverse but interdependent activities. The underlying situation may be taken to be one of optimal resource allocation, that is, the maximum achievement of some objective subject to constraints on the resources used. Under suitable hypotheses of convexity and differentiability, it is well known that optimality conditions can be stated in terms of

This chapter was written with Roy Radner. Reprinted from *Econometrica,* 47 (1979):361 – 385.

what the economist would call a price system and the mathematician a set of Lagrange parameters.

The constraint system, which represents the technology, may be very complicated indeed, so much so that it is unreasonable to suppose it known to any single individual or available in the memory of even the largest computer. On the other hand, each part of the technology is known to someone, the individual or individuals who have to use that part. Hence, the system as a whole has, in a certain sense, more knowledge than is possessed by any single member.

In a world of dispersed knowledge, obviously the constrained maximization cannot be carried out in the same way as if all the necessary information were concentrated. But the economics of socialism has thrived on the argument that, when production processes are additively separable, then the price system provides a means of arriving at the optimum without any process manager having to transmit a description of his entire production structure. In this model the decisions of the different processes are interdependent only because they compete for the same primary resources, directly or indirectly.

There is a large literature on the validity and limits of this proposition, and we do not wish to enter into that here. We wish rather to emphasize the somewhat implicit calculation of informational costs in the discussion. The price system appears as a process of successive approximations. A tentative price is announced, and the individual processes are supposed to respond with demand for inputs and offers of outputs. Hence at each stage, information is being supplied.

Now it is held to be a great advantage of the price system that the process manager need only transmit a vector instead of a description of the entire production structure. This argument presupposes that transmission of a vector is cheaper than transmission of a production possibility set or of a production function. This is clearly true if nothing is known a priori about the production structure; but as modern communication theory makes clear, the costs of transmission can be greatly reduced if advantage is taken of a priori knowledge. Thus, if a production function is known to be of the Cobb-Douglas form, then it is completely specified by a vector of parameters. Hence, the comparison of complete transmission of production structures with transmission of demands and supplies becomes a comparison of two finite-dimensional vectors.

A third and most important point is that the process of price adjustment requires in principle an infinite number of iterations. Therefore, the total transmission of information may be very large indeed, and it would require a more delicate measurement of communication costs to make clear whether decentralization is indeed superior to centralization.

Team theory (Marschak and Radner, 1972) introduces a new way of looking at the centralization-decentralization choice. On the one hand, it assumes fixed information and communication structures. In the simplest models there is an initial information pattern, which may be followed by one step in which some of this information is transmitted to some (possibly all) agents in the team. On the other hand, team theory relies more heavily on the a priori structure of the information concerning productive possibilities. Following the standard Bayesian approach, it assumes that there is a prior probability distribution over the production structures of all the processes. In the specific examples that have been worked out, a priori assumptions take the form of drawing the production structures from a finite-parameter family, with a probability distribution over the parameters. This prior distribution is known to the team when it is deciding on its decision and communication functions. At any given realization, each process manager knows the parameters which determine his production structure, but not anyone else's. A communication structure then determines that each firm manager transmits some of the parameters to some of the other agents. Each agent now has certain information, and takes the variables he does not observe to be distributed according to the conditional distribution obtained from the prior by conditioning on the information he has.

Suppose the production parameters for the processes are regarded as random drawings from the same distribution. If all information were conveyed to all agents (the equivalent of centralization), the optimal allocation to any agent would be determined by his parameters and by the realized (empirical) distribution of the parameters among the other processes (under suitable assumptions of convexity and symmetry). But if the number of processes is large, then the empirical distribution is essentially the distribution from which the random drawings were made and therefore is known, to a high degree of accuracy, a priori. It is the purpose of this chapter to examine this situation and deduce conditions under which limited communication yields almost as high a return as full communication.

The application of team theory to resource allocation has been developed in Radner (1972) and in Groves and Radner (1972). To represent joint resource constraints, we follow Radner in assuming that there is a resource manager who allocates the scarce resources. For our purposes, we confine ourselves to communication structures in which the process managers convey all their information to the resource manager. If the allocation of scarce resources completely determined the outputs of the individual processes, all such communication structures would be equivalent to complete centralization. However, it is assumed that each process manager must make another decision not subject to joint-resource constraints; for vividness, we call the second decision "labor" as contrasted with "resources." The two decisions are interrelated, in the sense that the production function for each process is not additively separable in the two variables. Then the optimal labor decision for each process depends on the resources allocated to it, and the latter in turn depends on the production parameters of all processes. Hence, it makes a difference whether or not each firm knows the production parameters of all other firms. Accordingly, we compare the payoffs to the following two communication structures: *full exchange of information* (FEI), in which every agent (all process managers and the resource manager) are supplied with the production parameters of every process; and *complete exchange with the center* (CEC), in which each process manager supplies the resource manager with his production parameters but there is no exchange of information among the process managers.

(Radner and Groves also considered two further communication structures, one in which no communication took place and one which turned out, in their context, to be equivalent to CEC. They also considered the possibility that the total resources might be initially uncertain, known in any realization to the resource manager but not to the process managers. In this chapter we do not consider these questions; in particular, total resource supply is assumed known to all a priori.)

Radner assumed that the output of each process was a concave quadratic function of the resource and labor decisions. Only the linear coefficients were uncertain. Among other results, he showed that as the number of firms became large, the difference in payoff between the FEI and CEC communication structures was bounded, but both payoffs were approaching infinity. Hence, he concluded, the value of the additional information in FEI becomes negligible as the number of firms becomes large. A careful look at the payoff formulas shows that these results hold even if total capital is held constant.[1] Now this result is clearly surprising; with limited resources one

---

1. See Radner (1972, eqs. (5.3), (6.6), (6.7), and (7.1), pp. 227, 229, and 231). The formulas have to be read carefully because of some notational assumptions; in effect, Radner's formulas have to be read as the difference in payoff between that with the actual distributions of the parameters and that which would hold if each firm received, with certainty, the mean values of the parameters. Hence, the dispersion of the production parameters is, by itself, producing an unboundedly increasing team output.

should get only finite output. (To be sure, labor is not limited in this model; but if one subtracts the output obtainable from labor in the absence of capital, the difference still approaches infinity with fixed total capital.) The difficulty is that the resource allocations were not constrained to be non-negative. Large differences in the productivity-of-capital parameter between processes could be exploited by giving a negative allocation to the inefficient process and a corresponding positive allocation to the efficient process.

Hence, the specific results of Radner's paper cannot be accepted in a resource allocation context. But, as already seen, the idea that the additional information in FEI over CEC may be unimportant for large numbers of firms is intuitively reasonable. It is the purpose of this chapter to establish this conclusion rigorously.

In the following section we illustrate the problem by a simple case, that in which each process is characterized by fixed coefficients. In the third section the model and its assumptions are presented, and the main result stated. The proof of the main result appears in the fourth section.

In the fifth section we consider the case in which the number of firms is large compared to the total quantities of resources to be centrally allocated. We formalize this by letting the number of firms increase without limit while the vector of total resources remains fixed. In this case, total output will remain bounded; we shall show that the loss in expected *total* output due to using a complete exchange of information with the center, instead of full exchange of information, tends to zero as the number of firms increases.

In the final section we briefly consider the case in which the production parameters of the firms are statistically dependent. In general, full information will remain definitely superior, as measured by expected output per firm, even as the number of firms increases without limit. This is explored by using the concept of an exchangeable sequence of random variables.

An Example

A simple example will serve to illustrate both the formulation of the problem and some of the technical difficulties. Suppose that for each firm there is a single output and two inputs. The first input, the "resource," is centrally allocated by the resource manager, and the second input, "labor," is determined locally by the firm manager. For each firm there is a fixed-coefficient production function. There is also a fixed wage rate for labor, the same for all firms. The "net output" of the firm is

$$(17\text{-}1) \qquad F(k,l,t) = \min{(tk,l)} - wl,$$

where k is the input of the resource, l is the input of labor, t is a parameter that may vary from firm to firm, and w, the wage rate, is a fixed parameter that is the same for all firms. Thus t is the output-resource ratio; it is also the labor-resource ratio if labor resources are used efficiently. Assume that $0 < w < 1$, and that t varies in the unit interval. The inputs k and l must be nonnegative numbers.

Let there be I such firms, with a total quantity $I\kappa$ of the resource to be allocated among them. For simplicity, we take $\kappa = 1$. Let θ_i denote the particular value of the parameter t for firm i. The numbers $\theta_1, \ldots, \theta_I$ are assumed to be independent and identically distributed according to some probability distribution P on the unit interval. The probability distribution P is known to all the managers. We denote by θ^I the I-tuple (θ_i), that is, the "random sample" of firm parameters.

The decision variable of firm manager i is the quantity l_i of his local input. The decision variable of the resource manager is the allocation $(k_1, \ldots, k_I)$ of the resource to the I firms. This allocation must be nonnegative, and the total quantity of the resource allocated must not exceed I, that is,

(17-2) $$\sum_i k_i \le I.$$

The corresponding average net output per firm for the I firms is

(17-3) $$\frac{1}{I} \sum_i F(k_i, l_i, \theta_i).$$

In the case of full exchange of information (FEI), every decision variable is allowed to depend on the complete I-tuple θ^I. If the goal is to maximize the total or average net output, then the optimal team decision function is easy to describe. First, for each firm, the quantity of local input should be adjusted optimally to its resource allocation, that is, $l_i = \theta_i k_i$. The resulting net output for firm i is

(17-4) $$G(k_i, \theta_i) = \theta_i k_i (1 - w).$$

Thus $G(k, t)$ is the maximum output of a firm with resource k and parameter t. Second, the total quantity, I, of the resource should be allocated among the firms so as to maximize

(17-5) $$\frac{1}{I} \sum_i G(k_i, \theta_i) = \frac{1}{I} \sum_i \theta_i k_i (1 - w).$$

This can be accomplished, for example, by allocating all of the resource equally among all of the firms with the largest parameter value; the resulting average net output per firm is

(17-6) $(1 - w) \max_i \theta_i.$

The expected value of (17-6) is the maximum expected average net output that is attainable under the full exchange of information; we denote this by

(17-7) $\omega_{FEI}(I) = (1 - w)E_{\theta^I} \max \{\theta_i : i = 1, \ldots, I\}.$

Note that $\omega_{FEI}(I)$ depends on I, the number of firms.

In the case of complete exchange with the center (CEC), the resource allocation is allowed to depend on the complete I-tuple, θ^I, but each firm's quantity of local input may depend only on its own parameter, θ_i. This represents the situation in which each firm reports its own parameter value to the resource manager before the latter determines his allocation, but each firm manager must decide on the quantity of his own local input before he knows how much of the resource he will get. The expected average net output under such an information structure may be represented as

(17-8) $E_\theta \dfrac{1}{I} \sum_i F[K_i(\theta^I), L_i(\theta_i), \theta_i],$

where the functions K_i and L_i are constrained to be nonnegative, and

(17-9) $\dfrac{1}{I} \sum_i K_i(\theta^I) \leqq 1,$

for every θ^I (or with probability 1). The maximum (or supremum) of (17-8), subject to these constraints, will be denoted by $\omega_{CEC}(I)$. If the probability distribution P is concentrated on finitely many t values, then there are only finitely many unknowns in (17-8), and the supremum ω_{CEC} will be attained; the problem of maximizing (17-8) can be formulated as a linear programming problem. (We do not know for what more general class of probability distributions P on the unit interval the supremum ω_{CEC} can actually be attained.)

Since the class of decision functions available to the team under CEC is essentially contained in the class of decision functions available under FEI, it is clear that $\omega_{CEC}(I)$ cannot exceed $\omega_{FEI}(I)$, and it will typically be strictly smaller. However, an implication of the main result of this chapter is that, as I increases without limit, $\omega_{CEC}(I)$ and $\omega_{FEI}(I)$ both approach the same limit. In other words, *for a sufficiently large number of firms, the loss in*

expected average net output per firm due to the incompleteness of informa-
tion inherent in CEC can be made negligible by a suitable choice of CEC
team decision functions.

We now sketch how this result can be proved in the context of the present
example. We shall consider two special cases regarding the probability
distribution P of the parameter t: (1) the probability distribution P is
concentrated on a finite number of t values; (2) P is the uniform distribution
on the unit interval.

For the first case suppose that P is concentrated on the (distinct) points
$t_1, \ldots, t_N$ in the unit interval, with corresponding (strictly positive)
probabilities $p_1, \ldots, p_N$. For simplicity, we assume that $t_N = 1$. As I
increases without limit,

$$E_\theta \max \{\theta_i : i = 1, \ldots, I\}$$

converges to 1; hence, from (17-7),

(17-10) $\lim_{I \to \infty} \omega_{FEI}(I) = 1 - w.$

We may interpret $(1 - w)$ as the maximum possible average output per firm
for an infinite population of firms in which the parameter t has the relative
frequency function (p_n), and the average resource per firm is constrained
not to exceed unity.

We shall now consider a particular sequence of CEC team decision
functions, and shall show that the expected average output per firm for this
sequence of decision functions also approaches $(1 - w)$ as I increases without limit. To motivate this particular choice of decision functions, we note
that in the case of the FEI information structure, if the relative frequency of
firms for which $\theta_i = t_N = 1$ is q_N^I, and q_N^I is strictly positive, then each such
firm will receive an allocation of the resource equal to $(1/q_N^I)$, and this will
also be equal to the quantity of the local input. For all firms with $\theta_i < 1$, the
resource and local inputs will both be zero (provided $q_N^I > 0$). By the Law of
Large Numbers, q_N^I converges to p_N as I increases without limit, so that "in
the limit" each firm for which $t = 1$ will have a local input equal to $(1/p_N)$.
This suggests the following sequence of CEC team decision functions. For
any fixed I,

(17-11a) $L_i(\theta_i) = \begin{cases} 1/p_N & \text{if } \theta_i = 1, \\ 0 & \text{if } \theta_i < 1; \end{cases}$

(17-11b)   the total resource is divided equally among all those firms, if any, for which $\theta_i = 1$; if there are no such firms, the resource is thrown away.

With this decision function, the average output per firm is

$$(17\text{-}12) \quad q_N^I \left[\min \left(\frac{1}{q_N^I}, \frac{1}{p_N} \right) - \frac{w}{p_N} \right] = \min \left(1, \frac{q_N^I}{p_N} \right) - \frac{q_N^I w}{p_N},$$

where it is understood that this is zero if q_N^I is zero. Appealing again to the Law of Large Numbers, we see that (17-12) converges (almost surely) to $(1 - w)$ as I increases without limit; hence so does its expected value (since it is bounded). Thus the expected average output per firm for the decision functions (17-11) converges to $(1 - w)$. But $\omega_{CEC}(I)$ is at least as large as the expected value of (17-12), and not greater than $\omega_{FEI}(I)$, so that $\omega_{CEC}(I)$ also converges to $(1 - w)$.

We turn now to the second case, in which P is the uniform distribution on the unit interval. Equation (17-7) is still valid for $\omega_{FEI}(I)$. Note, however, that for any I, there will be only one firm with the maximum parameter value in the sample (with probability 1), and the probability that this maximum is 1 is zero. Nevertheless, for the uniform distribution,

$$(17\text{-}13) \quad E_\theta \max \{\theta_i : i = 1, \ldots, I\} = \frac{I}{I+1},$$

so that (17-10) is valid for the uniform distribution, too. On the other hand, the interpretation of the limit in terms of an optimal allocation for an infinite population of firms is not so straightforward as in the case of a P with finite support. We might pose the problem for the infinite population as follows. Find a function $K(\cdot)$ on the unit interval that maximizes the integral

$$(17\text{-}14) \quad \int_0^1 tK(t)(1 - w)dt,$$

subject to the constraints

$$(17\text{-}15) \quad \int_0^1 K(t)dt = 1, \qquad K(\cdot) \geq 0.$$

Unfortunately, although the supremum of (17-14) subject to (17-15) exists and equals $(1 - w)$, this supremum is not attained by any function satisfying (17-15). We might say that, in the limit, "the firm with the maximum value of t (that is, $t = 1$) should get an infinite quantity of the resource."

Nevertheless, in this case, too, we can establish that

(17-16) $\lim_{I \to \infty} \omega_{CEC}(I) = 1 - w.$

The idea is similar to the one used in the case of P with finite support, but a suitable approximation must be made. Let c be a positive number less than 1, and let S denote the interval $[1 - c, 1]$. For any sample of I firms, let r^I denote the relative frequency of firms for which θ_i is in S. Consider the following sequence of team decision functions for the CEC information structure. For any fixed I,

(17-17a) $L_i(\theta_i) = \begin{cases} 1/c & \text{if } \theta_i \text{ is in } S, \\ 0 & \text{otherwise;} \end{cases}$

(17-17b) $K_i(\theta_i) = \begin{cases} 1/r^I & \text{if } \theta_i \text{ is in } S \text{ and } r^I > 0, \\ 0 & \text{otherwise.} \end{cases}$

The corresponding average output per firm, given $\theta^I = (\theta_1, \ldots, \theta_I)$, is

(17-18) $A_I^c \equiv \dfrac{1}{I} \sum_{\theta_i \in S} \left[\min\left(\dfrac{\theta_i}{r^I}, \dfrac{1}{c}\right) - \dfrac{w}{c} \right]$

$\geq \dfrac{1}{I} \sum_{\theta_i \in S} \left[\min\left(\dfrac{1-c}{r^I}, \dfrac{1}{c}\right) - \dfrac{w}{c} \right]$

$= r^I \left[\min\left(\dfrac{1-c}{r^I}, \dfrac{1}{c}\right) - \dfrac{w}{c} \right].$

By the Law of Large Numbers, r^I converges to c (almost surely), so that the last expression converges to

$c \left[\min\left(\dfrac{1-c}{c}, \dfrac{1}{c}\right) - \dfrac{w}{c} \right] = 1 - c - w.$

In other words,

$\liminf_{I \to \infty} A_I^c \geq 1 - c - w, \quad \text{almost surely.}$

Since A_I^c is bounded, it is also true that

(17-19) $\liminf_{I \to \infty} EA_I^c \geq 1 - c - w.$

But $\omega_{CEC}(I)$ is at least as large as EA_I^c, so we have shown that, for every $c > 0$,

(17-20) $\liminf_{I \to \infty} \omega_{CEC}(I) \geq 1 - c - w,$

or simply

(17-21) $\lim\limits_{I\to\infty} \inf \omega_{CEC}(I) \geqq 1 - w.$

Therefore, since $\omega_{CEC}(I)$ cannot exceed $\omega_{FEI}(I)$, we have again that

(17-22) $\lim\limits_{I\to\infty} \omega_{CEC}(I) = \lim\limits_{I\to\infty} \omega_{FEI}(I).$

Notice that the expected value of A_I^c could have been calculated exactly, but the inequality in (17-18) permitted us to avoid such an exact calculation. Another approximation serves the same purpose and is more suggestive of how to proceed in the more general case. Suppose that in the expression for A_I^c we replace every θ_i (in S) by 1; this will result in an error of at most c. For any t in S and any positive number r,

$$0 \leq \min\left(\frac{1}{r}, \frac{1}{c}\right) - \min\left(\frac{t}{r}, \frac{1}{c}\right) \leq \frac{c}{r}.$$

Hence

(17-23) $A_I^c \geq \dfrac{1}{I} \sum\limits_{\theta_i \in S} \left[\min\left(\dfrac{1}{r^I}, \dfrac{1}{c}\right) - \dfrac{w}{c} - \dfrac{c}{r^I} \right] = \min\left(1, \dfrac{r^I}{c}\right) - \dfrac{r^I w}{c} - c,$

which converges to the same limit as does (17-18). In fact, this same approximation could have been obtained by replacing each θ_i in S by any other point in S.

General Statement of the Main Result

The output of an individual firm is $F(k,l,t)$, where:

k is the vector of resources centrally allocated to the firm, a vector in the nonnegative part, K, of a Euclidean space, $\mathbb{R}^D$;

l is the local decision of the firm manager, a point in a closed convex subset, L, of a Euclidean space; $0 \in L$ (a convention);

t is the parameter that characterizes the individual firm's production function; t is a point in a compact metric space T;

F is the firm's production function, a real-valued function on $K \times L \times T$.

Let P be a probability measure on the Borel sets of T, such that T is the support of P. (All functions on T are to be understood to be Borel-measurable, and all probability measures on T to be on the Borel sets of T.)

For any vector, x, we define $\|x\| = \Sigma_i |x_i|$.

We shall make the following assumptions about F.

ASSUMPTION 1. *F is continuous on $K \times L \times T$.*

ASSUMPTION 2. *For every l in L and t in T, $F(\cdot ,l,t)$ is nondecreasing on K, and $F(\cdot , \cdot ,t)$ is concave on $K \times L$.*

ASSUMPTION 3. *For every k in K and t in T,*

$$G(k,t) \equiv \max_{l \in L} F(k,l,t)$$

exists; furthermore, this maximum is achieved at a point $\tilde{L}(k,t)$ in L such that $\|\tilde{L}(k,t)\| \leq \lambda \|k\|$, where λ is a positive number independent of k and t.

ASSUMPTION 4. *If $\|k_n\|$ diverges to $+\infty$, $k_n/\|k_n\|$ converges to $\bar{k}$, and t_n converges to $\bar{t}$, then $G(k_n,t_n)/\|k_n\|$ converges to a number that depends only on $\bar{k}$ and $\bar{t}$.*

Full Exchange of Information (FEI)

There are I firms, labeled $1, \ldots , I$, with respective parameters $\theta_1, \ldots , \theta_I$, where the latter are independently and identically distributed on T with common probability distribution P. There is a vector $I\kappa$ of total resources to be allocated among the I firms (κ, a known vector in K, represents the average resource per firm). A *team decision function* for FEI is a $2I$-tuple of functions $(K_1, \ldots ,K_I,L_1, \ldots ,L_I)$ on T^I such that each K_i takes values in K, each L_i takes values in L, and for every $\theta^I = (\theta_1, \ldots ,\theta_I)$ in T^I,

$$(17\text{-}24) \quad \sum_i K_i(\theta^I) \leq I\kappa.$$

The expected average output per firm for such a team decision function is

$$(17\text{-}25) \quad E_{\theta^I}\!\left(\frac{1}{I}\right) \sum_i F[K_i(\theta^I),L_i(\theta^I),\theta_i],$$

where the expectation is with respect to θ^I, that is, with respect to the product measure on T^I derived from P. Let $\omega_{FEI}(I)$ denote the maximum expected average output *per firm* that can be achieved using team decision functions for FEI.

Complete Exchange with the Center (CEC)

The situation with CEC is the same as in the case of FEI, except that each L_i

is further constrained to be a function of θ_i only, that is, each L_i is a function from T to L, and the expected average output is

$$(17\text{-}26) \qquad E_{\theta^I}\left(\frac{1}{I}\right) \sum_i F[K_i(\theta^I),L_i(\theta_i),\theta_i].$$

Let $\omega_{CEC}(I)$ denote the supremum of the expected average output per firm that can be achieved using only team decision functions for CEC.

Clearly, for every I,

$$\omega_{CEC}(I) \leqq \omega_{FEI}(I),$$

since the set of team decision functions for CEC is equivalent to a subset of team decision functions for FEI.

Our main result is as follows:

$$(17\text{-}27) \qquad \lim_{I\to\infty} \omega_{CEC}(I) = \lim_{I\to\infty} \omega_{FEI}(I).$$

In other words, *for large I, the information structure CEC is almost as good, per firm, as the complete information structure FEI.*[2]

The main result will be demonstrated by showing that each of the limits in (17-27) is equal to the solution of an auxiliary maximization problem, which can be interpreted as the maximum output per firm for FEI with "infinitely many" firms.

Recall that

$$(17\text{-}28) \qquad G(k,t) = \max_{l\in L} F(k,l,t).$$

The function G gives the output of a firm when the local decision is optimally adjusted to a given resource vector and parameter. We shall show that G is continuous on $K \times T$, that for every t, $G(\,\cdot\,,t)$ is concave and nondecreasing on K, and that there exist positive $\bar{a}$ and $\bar{b}$ such that

$$(17\text{-}29) \qquad G(k,t) \leqq \bar{a} + \bar{b} \cdot k.$$

We may write $\omega_{FEI}(I)$ in the form

$$(17\text{-}30) \qquad \omega_{FEI}(I) = E_{\theta^I} \max\left\{\frac{1}{I} \sum_i G(k_i,\theta_i): \frac{1}{I} \sum_i k_i \leqq \kappa, \; k_i \geqq 0\right\}.$$

By the symmetry among firms and the concavity of G in k, the maximum

---

2. Although (17-27) is stated in terms of expected values, we actually show that the average outputs under FEI and CEC converge to a common value almost surely.

in (17-30) can be achieved by allowing k_i to depend only on θ_i and the empirical distribution of $\theta_1, \ldots, \theta_I$, but not on i. That is to say, for any subset S of T, let $P_I(S;\theta^I)$ denote the relative frequency of firms i for which θ_i is in S; also, let $\mathcal{P}$ denote the set of all probability measures on T; then there is a function $\hat{K}_I$ from $T \times \mathcal{P}$ to K such that

$$(17\text{-}31) \qquad \omega_{FEI}(I) = E_{\theta^I}\left(\frac{1}{I}\right) \sum_i G\{\hat{K}_I[\theta_i, P_I(\,\cdot\,;\theta^I)], \theta_I\}.$$

This last can be rewritten formally as

$$(17\text{-}32) \qquad \omega_{FEI}(I) = E_{\theta^I} \int_T G\{\hat{K}_I[t, P_I(\,\cdot\,;\theta^I)], t\} P_I(dt;\theta^I).$$

Note that the expression

$$(17\text{-}33) \qquad \int_T G\{\hat{K}_I[t, P_I(\,\cdot\,;\theta^I)], t\} P_I(dt;\theta^I)$$

is the maximum average output per firm, given I, the number of firms, and $P_I(\,\cdot\,;\theta^I)$, the empirical probability measure corresponding to the "random sample" $\theta^I = (\theta_1, \ldots, \theta_I)$. The expression (17-33) is itself a random variable, since it depends on the random sample θ^I, and its expected value is equal to $\omega_{FEI}(I)$.

By analogy, let $\mathcal{H}$ denote the set of all nonnegative functions K from T to K such that

$$(17\text{-}34) \qquad \int_T K(t)P(dt) \leqq \kappa,$$

and define

$$(17\text{-}35) \qquad V(K) \equiv \int_T G[K(t), t]P(dt).$$

Equation (17-35) may be interpreted as representing the average output per firm for an infinite population of firms in which, for any measurable subset S of T, $P(S)$ is the relative frequency of firms whose parameter t lies in S, and $\int_S K(t)P(dt)$ is the average allocation of resources per firm for those firms.

By (17-29), for any K in $\mathcal{H}$,

$$(17\text{-}36) \qquad V(K) \leqq \bar{a} + \bar{b} \cdot \kappa.$$

Hence $V(K)$ is bounded on $\mathcal{H}$; let

(17-37) $\quad \omega \equiv \sup \{V(K): K \text{ in } \mathcal{H}\}.$

We shall prove the main result, (17-27), by showing that each side of (17-27) is equal to ω.

Proof of the Main Result

LEMMA 1. (a) *G is continuous on* $K \times T$; (b) *for every t,* $G(\cdot, t)$ *is concave and nondecreasing on* K; (c) *there are positive* $\bar{a}$ *and* $\bar{b}$ *such that, for all k and t,*

(17-38) $\quad G(k,t) \leqq \bar{a} + \bar{b} \cdot k.$

Proof. By Assumption 3, for every k and t,

$$G(k,t) = \max \{F(k,l,t): l \in L\}.$$

Hence, by one form of the "Theorem of the Maximum" (for example, Berge, 1966, p. 123), it follows from the continuity of F that G is continuous. Part (b) of the lemma is now immediate from the continuity of G and Assumption 2.

We now prove part (c). Let $\mathbf{1}$ denote the vector in $\mathbb{R}^D$ all of whose coordinates are unity. For every t, $G(\cdot, t)$ is concave and continuous; hence one can show that there exist $\alpha(t)$ in $\mathbb{R}$ and $\beta(t)$ in $\mathbb{R}^D$ such that

(17-39) $\quad G(k,t) \leqq \alpha(t) + \beta(t) \cdot k, \quad \text{for all } k \text{ in } K,$

(17-40) $\quad G(\mathbf{1},t) = \alpha(t) + \beta(t) \cdot \mathbf{1}.$

The pair $[\alpha(t),\beta(t)]$ corresponds to a hyperplane in $\mathbb{R}^{D+1}$ that is tangent to the graph of $G(\cdot, t)$ at the point $[\mathbf{1},G(\mathbf{1},t)]$. Since $G(\cdot, t)$ is nondecreasing, $\beta(t)$ is nonnegative. Since the vector 0 is in K, (17-39) implies that $\alpha(t) \geqq G(0,t)$. But $G(0, \cdot)$ is continuous on T, which is compact, and hence attains a minimum, say g_0, on T; hence

(17-41) $\quad \alpha(t) \geqq g_0, \quad \text{for all } t \text{ in } T.$

Similarly, $G(\mathbf{1},t)$ attains a maximum, say g_1, on T, so that from (17-40),

(17-42) $\quad \alpha(t) + \beta(t) \cdot \mathbf{1} \leqq g_1, \quad \text{all } t \text{ in } T.$

Combining (17-41) and (17-42) with the nonnegativity of $\beta(t)$, we see that the set of pairs $[\alpha(t),\beta(t)]$ is bounded. The proof of part (c) of the lemma is completed by taking

$$\bar{a} \equiv \sup_t \alpha(t), \qquad \bar{b}_j \equiv \sup_t \beta_j(t), \qquad \bar{b} = (\bar{b}_1, \ldots, \bar{b}_D).$$

LEMMA 2. *For every $\varepsilon > 0$ there is a $\delta_\varepsilon > 0$ such that, for every k in K, and every t and t' in T whose distance does not exceed δ_ε,*

(17-43) $|G(k,t) - G(k,t')| \leq \varepsilon \max (1, \|k\|).$

Proof. Suppose, to the contrary, that there exists a sequence (t_n, t'_n, k_n) such that the distance between t_n and t'_n converges to zero, but

(17-44) $|G(k_n, t_n) - G(k_n, t'_n)| > \varepsilon \max (1, \|k_n\|).$

Since T is compact, there is a subsequence for which both (t_n) and (t'_n) converge; thus, without loss of generality, we may assume that the original sequences (t_n) and (t'_n) both converge to, say, $\bar{t}$.

Case 1. $\|k_n\|$ *is bounded.* There is a subsequence for which k_n converges; then, for n in this subsequence, (17-44) contradicts the continuity of G on $K \times T$.

Case 2. $\|k_n\|$ *is unbounded.* Let $\mathcal{N}$ be a subsequence for which $\|k_n\|$ diverges to $+\infty$ but $k_n/\|k_n\|$ converges. By Assumption 4,

$$\lim_{n \in \mathcal{N}} \frac{G(k_n, t_n)}{\|k_n\|} = \lim_{n \in \mathcal{N}} \frac{G(k_n, t'_n)}{\|k_n\|},$$

which contradicts (17-44).

LEMMA 3. $\lim \sup_{I \to \infty} \omega_{FEI}(I) \leq \omega.$

Proof. By Lemma 2, for every $\varepsilon > 0$ there exists a *finite* partition $\{T^\varepsilon_n\}$ on T such that, for all n, and for all t and t' in T^ε_n,

$$|G(k,t) - G(k,t')| \leq \varepsilon \max (1, \|k\|), \quad \text{all } k \text{ in } K.$$

For each n, take a point t^ε_n in T^ε_n. For I firms with parameters $\theta_1, \ldots, \theta_I$, define

$$\tilde{\theta}_i \equiv t^\varepsilon_n, \quad \text{if } \theta_i \text{ is in } T^\varepsilon_n.$$

Hence, for any $k_1, \ldots, k_I$ in K for which $\Sigma_i k_i \leq I\kappa$,

$$\frac{1}{I} \sum_i [G(k_i, \theta_i) - G(k_i, \tilde{\theta}_i)] \leq \frac{\varepsilon}{I} \sum_i \max (1, \|k_i\|)$$

$$\leq \frac{\varepsilon}{I} \left[I + \sum_i \|k_i\| \right]$$

$$= \varepsilon(1 + \|\kappa\|),$$

which implies that

$$(17\text{-}45) \qquad \frac{1}{I} \sum_i G(k_i, \theta_i) \leq \frac{1}{I} \sum_i G(k_i, \tilde{\theta}_i) + \varepsilon(1 + \|\kappa\|).$$

As in the previous section, let $P_I(S; \theta)$ denote the relative frequency of firms i for which θ_i is in S, given $\theta^I = (\theta_1, \ldots, \theta_I)$, for any subset S of T. Define

$$(17\text{-}46) \qquad q_n^I \equiv P_I(T_n^\varepsilon; \theta^I),$$
$$q^I \equiv (q_1^I, \ldots, q_{N_\varepsilon}^I),$$

where N_ε is the number of elements in the partition $\{T_n^\varepsilon\}$. Thus q^I is a random probability vector, whose probability distribution depends on I, the number of firms.

For any N_ε-dimensional probability vector $q = (q_n)$, define

$$(17\text{-}47) \qquad W(q) \equiv \max \left\{ \sum_n q_n G(k_n, t_n^\varepsilon) : \sum_n q_n k_n \leq \kappa, k_n \geq 0 \right\}.$$

The first term on the right side of (17-45) does not exceed $W(q^I)$; hence, from (17-30),

$$(17\text{-}48) \qquad \omega_{FEI}(I) \leq EW(q^I) + \varepsilon(1 + \|\kappa\|).$$

Let p_n^ε denote $P(T_n^\varepsilon)$ and $p^\varepsilon = (p_n^\varepsilon)$. By the Strong Law of Large Numbers, q^I converges to p^ε almost surely. The function $W(\cdot)$ is continuous on a compact set, and therefore, by the Lebesgue Dominated Convergence Theorem,

$$(17\text{-}49) \qquad \lim_{I \to \infty} EW(q^I) = W(p^\varepsilon).$$

Suppose that $W(p^\varepsilon)$ is achieved by the N-tuple (k_n^ε), that is,

$$W(p^\varepsilon) = \sum_n p_n^\varepsilon G(k_n^\varepsilon, t_n^\varepsilon).$$

Define the simple function K^ε in $\mathcal{H}$ by

$$K^\varepsilon(t) = k_n^\varepsilon \quad \text{if } t \text{ is in } T_n^\varepsilon.$$

By an argument similar to the one leading to (17-45), one can show that

$$W(p^\varepsilon) \leqq \int G[K^\varepsilon(t),t]P(dt) + \varepsilon(1 + \|\kappa\|),$$

and the first term on the right side of this last expression does not exceed ω. Therefore

(17-50) $$W(p^\varepsilon) \leqq \omega + \varepsilon(1 + \|\kappa\|).$$

Combining (17-48), (17-49), and (17-50), we get the result that, for every $\varepsilon > 0$,

$$\limsup_{I \to \infty} \omega_{FEI}(I) \leqq \omega + 2\varepsilon(1 + \|\kappa\|),$$

from which the conclusion of Lemma 3 follows immediately.

Recall that

$$V(K) \equiv \int G[K(t);t]P(dt),$$
$$\omega \equiv \sup \{V(K) : K \text{ in } \mathcal{H}\}.$$

LEMMA 4. *For every positive ε there is a bounded function K_ε in $\mathcal{H}$ such that* $V(K_\varepsilon) \geqq \omega - \varepsilon.$

Proof. There is a sequence (K'_m) of functions in $\mathcal{H}$ such that $V(K'_m)$ converges to ω. For every pair of positive integers m and n define

$$K''_{mn}(t) = \min \{K'_m(t), n\kappa\},$$

where the minimum is taken coordinatewise. As n increases without limit, with m fixed, K''_{mn} converges to K'_m pointwise; also, since $G(\cdot, t)$ is nondecreasing on K,

$$G[K''_{mn}(t),t] \leqq G[K'_m(t),t].$$

Hence, by the continuity of $G(\cdot, t)$ on K and the Lebesgue Dominated Convergence Theorem, for every m,

(17-51) $$\lim_{n \to \infty} V(K''_{mn}) = V(K'_m).$$

For every positive number ε there is an m_ε for which

$$V(K'_{m_\varepsilon}) \geqq \omega - \frac{\varepsilon}{2},$$

and by (17-51) there is an n_ε such that

$$V(K''_{m_\varepsilon n_\varepsilon}) \geqq V(K'_{n_\varepsilon}) - \frac{\varepsilon}{2}.$$

Take $K_\varepsilon \equiv K_{m_\varepsilon n_\varepsilon}$. Then

$$V(K_\varepsilon) \geqq \omega - \varepsilon,$$

which completes the proof of Lemma 4. Note that K_ε is bounded above by $n_\varepsilon \kappa$.

LEMMA 5. $\lim \inf_{I \to \infty} \omega_{CEC}(I) \geqq \omega$.

Proof. Consider the sequence (K_ε) in Lemma 4, and fix ε. By Assumption 3 there is a function L_ε from T to L such that, for all t,

(17-52) $G[K_\varepsilon(t),t] = F[K_\varepsilon(t),L_\varepsilon(t),t]$,

(17-53) $\|L_\varepsilon(t)\| \leqq \lambda\|K_\varepsilon(t)\| \leqq \lambda n_\varepsilon \|\kappa\|$.

Let $\boldsymbol{K}_\varepsilon$ be the set of k in $\boldsymbol{K}$ with $\|k\| \leqq n_\varepsilon\|\kappa\|$, and let $\boldsymbol{L}_\varepsilon$ be the set of l in $\boldsymbol{L}$ with $\|l\| \leqq \lambda n_\varepsilon\|\kappa\|$. The function F is continuous on $\boldsymbol{K}_\varepsilon \times \boldsymbol{L}_\varepsilon \times \boldsymbol{T}$, and hence uniformly continuous. Hence, there is an $\eta_\varepsilon > 0$ such that, for all k in $\boldsymbol{K}_\varepsilon$ and l in $\boldsymbol{L}_\varepsilon$, and all t and t' in $\boldsymbol{T}$ whose distance does not exceed η_ε,

$$|F(k,l,t) - F(k,l,t')| \leqq \varepsilon.$$

Let $\{S_m\}$ be a finite partition of T such that no S_m has diameter greater than η_ε; also, let s_m be any point in S_m. (Note that $\{S_m\}$ and $\{s_m\}$ depend on ε.)

For any m for which $P(S_m) > 0$, define

$$k_m = \frac{1}{P(S_m)} \int_{S_m} K_\varepsilon(t)P(dt), \qquad l_m = \frac{1}{P(S_m)} \int_{S_m} L_\varepsilon(t)P(dt);$$

for other m choose (k_m,l_m) arbitrarily in $\boldsymbol{K}_\varepsilon \times \boldsymbol{L}_\varepsilon$. By the construction of $\{S_m\}$ and $\{s_m\}$, for every m and every t in S_m,

(17-54) $F[K_\varepsilon(t),L_\varepsilon(t),s_m] \geqq F[K_\varepsilon(t),L_\varepsilon(t),t] - \varepsilon$.

By the concavity of $F(\cdot, \cdot, s_m)$,

(17-55) $P(S_m)F(k_m,l_m,s_m) \geqq \int_{S_m} F[K_\varepsilon(t),L_\varepsilon(t),s_m]P(dt)$.

Hence, combining (17-52), (17-54), and (17-55), we get

(17-56) $\sum_m P(S_m)F(k_m,l_m,s_m) \geqq V(K_\varepsilon) - \varepsilon.$

We now proceed to construct a particular team decision function for the CEC information structure whose expected average output per firm will converge to something at least as large as the left side of (17-56) as the number of firms increases without limit. Let M be the number of elements in the partition $\{S_m\}$. For any M-dimensional probability vector $r = (r_1, \ldots, r_M)$, define $Z(r)$ to be an M-tuple $z = (z_m)$ that maximizes

$$\sum_m r_m F(z_m,l_m,s_m)$$

subject to the constraints

$$z_m \text{ in } K_\varepsilon \qquad (m = 1, \ldots, M);$$

$$\sum_m r_m z_m \leqq \kappa;$$

let $U(r)$ denote the corresponding maximum. For any I-fold sample $\theta^I = (\theta_1, \ldots, \theta_I)$, let r_m^I be the relative frequency of firms for which θ_i is in S_m, that is,

$$r_m^I = P(S_m;\theta^I),$$

and let $r^I = (r_1^I, \ldots, r_M^I)$. (Note that r^I depends on θ^I.)

Consider the following team decision function: for all θ_i in S_m,

(17-57) $K_i(\theta^I) = Z_m(r^I), \qquad L_i(\theta_i) = l_m.$

The corresponding average output per firm is

(17-58) $\dfrac{1}{I} \sum_m \sum_{\theta_i \in S_m} F[Z_m(r^I),l_m,\theta_i].$

By the construction of $\{S_m\}$ and $\{s_m\}$, (17-58) is at least as large as

$$\dfrac{1}{I} \sum_m \sum_{\theta_i \in S_m} \{F[Z_m(r^I),l_m,s_m] - \varepsilon\},$$

that is, at least as large as $U(r^I) - \varepsilon$. Hence

(17-59) $\omega_{CEC}(I) \geqq EU(r^I) - \varepsilon.$

Let $p_m = P(S_m)$ and $p = (p_m)$. By the Strong Law of Large Numbers, r^I

converges to p almost surely as I increases without limit. By the "Theorem of the Maximum" (again, see Berge, 1966, p. 123), U is continuous (on the compact set of M-dimensional probability vectors); appealing to Lebesgue once again, we have

$$(17\text{-}60) \qquad \lim_{I \to \infty} EU(r^I) = U(p).$$

But $U(p)$ is at least as large as the left side of (17-56). Hence, combining this fact with (17-56), (17-59), and (17-60), we have proved that, for every positive ε,

$$(17\text{-}61) \qquad \lim_{I \to \infty} \inf \omega_{CEC}(I) \geq U(p) - \varepsilon$$

$$\geq V(K_\varepsilon) - 2\varepsilon.$$

By letting $\varepsilon \to 0$ in (17-61), one completes the proof of the lemma.

Putting together Lemmas 3 and 5, we have

$$\lim_{I \to \infty} \sup \omega_{FEI}(I) \leq \omega \leq \lim_{I \to \infty} \inf \omega_{CEC}(I).$$

On the other hand, for every I,

$$\omega_{CEC}(I) \leq \omega_{FEI}(I).$$

It follows that

$$\lim_{I \to \infty} \omega_{CEC}(I) = \lim_{I \to \infty} \omega_{FEI} = \omega,$$

which is our main result, (17-27).

The Case in Which the Number of Firms Increases with Total Resources Fixed

We now consider the case in which the number of firms is large compared to the total quantities of resources to be centrally allocated. We formalize this by letting the number of firms increase without limit while the vector of total resources remains fixed. In this case, total output will remain bounded; we shall show that the loss in expected *total* output as a result of using a complete exchange of information with the center (CEC) instead of full exchange of information (FEI) tends to zero as the number of firms increases.

To simplify the argument, we restrict ourselves in this section to the case in which the set T of possible parameter values t is finite. Let $p(t)$ denote Prob $(\theta_i = t)$, and take $p(t) > 0$ for all t. As the number I of firms increases without limit, the number of firms of each type t, say, $N_t(t)$, will also increase without limit, by the Law of Large Numbers. Since all firms of the same type will get the same vector of resources,[3] this implies that, as I increases, the resource vectors allocated to individual firms will tend toward zero. Thus, when the number of firms is large, the total output for each type t will be determined by (1) the total number $N_t(t)$ of firms of that type, (2) the marginal productivity of the allocated resources *near zero input* (that is, at very small scale), and (3) the local decisions. In a sense, if the number of firms is large, each type will behave approximately like an industry with constant returns to scale.

We retain the model of the third section, except that the resource constraint (17-24) is replaced by

$$(17\text{-}62) \qquad \sum_{i=1}^{I} K_i \leq \kappa,$$

where κ is the same for all I, and the performance criterion is expected total output.

Full Exchange of Information

Let θ denote the *infinite* sequence $(\theta_1, \theta_2, \ldots)$ of random variables θ_i, independent and identically distributed on T (finite), with

$$(17\text{-}63) \qquad p(t) = \text{Prob } (\theta_i = t).$$

Define

$$(17\text{-}64) \qquad \Omega_I(\theta) \equiv \max \sum_{i=1}^{I} F(k_i, l_i, \theta_i),$$

subject to

$$k_i \in K, \qquad l_i \in L, \qquad \sum_{i=1}^{I} k_i \leq \kappa;$$

$$(17\text{-}65) \qquad \omega_{FEI}(I) = E\Omega_I(\theta).$$

---

3. Under assumptions of symmetry and concavity.

We maintain Assumptions 1–3. Hence, $\Omega_I(\theta)$ is well defined and is uniformly bounded, so that $\omega_{FEI}(I) < \infty$. Furthermore, for every θ, $\Omega_I(\theta)$ is nondecreasing in I. Hence,

(17-66) $\lim_{I \to \infty} \Omega_I(\theta) \equiv \Omega(\theta)$

exists for every θ, and is uniformly bounded, and hence,

(17-67) $\lim_{I \to \infty} \omega_{FEI}(I) = E\Omega(\theta).$

Indeed, we shall show that, almost surely, $\Omega(\theta) = E\Omega(\theta)$, that is, $\Omega(\theta)$ has the same value for almost all θ.

Let $N_I(t)$ denote the total number of firms among the first I for which $\theta_i = t$. Recall that we may take the values of k_i and l_i that achieve the maximum (17-64) to be the same, respectively, for all firms of the same type t. Denote such optimal values by $\hat{k}_I(t)$ and $\hat{l}_I(t)$, respectively. Keep in mind that $N_I(t)$, $\hat{k}_I(t)$, and $\hat{l}_I(t)$ are all random variables, that is, they depend on θ. Define

(17-68) $k_I(t) \equiv N_I(t)\hat{k}_I(t),$
            $l_I(t) \equiv N_I(t)\hat{l}_I(t),$
            $y_I(t) \equiv [k_I(t), l_I(t)].$

(We may interpret $k_I(t)$ as the total resource vector allocated to all firms of type t.) With this notation we may write

(17-69) $\Omega_I(\theta) = \sum_t N_I(t) F[y_I(t)/N_I(t), t].$

By the Law of Large Numbers,

(17-70) $\lim_{I \to \infty} \dfrac{N_I(t)}{I} = p(t) > 0,$

almost surely, so that, in particular,

(17-71) $\lim_{I \to \infty} N_I(t) = +\infty.$

The vectors $k_I(t)$ are uniformly bounded, and therefore, by Assumption 3, we may also take the vectors $l_I(t)$ to be uniformly bounded. It follows that, for every t, $y_I(t)/N_I(t)$ will converge to zero almost surely. Rewrite (17-69) as

(17-72) $\Omega_I(\theta) = \sum_t \|y_I(t)\| \dfrac{F[y_I(t)/N_I(t), t]}{\|y_I(t)/N_I(t)\|}.$

The sequence of vectors $y_I(t)$ will have a convergent subsequence (depending on θ) for which the corresponding vectors

(17-73) $y_I(t)$ and $\dfrac{y_I(t)/N_I(t)}{\|y_I(t)/N_I(t)\|}$

will also converge. This motivates the following assumption, which replaces Assumption 4.

Before stating the assumption we first point out that, for any y in $K \times L$ and t in T, the function f defined by

(17-74) $f(x) \equiv F(xy,t)$

is concave for x in the closed interval $[0,1]$. Therefore, if y is not 0, the limit

(17-75) $H(y,t) \equiv \lim\limits_{\substack{x \to 0 \\ x > 0}} \dfrac{F(xy,t)}{x\|y\|}$

exists (with $+\infty$ a possible value). For each t, the function $H(\,\cdot\,,t)$ is homogeneous of degree 0 (note that $H(0,t)$ is not defined).

ASSUMPTION 4′. *If* $\{y_n\}$ *is a sequence in* $K \times L$ *such that:*

(a) $y_n \to 0$,

(b) $\dfrac{y_n}{\|y_n\|} \to \bar{y}$,

then, for every t *in* T,

(17-76) $\dfrac{F(y_n,t)}{\|y_n\|} \to H(\bar{y},t) < \infty$.

It follows from Assumption 4′ that $H(\,\cdot\,,t)$ is continuous on $K \times L$ at every point $y \neq 0$; it further follows then that $H(\,\cdot\,,t)$ is uniformly bounded. If we make the convention that

(17-77) $\|y\|H(y,t) = 0$ if $y = 0$,

then the function

(17-78) $\sum\limits_{t} \|y(t)\|H[y(t),t]$

is continuous in the variables $y(t)$. Define

(17-79) $\omega = \max \sum\limits_{t} \|y(t)\|H[y(t),t]$, subject to:

(a)   for all t, $y(t) \in K \times L$,

(b) $\sum_t k(t) \leqq \kappa$.

For every θ there is a subsequence $\mathcal{J}(\theta)$ of I's such that the limits

(17-80) $\tilde{y}(t) \equiv \lim_{I \in \mathcal{J}(\theta)} y_I(t), \qquad \bar{y}(t) \equiv \lim_{I \in \mathcal{J}(\theta)} \frac{y_I(t)}{\|y_I(t)\|}$

exist for every t. By Assumption 4', and the definitions (17-66), (17-77), and (17-79),

(17-81) $\Omega(\theta) \equiv \lim_{I \to \infty} \Omega_I(\theta),$

$= \lim_{I \in \mathcal{J}(\theta)} \Omega_I(\theta),$

$= \sum_t \|\tilde{y}(t)\| H[\bar{y}(t), t],$

$= \sum_t \|\tilde{y}(t)\| H[\tilde{y}(t), t],$

$\leqq \omega.$

We have thus proved the following lemma.

LEMMA 6. *For every θ,*

(17-82) $\Omega(\theta) \leqq \omega.$

Complete Exchange with the Center

Suppose that the maximum, ω, in (17-79) is achieved at $\hat{y}(t) \equiv [\hat{k}(t), \hat{l}(t)]$. Consider the following CEC decision functions: for every θ and I, and every t for which $N_I(t) > 0$, let

(17-83) $K_i \equiv \dfrac{\hat{k}(t)}{N_I(t)}, \qquad L_i \equiv \dfrac{\hat{l}(t)}{Ip(t)}.$

The corresponding total output is

(17-84) $W_I(\theta) \equiv \sum_t N_I(t) F\left[\dfrac{\hat{k}(t)}{N_I(t)}, \dfrac{\hat{l}(t)}{Ip(t)}, t\right]$

$= \sum_t \left\|\left[\hat{k}(t), \dfrac{N_I(t)\hat{l}(t)}{Ip(t)}\right]\right\| \dfrac{F\left[\dfrac{\hat{k}(t)}{N_I(t)}, \dfrac{\hat{l}(t)}{Ip(t)}, t\right]}{\left\|\left[\dfrac{\hat{k}(t)}{N_I(t)}, \dfrac{\hat{l}(t)}{Ip(t)}\right]\right\|}.$

By the Strong Law of Large Numbers,

$$\left[\hat{k}(t), \frac{N_I(t)\hat{l}(t)}{Ip(t)}\right] \to [\hat{k}(t), \hat{l}(t)] \equiv \hat{y}(t) \quad \text{a.s.}$$

We may, without loss of generality, take $\hat{k}(t)$ to be nonzero, and thus $\hat{y}(t)$ to be nonzero. Therefore, a.s.,

$$\frac{\left[\dfrac{\hat{k}(t)}{N_I(t)}, \dfrac{\hat{l}(t)}{Ip(t)}\right]}{\left\|\left[\dfrac{\hat{k}(t)}{N_I(t)}, \dfrac{\hat{l}(t)}{Ip(t)}\right]\right\|} \to \frac{\hat{y}(t)}{\|\hat{y}(t)\|},$$

so that by Assumption 4' and the homogeneity of $H(\,\cdot\,,t)$, the second line of (17-84) converges for almost every θ to

$$\sum_t \|\hat{y}(t)\| H[\hat{y}(t)/\|\hat{y}(t)\|,t] = \sum_t \|\hat{y}(t)\| H[\hat{y}(t),t],$$

that is,

(17-85) $\lim\limits_{I\to\infty} W_I(\theta) = \omega, \quad \text{a.s.}$

Furthermore, $W_I(\theta)$ is uniformly bounded, so

(17-86) $\lim\limits_{I\to\infty} E_\theta W_I(\theta) = \omega.$

But, since $E_\theta W_I(\theta)$ is the expected total output for a particular CEC decision function,

(17-87) $E_\theta W_I(\theta) \leq \omega_{CEC}(I).$

Therefore, we have proved the following lemma.

LEMMA 7.

(17-88) $\liminf\limits_{I\to\infty} \omega_{CEC}(I) \geq \omega.$

Combining Lemmas 6 and 7 with (17-66) and (17-67), we have

(17-89) $\lim\limits_{I\to\infty} \omega_{FEI}(I) \leq \omega \leq \liminf\limits_{I\to\infty} \omega_{CEC}(I).$

On the other hand, $\omega_{CEC}(I) \leq \omega_{FEI}(I),$

(17-90) $\limsup\limits_{I\to\infty} \omega_{CEC}(I) \leq \lim\limits_{I\to\infty} \omega_{FEI}(I).$

Therefore,

(17-91) $\lim_{I \to \infty} \omega_{CEC}(I) = \lim_{I \to \infty} \omega_{FEI}(I) = \omega.$

Superiority of Full Information when Production Parameters Are Correlated

If the production parameters are independently distributed, then, for large teams, the empirical distribution is effectively known a priori, and the firm's knowledge of its own parameter, θ_i, defines its place in the general distribution, hence supplies all the information that could possibly be obtained. However, if the θ_i's are correlated but not perfectly, then the inferences of any one firm as to the empirical distribution of the others' parameters is less certain; it knows that they are drawn from the conditional joint distribution given its own parameter values, but since the latter is a random variable, so is the empirical distribution.

Retain the presupposition that production parameters of the firms are a priori indistinguishable from the viewpoint of other firms or of the resource managers. In a terminology introduced by de Finetti (1937, chap. 4), the production parameters of the different firms are taken to be *exchangeable* random variables: the (marginal) joint distribution of any finite subset of them is symmetric. Then, as shown by de Finetti (see also Hewitt and Savage, 1955), the joint distribution of an infinite sequence of exchangeable random variables can be represented as the distribution of an infinite random (independently and identically distributed) sequence from a distribution P which is itself a random variable. Formally, suppose $\tilde{T}$ is the infinite Cartesian power of T (the domain of the production parameter), Π the space of probability distributions of T, and σ the probability measure on $\tilde{T}$ for a sequence of exchangeable random variables. Then there exists a probability measure π on Π such that, for any sequence $\{A_i\}$, where A_i is a measurable subset of T,

$$\sigma(A_1 x A_2 x \ . \ . \ .) = \int_{\Pi} [P(A_1)P(A_2) \ . \ . \ .] \, d\pi(P).$$

We may interpret this as meaning that the actual θ for any firm is determined by the general conditions applicable to all firms, which are summed up in the parameters determining the distribution of P, and idiosyncratic conditions, represented by taking θ to be a random drawing from P. For a large team, therefore, the empirical distribution can be taken to be (approximately) P.

In the FEI case, P can, in the limit, be observed by all participants; hence, an optimizing policy will have the form of a pair of functions, $K_i(\theta,P)$, $L_i(\theta,P)$, not actually depending on i. If the optimal policy exists, then clearly $L_i(\theta,P)$ will in general depend genuinely on P. Even if there is no optimal policy, the sequence of approximately optimal policies will depend on P.

In the CEC case, P is observed by the center but not by the firms. Hence k can be chosen to depend on θ and P, but l must be chosen to be a function of θ only. This is a genuine restriction on the class of optimal policies. If the optimal policy for the FEI case really depends on P, then no policy in which the local decisions are independent of P can achieve the same level of aggregate output. Hence, the CEC case is not equivalent to the FEI case even in the limit.

We can illustrate this conclusion in the example studied in the second section. We assume that the team is large, effectively being at the limit. Take the case where the probability distribution of the parameter t is concentrated on a finite set. In the present context, we mean that there is a finite set of parameter values such that each P is concentrated on that set (or a subset thereof). As before, the largest possible value of t is $t_N = 1$. Assume that $P_N = P(t_N) > 0$ for all distributions P and that P_N takes on at least two different values as P varies. We can for simplicity assume that the probability distribution of P is concentrated on a finite set, each possible P having a positive probability.

If P is known to all managers, as it is under FEI, then as the second section shows, the optimal policy for large teams is to set $L_i(\theta_i) = 1/P_N$ if $\theta_i = 1$, and $= 0$ otherwise, the total resource being divided equally among the firms with $\theta = 1$. This yields a conditional expected average output of $1 - w$ for each P, and therefore an expected average output of $1 - w$ when P is considered as a random variable. If, for any P, any other policy were adopted, the expected average output would be less than $1 - w$ for that P.

This policy depends on P, through P_N, and is therefore not a CEC policy. A CEC policy must determine L_i as a function of θ_i, independent of P. It is impossible that $L_i(1) = 1/P_N$ for all P, since P_N takes on at least two different values. Therefore, for at least one P, the expected average output for the optimal CEC policy conditional on P must be less than the maximum attainable, $1 - w$. Since each possible value of P has a positive probability, the unconditional expected average output under the optimal CEC policy is less than $1 - w$, and therefore less than the expected average output under the optimal FEI policy.

It might be asked if a modicum of information can be added to the CEC case to realize the same average output level as the FEI case. Clearly, it is sufficient to identify P in the class of admissible P-values, and any statistic which will accomplish that is enough. If, for example, $E(\theta|P)$ varies with P, the sample arithmetic mean of the θ's (or even of a random sample of the actual θ's, but one which goes to infinity in size with the number of firms) is sufficient. In particular cases, less information would suffice, since all that is really needed is to identify the function $L_i(\theta,P)$ which gives the optimal FEI local decision. Thus, in the preceding example, it is enough to have a consistent estimate of P_N, since the other aspects of P distributions are irrelevant to the asymptotically optimal FEI policy.

References

Berge, C. *Espaces Topologiques,* 2nd ed. Paris: Dunod, 1966.

DeFinetti, B. "La Prévision, ses lois logiques, ses sources subjectives," *Annales de L'Institut Henri Poincaré,* 7 (1937), 1–68.

Groves, T. E., and R. Radner. "Allocation of Resources in a Team," *Journal of Economic Theory,* 3 (1972), 415–441.

Hewitt, E., and L. J. Savage. "Symmetric Measures on Cartesian Products," *Transactions of the American Mathematical Society,* 80 (1955), 470–501.

Marschak, J., and R. Radner. *Economic Theory of Teams.* New Haven: Yale University Press, 1972.

Radner, R. "Allocation of a Scarce Resource under Uncertainty: An Example of a Team," chap. 11 of *Decision and Organization,* ed. C. B. McGuire and R. Radner. Amsterdam: North-Holland, 1972.

18 On Partitioning a Sample with Binary-Type Questions in Lieu of Collecting Observations

In the course described in the headnote to Chapter 17, I found myself under the necessity of making up interesting examination questions. Since I prefer open-book examinations in an advanced course, these questions had to be essentially miniature research studies. I had the idea of showing the power of sequential decision procedures in a context suggested by Shannon's measure of the cost of communication: that is, in seeking a best element from a set, one could at each stage only dichotomize the set. The dialogue could be regarded as a special case of the Lange-Lerner process of achieving an optimal resource allocation. What was surprising was that, under the assumed conditions, the expected number of steps needed to achieve the exact optimum was finite, in fact less than three. What I did was to exhibit a method to achieve this. Later Leon Pesotchinsky and Milton Sobel showed how to find the optimal solution, a considerably more difficult step.

In effect, this provides an excellent iterative procedure for allocating one scarce resource, when one considers the costs of communication. However, it is clear that the method does not work in the same way for two or more scarce resources. Then one must have shadow prices; and this introduces a cardinal element to a problem which is essentially ordinal in the single-resource case.

This chapter was written with Leon Pesotchinsky and Milton Sobel. Reprinted from *Journal of the American Statistical Association,* 76 (1981): 402–409.

This problem originated in research on the optimal design of organizations, though it clearly has many other applications. Consider the simplest problem of resource allocation, in which there is one input to be allocated among many possible users. All users produce the same one product, and each user is characterized by an output-input ratio independent of the scale of operations. Optimal resource allocation would require allocating the entire input to the user with the highest output-input ratio.

Suppose there is a large number of users. In the first instance, each user knows his or her own ratio, but the center (the agent performing the allocation) does not. The center must acquire the information by questioning the users. However, in the spirit of information theory, the more exact the required answer, the more costly is its transfer. We can reduce the problem to that of asking dichotomous questions, such as whether an individual's ratio, say X, is larger or smaller than some specified number c. Since the center does not know the individual values of the output-input ratio, it may treat them as members of a random sample from a distribution. In this chapter we assume the distribution to be known.

There are many other situations in which the choice of the largest element from a sample may reasonably be made by binary-type questions. For instance, the data to be collected may be of a confidential or semiconfidential nature, and people may be reluctant to furnish information on age or salary or even on the amount of money now in their wallets. On the other hand, people may be willing to state that the quantity X in question (that is, X equals age) is greater than 30 and, if necessary, later state that it is under 45, and so on. The problem (or goal) is to continue such questions with the n people (or a subset of them) to find the one whose X characteristic is the most extreme in a given direction (say, the largest), but not necessarily to find its value. A more general goal would be to find the t largest (smallest) of n with or without respect to order. For the latter goal with ordering, the case $t = n - 1$ (or n) would correspond to a complete ordering of the people in the sample; this is an important special case. Clearly, for the case $t = 1$ the latter goal reduces to the former goal.

A related problem would be to search for any particular quantile such as the median, that is, to look for the median subject without knowing his X value. These problems can be handled similarly, but the results are quite different. Thus, the expected number of questions is not bounded by a uniform constant for all n (as in the search for the t largest for fixed t) but is rather an increasing function of n (see the corresponding remark at the end of the next section).

The criterion to be used must be specified exactly in order to either find the optimal procedure or decide whether a given procedure is optimal. The main criterion noted in this chapter is the expected number of questions that must be asked. We are also interested in criteria such as "maximizing the probability of terminating in r steps." For most of our goals, the latter criterion with $r = 1$ and the main criterion (expectation) give results that are in close proximity from the point of view of applications.

Several things should be noted.

1. We are not allowing paired comparisons; we do compare all n of the x's in a specified subset with a single specified constant and call this one question. In the applications we have in mind, it makes sense to call this one question rather than n questions, as in a classroom setup in which the major cost in time and energy required to get an answer is roughly equivalent to the cost of asking one question in other types of sampling surveys. On the other hand, one could, if it were desirable and appropriate, consider the corresponding model in which one regards this as n questions when the set involved contains n subjects; this latter model will be referred to in the final section, since it opens up a new set of problems related to corresponding problems dealing with pairwise comparisons.

We restrict our attention to procedures that compare the whole of a previously formed subset (and not a proper subset of it) with a specified constant. Thus, suppose we already have a disjoint partition into S sets S_1, S_2, . . . , S_S such that every x in S_i is greater than every x in $S_{i+1}(i = 1,2,$ . . . , $s - 1$), and we are restricting ourselves to this type of sampling. Then the further refinements of each of the sets S_i are separate problems in the sense that (1) there is no loss of efficiency in first considering all the refinement needed for S_1, then doing all that is needed for S_2, and so on, and (2) any application of a question to a proper subset of one of the S_i is clearly less efficient and cannot improve the efficiency. In fact, the omission of even a single subject has a positive probability of increasing the expected number of questions required to reach the goal. These remarks on optimality are a consequence of the above postulate that a single query of n people is to be regarded as one question; they would not necessarily hold if we counted the query as n questions.

2. We assume in our illustrations that the X characteristics of the n people, $x_1, x_2, . . . , x_n$, are independent and identically distributed (iid), or at least exchangeable with cdf $F(x)$, which is known to us.

3. We assume that the observations (x's) are continuous, so that with probability one we can assert that no two are exactly equal. We recognize

that this may not be strictly true in the applications noted earlier, and that practical modifications will be necessary to handle ties (for example, two people may both be 45 years old, and the data available to us do not give ages finer than to the nearest year). However, the theoretical analysis will not take this into account; it simply uses the fact that with probability one under very weak restrictions (independence being more than sufficient), no two x's will be exactly equal. (Moreover, there will usually be a practical lower bound to the fineness of the data, say ϵ, that encourages ties for large sample sizes. If we expect ties in the sample we modify our procedure by not allowing in our questions [which are of the form: "Is your X larger than c?"] two constants within ϵ of each other. Then it is easy to show that the results we give later on expectation are upper bounds for this new modified procedure, even if the probability of ties is not small.)

Our solutions (for the case of known cdf $F(x)$) are strongly dependent on the given cdf $F(x)$ (that is, when the true cdf $F(x)$ is completely specified). However, the solutions are nonparametric in the sense that the instructions and tables needed to carry out the procedures are the same regardless of the particular assumed $F(x)$. Thus, our tables would specify a value of p, and the procedure (at the first step) might be to solve $F(c) = p$. An equivalent way to state this is that the problem has been reduced to that of the uniform $(0,1)$ distribution.

The results obtained are striking. Thus, in the basic illustration ($t = 1$), the minimal expected number of questions required is less than 2.5, namely 2.42778. The result above holds for any starting sample size n and for any known cdf $F(x)$. The procedure that maximizes the probability of terminating on the very next step (the second criterion with $r = 1$) has a result not far removed, namely, the corresponding expected number of questions required is 2.44144. The optimal procedure in the latter sense is simpler because it does not require the use of any table of optimal p (or c) values.

Of course, there could be other ways of asking group questions; for example, rather than asking a binary-type question leading to a yes or no answer (such as "raise your hand if your X is larger than c and do not raise otherwise"), we could allow questions with three possible answers (such as "raise your right hand [or red flag] if $X > c_2$, your left hand [or blue flag] if $X \leq c_1$, and no hand [flag] otherwise"). Then, with $c_1 < c_2$ we can partition the sample with one question into at most three disjoint sets: $X \leq c_1$, $c_1 < X \leq c_2$, $X > c_2$. In the same way, questions with $k_0 (>3)$ possible answers may be allowed, and of course we should make every attempt to use such questions if we wish to attain an optimal solution. (The reason for this is that for $k_2 > k_1 \geqq 2$, an optimal procedure with "k_2-way" questions generally gives better results than an optimal procedure with "k_1-way" questions.) In the illustrations given below, only binary-type questions are allowed; however, the same approach could be implemented in the case of more complicated sampling procedures (we refer to the type of question allowed as a part of our "sampling procedure").

We regard our problem as the partial or complete ordering of a sample without the necessity of knowing any particular values of the observations in the sample. In the next section we consider the problem of selecting without order the t largest of n observations in a random sample; the same problem with ordering is discussed at the end of the third section. The main part of the third section deals with the problem of a complete ordering of the sample.

Selecting without Order the t Largest Observations

Preliminaries

Consider the problem of selecting without order the t largest observations in a sample (say, of people) of size n when the above type of sampling is available to us; that is, we can ask any subset, S_i, $i = 1, 2, \ldots, s$, of people to each raise a hand if (and only if) their $X > c$, where c is at our disposal to select. In this way, we partition S_i into two new subsets (that is, those whose X's are larger than c and those for whom $X \leqq c$). We terminate when (and only when) we definitely have the t largest separated from all the others. (The modifications required in the case of ties will be evident in the light of a remark made in the previous section.)

It should be understood from the description of considered procedures that if we obtain a subset of size k that is less than t as a result of the first question, then we continue looking for $t - k$ from the batch of size $n - k$; if $k > t$, then we continue looking for t from the reduced batch of size k.

Let $\pi_{i,j}$ denote the probability that j people out of i will respond affirmatively to a single question. In fact, these $\pi_{i,j}$ values can in the most general setup depend on the entire history of the procedure. In other words, if $\{\omega\}$ denotes the space of trajectories of a random process associated with our procedure, then after w questions have been asked (or at a moment w), $\pi_{i,j}(\omega) = \pi_{i,j}(\omega_s, s \leqq w | \omega_w = i)$. However, using the assumption that $\pi_{i,j} > 0$ for $j \leqq i$, it can be shown in a manner completely analogous to that given by Ross (1970, chap. 6) that if the X's are independent (or at least exchangeable), then the optimal solution for our principal criterion (minimum expected number of questions) is obtained by a stationary Markov decision procedure, that is, with transition probabilities $\pi_{i,j}$ not depending on ω. (Although the probabilities remain the same, the choice of question, that is, the c value, obviously will change and depends on the distribution of the x's in the subset to which we pose the next question.)

Illustrative Example. Let us consider a search for three "candidates" with the highest scores from a group of nine candidates, with the scores assumed to be independently and uniformly distributed on (500, 980]. For simplicity we ignore the ties and assume that the distribution is continuous uniform. For the first question we choose $c_1 = 820$ (which actually corresponds to the t/n procedure defined in this section), so that $\pi_{9,3} = \binom{9}{3}(3/9)^3(6/9)^6 = \max_p \binom{9}{3}p^3(1-p)^6$. Suppose that only one candidate has a score greater than 820. Then we look for the best two candidates from a group of eight with the scores uniform on (500, 820] (conditional distribution of the scores of the rest of the candidates), and our next $c_2 = 740$ with $\pi_{8,2} = \binom{8}{2}(2/8)^2(6/8)^6 = \max_p \binom{8}{2}p^2(1-p)^6$. Suppose now that none of the candidates has a score in (740, 820]. Then we have the same problem as before, but on the interval (500, 740]. Our $c_3 = 680$ and $\pi_{8,2}$ is exactly the same as before. If this time three candidates have scores larger than 680, we search for the two best out of three in the interval (680, 740] and our next $c_4 = 700$, and so on.

In the important special case where $x_1, \ldots, x_n$ are obtained from continuous iid random variables, the transition probabilities $\pi_{n,j}$ are binomial, namely $\pi_{n,j} = \binom{n}{j}p_n^j(1-p_n)^{n-j}$, where $p_n = 1 - F(c_n)$ and c_n is a value that defines the initial question for the sample of size n. It is clear that for the optimal solution the p_n's do not depend on F (otherwise, if for some cdf F_0 we had $p_n(0)$'s and $c_n(0)$'s yielding a better result than for another cdf F_1, we could use $p_n(0)$'s for F_0 defining $c_n(1)$'s for F_1 from $1 - F_0(c_n(0)) = 1 - F_1(c_n(1)) = p_n(0)$ and obtain the same expected number of questions). Therefore, we may assume that F is uniform on [0, 1] and denote by $\mu_n^{(t)}(p)$ the expected number of questions required for the search of the t largest x's if the original $p_n = p$. Since the conditional distribution of the x's less than p (or larger than p) is also uniform on $[0,p]$ (or on $[p,1]$), we may write that for our procedure

$$(18\text{-}1) \qquad \mu_n^{(t)}(p) = \sum_{j=0}^{t-1} \pi_{n,j}\mu_{n-j}^{(t-j)} + 1 + \sum_{j=t+1}^{n} \pi_{n,j}\mu_j^{(t)},$$

where $\pi_{n,j}$ are binomial probabilities and $\mu_k^{(s)} = \min_p \mu_k^{(s)}(p)$, $k \leq n$, $s \leq t$. From (18-1) we obtain

$$(18\text{-}2) \qquad \mu_n^{(t)}(p) = \frac{1 + \sum_{j=t+1}^{n-1} \pi_{n,j}\mu_j^{(t)} + \sum_{j=1}^{t-1} \pi_{n,j}\mu_{n-j}^{(t-j)}}{1 - \pi_{n,0} - \pi_{n,n}}.$$

A sufficient condition for the expected time of absorption (equivalent to the expected number of questions needed in our problem) to be finite and hence for both sides of (18-2) to be finite is that the $\pi_{i,j}$ be bounded away from zero; more precisely, that $\pi_{i,j} > \delta$ for all i and j ($j \leq t < i \leq n$) for some $\delta > 0$. (This sufficient condition can be shown to hold for our optimal procedure.) Another way to show that $\mu_n^{(t)}$ are all finite for the case of the optimal procedure is to find some other (that is, any) procedure for which the expected times of absorption are finite for all n. In fact, it will be shown that an optimal procedure in the sense of our second criterion with $r = 1$ yields finite values for all $\mu_n^{(t)}$.

The optimal solution is given by a sequence of values $p_k^{(\tau)}$, $k \geq \tau + 1$, $\tau \leq t$, which can be obtained from (18-2), viewing it as a recurrence relation, through minimization of $\mu_n^{(t)}(p)$. Clearly, the $\mu_n^{(t)}$ also do not depend on F, since in using the same $p_k^{(\tau)}$ we will get the same $\mu_k^{(t)}$ for all F's.

In a more general setting, $p_k^{(t)}$'s themselves can be functions of some parameters $v_1(k,\tau), \ldots, v_{m(k,\tau)}(k,\tau)$. Then the optimal values of these parameters can also be found recurrently from (18-2) through minimization of $\mu_n^{(t)}(v_1, \ldots, v_m)$.

For our second criterion with $r \geq 2$ (that is, maximization of $P_{n,t}(r)$ for a specific r), we can write

$$(18\text{-}2') \qquad P_{n,t}(r) = \sum_{j=t+1}^{n} \pi_{n,j} P_{j,t}(r-1) + \sum_{j=0}^{t-1} \pi_{n,j} P_{n-j,t-j}(r-1),$$

where $P_{n,t}(r)$ denotes the probability of terminating in exactly r steps if we start with n and our goal is to find the top t unordered. Equation (18-2') can be treated in a manner analogous to that of (18-2), assuming that the $P_{i,j}(\tau)$ have been found for all $i \leq n$, $s \leq t$, and $\tau \leq r - 1$. For $r = 1$ the solution in the last case is obtained simply by maximization of the single coefficient $\pi_{n,t} = \binom{n}{t}p_n^t(1 - p_n)^{n-t}$; it is easily shown that the sequence $\tilde{p}_n = t/n$ is optimal in the sense of this criterion. We can see that $\pi_{n,t} \downarrow t^t e^{-t}/t!$ as $n \to \infty$ for fixed t, and hence in the associated Markov chain the absorption time $\tilde{\mu}_n^{(t)} \leq (\lim \pi_{n,t})^{-1} = t! e^t/t^t$ and hence $\tilde{\mu}_\infty^{(t)} = \overline{\lim} \, \tilde{\mu}_n^{(t)}$ satisfies the same inequality. Thus for each t the quantity $t!(e/t)^t$ is an upper bound on the optimal $\mu_n^{(t)}$ for any n; this upper bound holds both for optimality of the second criterion with $r = 1$ and for that of the basic criterion.

In the next subsection we use (18-2) to derive some results for the optimal procedure with respect to the basic criterion.

The Optimal Procedure for the Basic Criterion

THEOREM 1. *Let* $\{p_n^{(t)}\}$ *be optimal in the sense of our basic criterion and* $\mu_n^{(t)}$ *denote the corresponding expectations. Then*

(a) $\mu_n^{(t)}$ *increases with* n *(for any fixed* t*)*
$$\mu_n^{(t)} \leq \mu_\infty^{(t)} < \tilde{\mu}_\infty^{(t)} < \sqrt{2\pi t}\, e^{1/12t};$$

and

(b) $t/n \leq p_n^{(t)} < (t + 1)/(n + 1)$ *for* $t < (n + 1)/2$
$$\lim_{n \to \infty} np_n^{(t)} = \theta_t, \text{ exists } (t < \theta_t < t + 1).$$

Proof. For simplicity, let us first take $t = 1$ and write p instead of p_n (or $p_n^{(t)}$), q instead of $1 - p$, and μ_n instead of $\mu_n^{(t)}$. Then (18-2) can be written as

$$(18\text{-}3) \qquad \mu_n(p) = \frac{1 + \sum_{j=2}^{n=1} \binom{n}{j} p^j q^{n-j} \mu_j}{1 - p^n - q^n},$$

which defines an analytic function of p on $(0,1)$ so that for the optimal p (that is, $p = p_n^{(1)}$) we have $d\mu_n(p)/dp = 0$, which gives us, after some algebra,

$$(18\text{-}4) \qquad \sum_{j=2}^{n-1} \binom{n}{j} p^{j-1} q^{n-1-j}(j - np)\mu_j = n(q^{n-1} - p^{n-1})\mu_n.$$

Using the identity $j - np = nq - (n - j)$ in the left-hand side of (18-4) we then rewrite (18-4) in the form

$$(18\text{-}5) \qquad \frac{n}{p}\left\{\sum_{j=2}^{n-1} \binom{n}{j} p^j q^{n-j} \mu_j - \sum_{j=2}^{n-2} \binom{n-1}{j} p^j q^{n-1-j} \mu_j - p^{n-1}\mu_{n-1}\right\}$$
$$= n(q^{n-1} - p^{n-1})\mu_n.$$

Since p_{n-1} was chosen so that $\mu_{n-1}(p)$ has a minimum over all values of p, it is clear from (18-3) that for any p and the optimal μ_{n-1},

$$(18\text{-}6) \qquad \mu_{n-1} \leq \left(1 + \sum_{j=2}^{n-2} \binom{n-1}{j} p^j q^{n-1-j} \mu_j\right)(1 - p^{n-1} - q^{n-1})^{-1}.$$

Hence we obtain from (18-3), (18-5), and (18-6)

(18-7) $\mu_n(pq^{n-1} - p^n) \leq \mu_n(1 - p^n - q^n) - \mu_{n-1}(1 - q^{n-1}),$

which yields

(18-8) $\mu_{n-1} \leq \mu_n.$

This, with the previous remark, proves part (a) for the case $t = 1$.

Now, in the first line of (18-4) we expand $j - np$ as two separate terms and use (18-3) on the second sum. Equating this to the third term in (18-4) we obtain, for any p_r that satisfies $(d\mu_n(p))/(dp) = 0,$

(18-9)

$$[\mu_n(p_r) - \mu_n](1 - p_r^{n-1}) = 1 - \mu_n + \sum_{j=2}^{n} \binom{n-1}{j-1} p_r^{j-1} q_r^{n-j} \mu_j.$$

By virtue of (18-8) the right side of (18-9) is an increasing function of p_r, and hence by (18-9) $\mu_n(p_r)$ is also; that is, if there are two solutions p_1, p_2 with $p_1 < p_2$ then $\mu_n(p_1) \leq \mu_n(p_2)$. Since $\mu_n(p)$ is an analytic function in $(0,1)$ and tends to infinity as $p \to 1$ from the left and also as $p \to 0$ from the right, there cannot be two such p values that are both local minima. Hence the minimum must be unique, and there is no analytical maximum in $(0,1)$.

The next task is to locate this unique minimum. From (18-4) we obtain

(18-10) $$\frac{d\mu_n(p)}{dp} = \frac{\sum_{j=2}^{n-1} \binom{n}{j}(j - np)p^{j-1}q^{n-1-j}\mu_j - n\mu_n(p)(q^{n-1} - p^{n-1})}{1 - p^n - q^n},$$

and we can show that for every n the derivative is negative at $p = 1/n$ and positive at $p = 2/(n + 1)$. Thus

(18-11) $1/n \leq p_n^{(1)} < 2/(n + 1),$

and the equality holds only for $n = 2$. The inequality (18-11) enables us to take limits in (18-3) in accordance with two subsequences converging respectively to $\underline{\lim}\, np_n^{(1)}$ and $\overline{\lim}\, np_n^{(1)}$ (using the Poisson approximation to the binomial distribution). The Poisson approximation and the monotonicity of $\mu_n^{(1)}$ imply that $\underline{\theta}_1 = \underline{\lim}\, np_n^{(1)} = \overline{\lim}\, np_n^{(1)} = \overline{\theta}_1 = \theta_1$ (say). A new equation can now be written instead of (18-3), namely,

$$\mu_\infty^{(1)} = \left\{ 1 + e^{-\theta_1} \sum_{i=2}^{\infty} \frac{(\theta_1)^i}{i!} \mu_i^{(1)} \right\} (1 - e^{-\theta_1})^{-1},$$

which is more convenient for the numerical search for θ_1. This completes the proof for $t = 1$.

For $t > 1$ the proof of Theorem 1 follows essentially in the same manner, and hence we omit the detail.

It is easy to show that the equality in

$$t/n \leq p_n^{(t)} < (t+1)/(n+1)$$

holds only if $n = 2t$. Indeed, if $n = 2t$, we obtain from (18-2) (taking into account that $\mu_{2t-k}^{(t-k)} = \mu_{2t-k}^{(t)}$) that

$$(18\text{-}12) \quad \mu_{2t}^{(t)}(p) = \frac{1 + \sum_{k=1}^{t-1} \mu_{t+k}^{(t)}(\pi_{2t,t+k} + \pi_{2t,t-k})}{1 - p^{2t} - q^{2t}},$$

and the monotonicity of $\mu_{t+k}^{(t)}$ in k implies that $p = \frac{1}{2}$ yields the minimum for $\mu_{2t}^{(t)}(p)$.

Approximation to the Optimal Procedure

The results given above enable us to prove that the proximity of t/n and $p_n^{(t)}$ implies the same for $\mu_n^{(t)}$ and $\tilde{\mu}_n^{(t)}$; the latter refers to the second criterion discussed earlier in the section on preliminaries.

THEOREM 2. *There exists an $\epsilon > 0$ such that for all $n \leq \infty$ (since n can be finite or infinite) and $t < (n+1)/2$*

$$\tilde{\mu}_n^{(t)} - \mu_n^{(t)} \leq \epsilon.$$

Proof. We can write that

$$(18\text{-}13) \quad \tilde{\mu}_n^{(t)} - \mu_n^{(t)} = \{\tilde{\mu}_n^{(t)} - \overline{\mu}_n^{(t)}\} + \{\overline{\mu}_n^{(t)} - \mu_n^{(t)}\},$$

where $\overline{\mu}_n^{(t)}$ is defined by (18-2) with the optimal $\mu_s^{(u)}$, $u \leq t$, $s \leq n-1$, and $p = t/n$. The first term in (18-13) is an "improvement" introduced to the optimal procedure in the sense of the second criterion with $r = 1$ by substituting $\tilde{\mu}_s^{(u)}$ for the smaller values $\mu_s^{(u)}$, and the second term is an "improvement" to $\overline{\mu}_n^{(t)}$ due to the optimal choice of p.

Let us suppose now that the statement of the theorem holds for all $u \leq t-1$. Then we get from (18-12) (taking into account that $p_{2t}^{(t)} = \frac{1}{2}$ and denoting $\sup_{2u-1 < s; u \leq t-1} \{\tilde{\mu}_s^{(u)} - \mu_s^{(u)}\}$ by ϵ_{t-1}) that

$$\tilde{\mu}_{2t}^{(t)} - \mu_{2t}^{(t)} = \tilde{\mu}_{2t}^{(t)} - \overline{\mu}_{2t}^{(t)} = \frac{\sum_{k=1}^{t-1} (\tilde{\mu}_{t+k}^{(k)} - \mu_{t+k}^{(k)})(\pi_{2t,t+k} + \pi_{2t,t-k})}{1 - p^{2t} - q^{2t}}$$

$$\leq \epsilon_{t-1}\left(1 - \frac{\binom{2t}{t}2^{-2t}}{1 - 2^{-2t+1}}\right).$$

The inequality above serves as the basis for the induction. Using the induction and some algebra, we can show that

$$\tilde{\mu}_n^{(t)} - \mu_n^{(t)} \leq \epsilon$$

if

$$\epsilon\binom{n}{t}\left(\frac{t}{n}\right)^t > t,$$

or if

$$\epsilon > \alpha_t = \sqrt{2\pi}\, t^{3/2}e^{-t} > \binom{n}{t}^{-1}n^t t^{-t+1}.$$

Since $\alpha_t \to 0$ as $t \to \infty$, the ϵ can always be chosen to satisfy the statement of the theorem.

The calculations presented in Table 18.1 show that for $t \leq 7$ we have $\epsilon_t \leq \epsilon_1 \leq 0.014$, and since $\alpha_8 < 0.014$ we have $\epsilon = \epsilon_1 \leq 0.014$.

From Theorem 2 and Table 18.1 we can see that from a practical point of view, the optimal procedure for the second criterion (with $r = 1$) is nearly optimal in the sense of the first criterion. Clearly, the so-called t/n procedure does not require specific tables for determining the $p_n^{(t)}$'s. The tables assess the closeness of these two procedures.

The results of this section can also be applied to the search for, say, the sample median. Suppose, for example, that $n = 2t - 1$. Then the expected minimal number of steps required for the search for the median, say, $\mathcal{M}_{2t-1}$, is not smaller than $\mu_{2t-1}^{(t)}$. At the same time we can suggest the following procedure: determine in the beginning the t largest (with the expected number of steps $\mu_{2t-1}^{(t)}$) and then find the smallest of them (with the expected number of steps $\mu_t^{(1)}$). This gives us the bounds for $\mathcal{M}_{2t-1}$:

$$\mu_{2t-1}^{(t)} \leq \mathcal{M}_{2t-1} \leq \mu_{2t-1}^{(t)}\mu_t^{(1)}.$$

Clearly, this procedure is a good approximation for the optimal one (at least for large t) since $\mu_t^{(1)}$ is bounded by $\mu_\infty^{(1)} = 2.44144$ and $\mu_{2t-1}^{(t)}$ increases with t. For smaller values of t one can write analogues of (18-2) for the search for the median and the sample quantiles. For example, if $n = 3$ the equation for $\mathcal{M}_3(p)$ is

$$\mathcal{M}_3(p) = \frac{1 + \pi_{3,1}\mu_2^{(1)} + \pi_{3,2}\mu_2^{(1)}}{1 - \pi_{3,0} - \pi_{3,3}} = \frac{1 + 6pq}{3pq},$$

and $\min_p \mathcal{M}_3(p) = \mathcal{M}_3(0.5) = 10/3$. The approximate procedure described above gives us the expected number of steps $\mu_3^{(1)} + \mu_2^{(1)} = 4.16507$.

Table 18.1 Selecting without order the t largest

t	n	$p_n^{(t)}$	$\mu_n^{(t)}$	$\tilde{\mu}_n^{(t)}$	ϵ_t
	2	0.5	2.0	2.0	0
	3	0.34627	2.16507	2.16667	.00160
	4	0.26557	2.23783	2.24138	.00355
1	10	0.11111	2.35625	2.36524	.00899
	50	0.02281	2.41389	2.42676	.01287
	∞	1.14852[a]	2.42778	2.44144	.01366
	6	0.5	2.59500	2.59706	.00206
	7	0.43187	2.66373	2.66642	.00269
3	8	0.38017	2.70961	2.71295	.00334
	10	0.30683	2.76729	2.77175	.00446
	50	0.06326	2.91523	2.92435	.00912
	∞	3.18865	2.94586	2.95512	.00926
	10	0.5	2.84750	2.85131	.00381
	11	0.45603	2.88829	2.89246	.00417
5	12	0.41919	2.91945	2.92397	.00452
	15	0.33748	2.98061	2.98601	.00540
	50	0.10317	3.11403	3.12240	.00837
	∞	5.20228	3.15957	3.16726	.00769
	14	0.5	3.0083	3.00579	.00496
	15	0.46751	3.02909	3.03427	.00518
7	20	0.35294	3.11390	3.12003	.00613
	30	0.23691	3.18262	3.18984	.00722
	50	0.14295	3.22936	3.23751	.00815
	∞	7.20982	3.28944	3.29631	.00687

a. For $n = \infty$ the entry in the $p_n^{(t)}$ column represents $\lim_{n\to\infty} np_n^{(t)}$.

The Complete Ordering of a Sample

Let us denote by G_n the expected number of required steps. Then in the same manner as earlier for $\mu_n^{(t)}$ and for the same class of procedures, we can write

$$(18\text{-}14) \quad G_n(p) = \frac{1 + \sum_{r=2}^{n-2} \binom{n}{r} p^r q^{n-r}(G_r + G_{n-r}) + npq(q^{n-2} + p^{n-2})G_{n-1}}{1 - p^n - q^n},$$

and the minimization of (18-14) will provide the optimal result in the sense of expectation.

We can show algebraically that for $n \leq 5$ the optimal value of p_n is $\frac{1}{2}$. For many values of $n \geq 6$ it is no longer true; however, the procedure with $p_n = \frac{1}{2}$ for all n serves in this case as an approximation to the optimal procedure, just as the t/n-procedure from the previous section does in the case of selecting without order the t largest. In contrast to the previous problem, we have not obtained exact analytic results on the limiting approach of the "$\frac{1}{2}$-procedure" to the optimal procedure, but we do have considerable empirical information on this which we will describe later. We have obtained an explicit upper bound for $n \geq 6$ for the optimal procedure based on the $\frac{1}{2}$-procedure. Furthermore, the numerical results in Table 18.2 indicate that the difference between the G_n results for $p = \frac{1}{2}$ (denoted by $\tilde{G}_n$) and the optimal G_n value is extremely small.

THEOREM 3.   *For the $\frac{1}{2}$-procedure we have the exact result*

$$(18\text{-}15) \qquad \tilde{G}_n = \sum_{r=2}^{n} (-1)^r \binom{n}{r}(r-1)(1-2^{1-r})^{-1} = \frac{n-1}{\ln 2} + \alpha_n,$$

where $0 \leq \alpha_n \leq \frac{1}{2}$ $(n = 2,3 \ldots)$.

Proof. From (18-14) with $p = \frac{1}{2}$ we have

$$(18\text{-}16) \qquad 2^n \tilde{G}_n = 2^n + 2 \sum_{r=0}^{n} \binom{n}{r}\tilde{G}_r - 2(\tilde{G}_0 + n\tilde{G}_1),$$

where for convenience we define $\tilde{G}_0 = \tilde{G}_1 = 1$ in order for (18-16) to hold for $n = 0$, 1. Multiplying through by $z^n/n!$, we let $y(z) = \sum_{n=0}^{\infty}(G_n/n!)z^n$ and obtain

$$(18\text{-}17) \qquad y(2z) = e^{2z} + 2y(z)e^z - 2 \sum_{n=0}^{\infty} \frac{n+1}{n!} z^n$$

$$= e^{2z} + 2y(z)e^z - 2(z-1)e^z.$$

Multiplying (18-17) by e^{-2z}, we let $F(z) = e^{-z}y(z) = \sum_{n=0}^{\infty}(A_n/n!)z^n$ and obtain

$$(18\text{-}18) \qquad F(2z) = 2F(z) + 1 - 2(z+1)e^{-z},$$

$$(18\text{-}19) \qquad \sum_{n=0}^{\infty} \frac{A_n(2z)^n}{n!} - 2 \sum_{n=0}^{\infty} \frac{A_n z^n}{n!} = 1 + 2 \sum_{n=0}^{\infty} (-1)^n \frac{(n-1)z^n}{n!}.$$

Equating coefficients, we obtain for $n \geq 2$

$$(18\text{-}20) \qquad A_n = \frac{(-1)^n(n-1)}{2^{n-1} - 1},$$

Table 18.2 Complete ordering

n	Optimal p_n	Optimal G_n	$\frac{1}{2}$-procedure $\tilde{G}_n$	Asymptotic difference $\frac{n}{\ln 2} - 1$	$\frac{n}{\ln 2} - 1 - G_n$
2	0.50000	2.00000	2.00000	1.88539	−0.11461
3	0.50000	3.33333	3.33333	3.32808	−0.00525
4	0.50000	4.76190	4.76190	4.77078	0.00888
5	0.50000	6.20952	6.20952	6.21347	0.00395
6	0.53686	7.65650	7.65653	7.65617	−0.00033
7	0.61306	9.09874	9.10046	9.09887	0.00013
8	0.63462	10.54059	10.54268	10.54156	0.00097
9	0.64504	11.98319	11.98451	11.98425	0.00106
10	0.50000	13.42597	13.42660	13.42695	0.00098
11	0.50000	14.86811	14.86909	14.86965	0.00154
14	0.50000	19.19579	19.19775	19.19773	0.00194
15	0.50000	20.63847	20.64062	20.64042	0.00195
16	0.58992	22.08108	22.08341	22.08312	0.00204
17	0.62204	23.52360	23.52610	23.52582	0.00222
22	0.67052	30.73636	30.73914	30.73930	0.00294
23	0.68381	32.17894	32.18179	32.18199	0.00305
24	0.50000	33.62148	33.62447	33.62468	0.00320
25	0.50000	35.06402	35.06719	35.06738	0.00336
30	0.50000	42.27682	42.28092	42.28085	0.00403
31	0.50000	43.71939	43.72366	43.72355	0.00416
32	0.55179	45.16196	45.16639	45.16625	0.00429
33	0.57485	46.60452	46.60911	46.60894	0.00442
47	0.67849	66.80036	66.80650	66.80666	0.00630
48	0.68690	68.24292	68.24919	68.24936	0.00644
49	0.50000	69.68549	69.69188	69.69206	0.00657
50	0.50000	71.12804	71.13458	71.13475	0.00671
62	0.50000	88.43877	88.44721	88.44709	0.00832
63	0.50000	89.88133	89.88992	89.88978	0.00845
64	0.55377	91.32390	91.33264	91.33249	0.00859
65	0.57481	92.76646	92.77535	92.77518	0.00872
90	0.67282	128.83047	128.84238	128.84255	0.01208

where A_0 and A_1 will be found later. Hence it follows that

(18-21) $y(z) = \sum_{B=0}^{\infty} \frac{A_B}{B!} z^B \cdot \sum_{\alpha=0}^{\infty} \frac{z^\alpha}{\alpha!} = \sum_{n=0}^{\infty} \frac{z^n}{n!} \sum_{r=0}^{n} \binom{n}{r} A_r.$

Using (18-20) and the definition of $y(z)$, we obtain

(18-22) $\tilde{G}_n = \sum_{r=0}^{n} \binom{n}{r} A_r.$

From (18-22) for $n = 0$ and 1 we find that $\tilde{G}_0 = A_0 = 1$ and

(18-23) $\tilde{G}_1 = 1 = A_0 + A_1 = 1 + A_1 \Rightarrow A_1 = 0.$

Hence we obtain the final result from (18-20), (18-22), and (18-23):

(18-24) $\tilde{G}_n = 1 + \sum_{r=2}^{n} (-1)^r \binom{n}{r} \frac{r-1}{2^{r-1} - 1}$

$= \sum_{r=2}^{n} (-1)^r \binom{n}{r} \frac{r-1}{1 - 2^{-r+1}}.$

(In (18-24) we used the identity $\sum_{r=2}^{n} (-1)^r \binom{n}{r}(r-1) = 1$.)

Asymptotic evaluation of $\tilde{G}_n$. From (18-24) we also obtain for $\Delta\tilde{G}_n = \tilde{G}_n - \tilde{G}_{n-1}$ for $n > 2$

(18-25) $\Delta\tilde{G}_n = \sum_{r=2}^{n} \frac{(-1)^r (r-1)}{1 - 2^{1-r}} [\binom{n}{r} - \binom{n-1}{r}]$

$= \sum_{s=0}^{n-2} \frac{(-1)^s (s+1)}{1 - (\frac{1}{2})^{s+1}} \binom{n-1}{s+1}$

$= (n-1) \sum_{s=0}^{n-2} (-1)^s \binom{n-2}{s} [1 + (\frac{1}{2})^{s+1} + (\frac{1}{2})^{2s+2} + \ldots]$

$= (n-1) \sum_{\alpha=1}^{\infty} \frac{1}{2^\alpha} \left(1 - \frac{1}{2^\alpha}\right)^{n-2};$

and we obtain from (18-25)

(18-26) $\tilde{G}_n - 1 = \sum_{\alpha=1}^{\infty} \frac{1}{2^\alpha} \sum_{i=2}^{n} (i-1) \left(1 - \frac{1}{2^\alpha}\right)^{i-2}.$

We now use the Euler-MacLaurin sum formula for (18-26) and obtain that

(18-27) $\tilde{G}_n = \frac{n-1}{\ln 2} + v_n,$

where the nonnegative remainder term is bounded by $\frac{1}{2}$. Hence the asymptotic result for $\tilde{G}_n$ is

$$(18\text{-}28) \qquad \tilde{G}_n \approx \frac{n}{\ln 2} - 1 \approx 1.44269n - 1,$$

where the adjusted constant is based on empirical results. (For $n = 50$ this gives 71.1345, and the exact result for $\tilde{G}_{50}$ is 71.1342, an error of less than 1/200 of 1 percent. The optimal result for $n = 50$ is 71.1280, an error in $\tilde{G}_n$ of about 1/100 of 1 percent.)

In this problem we need a minimum of at least $n - 1$ questions to separate all the n observations, and (18-28) shows that for the "$\frac{1}{2}$-procedure" we need *on the average* only about 44 percent more than this minimum.

We should mention here that from a computational point of view the search for the optimal solution in our last setting represents a significant problem. The problem is that G_n as a function of n is so closely approximated by a linear function of n, and that for the fixed n, $G_n(p)$ is almost constant, so that the search for p which yields the minimum to $G_n(p)$ is quite difficult. Thus, for $n \geq 10$ the variation of p in the interval $[0.5, 0.7]$ does not change the first two decimals in $G_n(p)$. However, the differences $n(\ln 2)^{-1} - 1 - G_n$ (which show up in the third decimal) tend to grow very slowly with n so that the correction term, namely the constant 1 in $G_n \cong n(\ln 2)^{-1} - 1$, should actually be larger than one, say of the form $1 + \beta_n$, where β_n is a very slowly increasing function of n.

From Table 18.2 we empirically observe a cyclic pattern for the optimal p value which ought to be described. The optimal p value is always between 0.5 and a constant that appears to be close to $\ln 2 = 0.693. \ldots$ For $2 \leq n \leq 5$ the optimal p is 0.5; for $6 \leq n \leq 9$ it increases; for $10 \leq n \leq 15$ it is again 0.5; for $16 \leq n \leq 23$ it increases; for $24 \leq n \leq 31$ it is again 0.5; for $32 \leq n \leq 48$ it increases; for $49 \leq n \leq 63$ it is again 0.5; and it increases for $n > 64$. For large r we conjecture that the optimal p will be $\frac{1}{2}$ for $3 \cdot 2^{r-2} \leq n \leq 2^r - 1$, that it will increase between $\frac{1}{2}$ and some constant close to $\ln 2$ for $2^r \leq n < 3 \cdot 2^{r-1}$, and that it will follow this type of cyclic pattern indefinitely. Furthermore, we conjecture that the small variation in the optimal G_n as p varies from 0.5 to 0.7 will persist for large values of n, so that the $\frac{1}{2}$-procedure will always give an answer equal to the optimal G_n value to two or three decimal places.

It is interesting to mention here that the natural generalization for the problem of complete ordering of the second optimality criterion from the selection problem (namely, maximizing the probability of a complete ordering in $n - 1$ steps) leads for $n \geq 2$ to the equation

$$(18\text{-}29) \quad P_n(p) = \sum_{k=1}^{n-1} \pi_{nk} P_k P_{n-k}$$

$$= \sum_{k=2}^{n-2} \pi_{nk} P_k P_{n-k} + (\pi_{n1} + \pi_{n,n-1}) P_{n-1},$$

where P_k denotes the probability of the complete ordering of a sample of size k in $k - 1$ steps and the π_{nk} are binomial probabilities: $\pi_{nk} = \binom{n}{k} p^k (1 - p)^{n-k}$. For $n \leq 6$ the optimal p (which yields the maximum for $P_n(p)$) is $\frac{1}{2}$; in the same way as above, we consider a $\frac{1}{2}$-procedure and denote by $\tilde{P}_n$ the corresponding probabilities and by P_n the maximal values over p of $P_n(p)$. It is easy to show that (18-29) implies for $n \geq 2$ the inequalities

$$(18\text{-}30) \quad \tfrac{1}{2}(\tfrac{2}{3})^{n-2} \leq \tilde{P}_n \leq P_n \leq \tfrac{1}{2}(\tfrac{3}{4})^{n-2}.$$

For the problem of the selection of the t largest with ordering out of n, we can easily write the equation for the expectation of the number of questions:

$$(18\text{-}31) \quad G_n^{(t)}(p) = \frac{1 + \sum_{k=1}^{t} \pi_{nk}(G_k + G_{n-k}^{(t-k)}) + \sum_{k=t+1}^{n-1} \pi_{nk} G_k^{(t)}}{1 - p^n - q^n},$$

where G_k denotes the minimal expectation for the problem of complete ordering, $G_k^{(t)} = \min_p G_k^{(t)}(p)$, and π_{nk} are binomial probabilities as before.

It is easy to see that

$$(18\text{-}32) \quad G_t \leq G_n^{(t)} \leq G_t + \mu_n^{(t)},$$

where the right-hand side corresponds to the expected total number of steps in the procedure "μ/G" in which we first select the t largest and then order them. Since G_t is of order t and $\mu_n^{(t)}$ is of order $\sqrt{t}$ or less, with large values of t the optimal procedure for this problem of selection with ordering does not give the qualitative improvement over the procedure "μ/G" described above. However, our conjecture is that the optimal value of $p_n^{(t)}$ for the selection with ordering is between $t/2n$ and t/n, and that there exists a constant v such that $G_n^{(t)} - G_t \leq v$ for all n and t.

Relation of Our Procedure to That of Pairwise Comparisons for the Same Goal

The model in which the cost of a question is equal to the number of people addressed raises some interesting problems, particularly as to how our method (for selecting the t largest or the tth largest, or for the complete ordering by comparisons with calculated c values) compares with known results about the method of pairwise comparisons of the data for the same goals. At this point we wish to give only a preliminary survey of the results obtained, comparing our results with those of Floyd and Rivest (1973).

Using the $\frac{1}{2}$-procedure from the previous section for the complete ordering problem, we find that the expected number of "single" comparisons of X's with c values is asymptotically of the order $n \log_2 (n-1) + n(1 + (\ln 2)^{-1})$. The corresponding asymptotic result using pairwise comparisons for the same goal obtained by Hadian and Sobel (1970) is $n(1 + \{\log_2 n\})$, where $\{x\}$ is the smallest integer not less than x. These results are not claimed to be optimal overall, but in the last reference optimality is claimed within a relevant subclass of procedures.

For the goal of finding the t largest (or the tth largest) for $n \gg t$ and with the new optimality criterion, our procedure from the second section with the p value $2 \ln n/n$ yields asymptotically an expected number $E_{n,t}$ of "single" comparisons equal to $n + 8 \ln n + o(\ln n)$. Also, for the same procedure and for any τ, $0 < \tau < 1$, the probability is larger than $1 - \tau$ that the required number of steps is asymptotically of order $n + c \ln n$ (where c depends on τ). These results can be compared to the results of Sobel (1968), Hadian and Sobel (1970), Blum and colleagues (1973), and Floyd and Rivest (1973). In the first two of these papers it was shown that for the search for the two largest by their procedure,

$$n + 2 \ln \ln n + O(1) \leqq E_{n,2} \leqq n - 1 + \{\log_2 n\},$$

where both bounds are attained for different n. Floyd and Rivest proved that for their algorithm SELECT (which chooses the tth largest), $E_{n,t} \leqq n + \min (t, n - t) + O(\sqrt{n})$.

For the maximum number of comparisons, say $M_{n,t}$, Hadian and Sobel (1970) proved for their procedures that for the search for the t largest,

$$M_{n,t} = n - t + (t - 1)\{\log_2 (n - t + 2)\},$$

and for the tth largest,

$$M_{n,t} = n - t + \sum_{j=n-t+2}^{n} \{\log_2 j\}.$$

Blum and colleagues (1973) established a uniform linear bound on $M_{n,t}$ (algorithm PICK) $M_{n,t} \leqq 5.4305n$ for all t; for the search for the tth largest this is an improvement over the results given above for the mid-interval values of t (that is, t close to $n/2$).

With the goal of searching for the median, we conjecture that the result of our procedure is similar to that of Floyd and Rivest (1973), namely, $E_{n,t} = 3n/2 + O(n^{1/2})$. For further discussion on these problems the reader is referred to Knuth (1973).

In summary, the results show that our methods are asymptotically comparable with the best-known methods for ordering by using pairwise comparisons, provided the distribution of the X's is known. Moreover, the implementation of our algorithm is an easy one, and the actual time required for, say, computing a c value and comparing n of the X values with it might be smaller than the time needed to carry out n pairwise comparisons.

References

Blum, M., Floyd, R. W., Pratt, V., Rivest, R. L., and Tarjan, R. E. (1973), "Time Bounds for Selection," *Journal of Computer and System Science,* 1, 448–461.
Floyd, R. W., and Rivest, R. L. (1973), "Expected Time Bounds for Selection," Technical Report CS 73 349, Stanford University, Dept. of Computer Science.
Hadian, A., and Sobel, M. (1970), "Ordering the *t* Largest of *n* Items Using Binary Comparisons," Technical Report no. 136, University of Minnesota, School of Statistics.
Knuth, D. E. (1973), *The Art of Computer Programming,* vol. 3, Reading, Mass.: Addison-Wesley.
Ross, S. M. (1970), *Applied Probability Models with Optimization Applications,* San Francisco: Holden-Day.
Sobel, M. (1968), "On an Optimal Search for the *t* Best Using Only Binary Errorless Comparisons: The Selection Problem," Technical Report no. 114, University of Minnesota, School of Statistics.

Index